Advance Praise for

RELEASING
THE BONDS

"Hassan's new book lays out with clarity, precision, vast personal illustrations, and no hysteria, the best analysis of the mind control used by every destructive religious group. He follows with a clear prescription for families and professionals showing how they can get help and deal with these human tragedies. An absolutely necessary tool for student personnel workers, clergy, and others who have faced destructive cults."

Robert Watts Thornburg, Dean, Marsh Chapel, Boston University

"The essence of Steve Hassan's work is the liberation of the human potential in all of us. Can anyone of us be really free when others are enslaved? Steve's emphatic 'no' to this agonizing question makes *Releasing the Bonds* a vibrant tool for so many of us in the helping professions. As a rabbi and teacher, I am always inspired by Steve Hassan's integrity and determination. Let it continue for many years."

Rabbi Moshe Waldoks, Ph.D., Author of *The Big Book of Jewish Humor*

"With *Releasing the Bonds*, Steve Hassan has provided a reasoned, principled, and highly readable approach to attacking a serious social problem. We need this book!"

Robert B. Cialdini, Ph.D., Arizona State University, Author of
Influence: The New Psychology of Modern Persuasion

"When Steve Hassan was still a high ranking member in the Unification Church, I participated in an unsuccessful voluntary deprogramming of my daughter, Barbara. For two days the team leader pounded at the cult member and her group. Deliberately, he insulted them using bathroom language on the theory that the cult member would 'snap'. We failed. As she returned to her group the cultist remarked, 'Where was the love?' If the team leader and the cult member had had the opportunity to read Hassan's *Releasing the Bonds*, the results might have been quite different. Hassan has skillfully condensed his twenty-five years of experience in liberating members of destructive groups into a valuable workbook for counselors, cult members and their families, and mental health professionals. His formula, the Strategic Interaction Approach, stresses love, respect, freedom of choice, customized planned action fitted to the individual with the family as key participants, psychotherapy, and applied social psychology."

Arthur A. Dole, Ph.D, ABPP, Editorial Advisory Board for the
Cultic Studies Journal, American Family Foundation

"For sixteen-hours a day and a paycheck averaging $40 a week I gave more than a decade of my youth to a cult. Although it is eighteen years since I have left the cult, Steve Hassan's book *Releasing the Bonds* has provided me with new insights and additional healing. His book offers fresh perspectives and tools that can lead to letting go of the shame, recognizing one's personal goodness, and appreciating one's strength and integrity. I urge every former cult member to read *Releasing the Bonds*. Hassan's book will also be a reassuring message for families and friends who have suffered the loss of a loved one to a cult as well as offering a basic introduction to cult issues."

Ginger Ross Breggin, Executive Director of the International Center
for the Study of Psychiatry and Psychology

"*Releasing the Bonds* is a compassionate and intelligent guide for anyone who has ever been caught up in a cult or cult-like organization. Hassan offers perceptive and non-coercive guidance to family and friends of those whose idealism or vulnerability has led them to become cult members. Further, the book provides valuable insights into the control and manipulation that can occur in abusive personal relationships such as those expe-

rienced by battered women. It is a vital tool for professionals and layper-
sons alike."

Peter R. Breggin, M.D., Author of *Your Drug May Be Your Problem:
How and Why to Stop Taking Psychiatric Drugs*

"Steve Hassan is one of the very few people to understand the mechanics
of manipulation. He sheds a rare light on the mysterious processes used to
overwhelm independent thought and behavior in totalist groups. Steve is
a truly insightful commentator whose work always stimulates. His experience is vast and his prose is lucid. Steve's work is a must read for anyone
who wants to comprehend indoctrination and understand how to undo
it."

Jon Atack, Author of *A Piece of Blue Sky: Scientology, Dianetics and
L. Ron Hubbard Exposed*

"At the time I left the headquarters of Jehovah's Witnesses in New York,
after having worked for $14 a month for six years, I was able through
much inner soul-searching to extricate myself on my own. Had I possessed the information in *Releasing the Bonds*, more than likely it would
have greatly shortened the amount of time spent still searching for
answers. When you are the one being manipulated by controlling leadership, you are least likely to understand the motives behind that leadership,
as it is carefully cloaked behind doctrine, fear and guilt. Now one can
shortcut the process significantly and recover without fear of returning to
the group, or of being caught up in another high-control group."

Randall Watters, Author of *Thus Saith the Governing Body
of Jehovah's Witnesses*

"Congratulations, Steve! You have a unique handbook/guidebook here
which, if followed carefully, should result in freeing many cult members
from the bondage of mind control. It will give hope and motivation to
their many relatives and friends who feel helpless and hopeless and are
desperate to discover some means of reaching their loved ones. I remember the dark depressive cloud of despair which settled on me when I first
heard of my son Peter's involvement in Scientology. What a tremendous
relief it was when his wife Mary Jo reassured us that he had responded
positively to your counseling and had re-entered the real world. It is good
that you affirm consistently the importance of an individual's faith — you

make it clear that no Christian should fear that your methods or techniques would impact the cult member's religious faith negatively. You are unselfishly sharing what you know with others, and encouraging them to try it. The Moonies would have undoubtedly left you alone, had they any idea what your indoctrination would eventually lead to! God works in mysterious ways."

Joyce Farrell

"Steven Hassan has called upon his twenty-three years of expertise in the cult field to write this excellent, highly readable and extremely practical manual. Reading this book and implementing Hassan's advice will hopefully help everyone affected by a mind-control situation to understand and re-evaluate an unhealthy involvement."

Marcia R. Rudin, Founding Director, International Cult Education Program of the American Family Foundation

"Steven Hassan is one of our most eloquent defenders of freedom of the mind. For decades he has labored mightily on behalf of the majesty of the human spirit. His good work has brought psychological and spiritual relief to countless victims and families who have unknowingly stumbled into the clutches of mind control perpetrators. As a spokesperson for the individual's right to be the master of his or her own thoughts and choices, Hassan has resisted the dangers and threats manufactured by manipulators who have sought to silence his courage. His new book will bring special hope for current victims, but it should be read by anyone who values individuality."

Alan W. Scheflin, Professor of Law; Santa Clara University
Co-author of *The Mind Manipulators*, Recipient of seven awards in the field of mental health.

RELEASING THE BONDS

Empowering People to Think for Themselves

RELEASING THE BONDS

Empowering People to Think for Themselves

Freedom of Mind Press
Somerville, MA
2000

A Freedom of Mind Press Book

Published by Aitan Publishing Company
62 East Starrs Plain Road
Danbury, CT 06810

ISBN: 0-9670688-0-0
Library of Congress catlog card number: 99-68918

Hassan, Steven
Releasing the Bonds: empowering people to think for
themselves!/Steven Hassan—1st ed.
P. cm
Includes bibliographical references and index.

1. Cults 2. Deprogramming 3. Cults-Psychology 4. Brainwashing
5. Ex-Cultists—Counseling of. I. Title

BP603.H37 2000   305.6'2999
QB-I99-500583

Readers can reach Steven Hassan or The Freedom of Mind
Resource Center at http://www.freedomofmind.com
9 8 7 6 5 4 3 2 1
Manufactured in the United States of America

I dedicate this book to the spirit of

Lisa McPherson (1959-1995)

and to everyone who has yearned to be free.

TABLE OF CONTENTS

Acknowledgments

First, and foremost, I would like to thank my parents, Milton and Estelle Hassan, for their love and support throughout my forty-five years. In May of 1976, they risked everything to rescue me from the Moon cult after a serious van crash. If they had not intervened, it is possible I might still be in the cult today. I want to thank Gary R., Michael S., Nestor G., and Gladys R. for helping to "wake me up" during that fateful week of my deprogramming.

It seems like eons have passed since 1988 when I wrote *Combatting Cult Mind Control*. While it was always my intention to write other books, it took my sister, Thea Luba, to get this book project going. She took it upon herself to make sure the developments of my counseling approach over the past twelve years were written down and shared with a wider audience. She transcribed many hours of audio tapes of sessions with clients, read cult-related books, repeatedly interviewed me and former members and activists, attended conferences and generally threw herself into understanding "my world." As the project developed, and as I was able to devote more time to the writing, Thea continued to shape the material, making fundamental conceptual contributions: it was her idea to use the term "interaction" approach, instead of "intervention." By encouraging me to explain what I did, and why I did it, Thea helped to develop the Strategic Interaction Approach. She went beyond what a brother could ask, and I thank her deeply. She has since gone on to develop her own web-based music publishing and teaching course, which should attract thousands of students world-wide.

To help organize the many hundreds of pages of text into a book, I turned to Richard N. Côté and Duncan Greene. Working with extensive editorial guidance from my wife, Misia Landau, and myself, they produced a commendable draft which, over the following months, I reworked into the present manuscript. Misia spent many hours turning my words and concepts into their present polished form. Thankfully, she is not only incredibly bright and beautiful, and a gifted writer, she is also committed to helping my life's work. She has contributed tremendously to this book and to my life. I love her more than words can ever say.

Before its publication, the book has had numerous people read it and offer constructive feedback. I would especially like to thank Thea Luba, for her perceptive comments throughout and for pushing me to revise chapters 12 and 13, and Elyse Hirschorn and Janet Crane for an amazing copy edit. I also thank Marc Hirschorn, Alan Scheflin, Keith Holden, Jon Atack, Monica Pignotti, Cathleen Mann, Kelton Rhoads, David Anderson and Reb Moshe Waldoks for their constructive suggestions.

Setting up an independent press has been quite a project. I am especially grateful to Marc Hirschorn, Hank Greenberg, my business managers Neil Reshen and Dawn Reshen-Doty, David Korzenick, Scott Spiewak, Janice Hoffman, Peter McWilliams, Bob Minton, Sue Auclair, Terra Frederichs, Mike Doughney, Larry Flusser, Bob Aulicino, Kurt Aldag and Peter Fulton.

I am also very grateful for the support of many family and friends who have helped me along the way: Doug and the entire Luba family, the Freese family, Phyllis and Morty Slotnick, Mark and Steffie Slotnick, Debbie and Mike Miron, Madeline and Victor Lipschutz, Lauren and Danny Broch, Ricki and Dennis Grossman, Michael Stone and Stephen Kelley, Steve Morse, Monica Weiss and Danny Hanson, Russell Backer, Susan Mayer, Gary Birns, the Bar-Yam family, Amy Elizabeth Fox, Eric and Susan Rayman, Elissa Weitzman and Shep Doeleman, Elliot Baker, The String Cheese Incident for inspiration to go for it, Tina and Carla DeLillis and everyone at Johnny D's. I apologize if I have forgotten to mention anyone. You know who you are—and thanks so much!

Introduction

Like most people, I knew nothing about mind control when I was deceptively recruited into the "One World Crusade," a front group for the Unification Church — better known as the "Moonies." I was nineteen and a junior at Queens College. That fateful February in 1974, I had just broken up with my girlfriend and was an appealing target: bright, educated, from a solid family, idealistic, and especially vulnerable at that moment to the smiles of three attractive women who flirted with me and invited me over "for dinner."

Dinner led to other longer meetings. After an intense three-day "workshop," I became convinced that God wanted me to drop out of school, quit my job, turn over my bank account, and follow the "Messiah," and my "true father," Sun Myung Moon. Within a few short weeks, I came to believe that Armageddon was at hand, that World War III would start in 1977, and that we alone were personally responsible for defeating Satan and erecting the Kingdom of Heaven on earth.

I worked eighteen to twenty hours a day, seven days a week, fundraising, recruiting and indoctrinating new members, undertaking public relations and political campaigns, and meeting regularly with Moon and his highest-ranking lieutenants. As an American, I had no real power, just position. The upper echelons of the hierarchy were composed exclusively of Koreans and Japanese, with the Koreans in the position of the "master race." Moon had moved to the United States, and he needed American front men who were intelligent, passionate and dedicated. Over a matter of months, I went from being founder of a recruiting front group, C.A.R.P.,[1] at my former college, to the rank of Assistant Director of the

Unification Church at National Headquarters in Manhattan. I was highly praised by Moon himself and at one point was held up to the membership as a "model member."

Had it not been for a miracle, I might still be a cult member today. In 1976, after three days without sleep, I nodded off at the wheel of a Moonie fundraising van and crashed into the back of an eighteen-wheeler. This near-fatal accident gave my family the opportunity to help me leave the cult. At that time, the only means available to my parents was a forceful rescue method called "deprogramming," which typically involves holding the cult member against his will.[2] On the second day of my deprogramming, I threatened my father with violence, at which point he broke down into tears, asking me what I would have done if I were in his position. His sincerity touched me and, for a brief moment, I was able to see from his perspective and feel his pain. I reluctantly agreed to meet with a team of former members for five days, without contacting the cult or trying to escape.

As a devoted Moonie, I did my best to fight the deprogramming process, but the information that was presented gradually began to sink in. In the days that followed, I came to understand what "brainwashing"—as practiced by Mao Tse Tung in his Communist political "re-education" centers—was all about. Robert Jay Lifton's *Thought Reform and the Psychology of Totalism* (Norton, 1961) helped me realize that the techniques we used in the Moonies were so much like those used to "brainwash" political prisoners. Eventually, I came to the painful realization that I had not only been subjected to mind control processes, but that I had recruited others into the Moonies, too.

After my deprogramming, I returned to college and went on to complete a master's degree in counseling psychology. Realizing my unique position as a former cult member and counselor, I dedicated myself to helping others escape and recover from destructive mind control situations. Since 1979 I have taken many avenues to educate people about the dangers of mind control groups. That year, following the mass suicide of the followers of Jim Jones at Jonestown, Guyana, I founded Ex-Moon Inc., a nonprofit educational organization made up of ex-members of Moon's Unification Church. I published a newsletter, held media conferences, and established a clearinghouse for information about the Moon organization. I later served for a year as the national coordinator of FOCUS, a support and information network of former members of destructive cult groups. Now, I have founded Freedom of Mind Institute and Freedom of Mind Resource Center, Inc. (http://www.freedomofmind.com), with its Internet web site dedicated to informing the public about destructive mind control and deceptive cult practices.

In 1988 I wrote *Combatting Cult Mind Control: The #1 Best-selling Guide to Protection, Rescue, and Recovery from Destructive Cults* (Park Street Press). The publication of this book allowed me to share my experiences as a cult counselor with people all over the world. The book was translated into Spanish, French, German, Japanese, Italian, Polish and Czech. *Combatting* was based on my work in the field of "exit-counseling," a rescue method that was developed as a legal, non-coercive alternative to the intrusive and often illegal method of deprogramming.

Changes over the past twelve years have caused me to develop my approach and refine my techniques. In the early 1990s, I learned that the leaders of many of the larger cults had started buying copies of *Combatting* so that they could learn how to prepare their members to resist the exit counseling process. Kip McKean, who founded the International Churches of Christ, reportedly held my book up at a general assembly meeting and told some 15,000 members that they would be in sin if they met with me or even read my book.[3] In this way, cult leaders were able to impede the efforts of many families by preventing members from meeting with people outside the group.

I now know that this roadblock was actually a blessing in disguise because it forced me to develop more effective ways of teaching family members and friends how to think strategically and interact with their loved one in creative ways. I began to see that all of a cult member's friends and family are traumatized by the situation, in some cases quite profoundly. I realized that to mobilize them into a resourceful mode, I had to find ways to empower them, both as individuals and as a team of concerned, loving adults. These revelations have become the cornerstones of the method I currently use, which I call the Strategic Interaction Approach.

This book is the culmination of my twenty-five years of experience in helping thousands of people all over the world and describes a practical, hands-on approach to helping those affected by mind control processes. In addition, the development of the Internet, which provides fast and economical access to information about particular cult groups, has played an enormous role in the development of my new approach. Indeed, this book could not have been written prior to the development of the Internet.

The Strategic Interaction Approach (SIA) is a dramatic evolution of and improvement upon exit counseling and promotes a family-centered, non-coercive course of therapy. Strategic Interaction therapy provides the friends and family of the cult member with a much greater understanding of cults, their methods, and the effects of the indoctrination process. It offers new insight into cult-induced phobias and effective tools for overcoming them.

The SIA is designed to help the cult member recognize that he has been under the influence of mind control, and consequently has surrendered personal power to the group and its leader. With continued work and application of this approach, he recognizes the pervasiveness of the group's control over his life. Once the former member has experienced such an awakening, my methods help him regain a sense of personal power, integrity, and direction. Although cult members are indoctrinated to fear change, most with whom I have worked have experienced emotional, psychological and even spiritual rebirth. They were able to return to their families and were spared further injury, in some cases, even death.

This goal-oriented communication course is designed for use by a professional therapist, although it can also be initiated and implemented by motivated family members and friends. This book is not meant to replace professional counseling, nor is it meant to solve every problem faced by the family and friends of a loved one involved in a cult. It is written for intelligent people who find themselves in an extreme situation and don't know what to do. It is also written for the many hundreds of people who have contacted me after reading *Combatting Cult Mind Control*, asking what *more* they could do to help loved ones affected by mind control.

Since you are reading this introduction, I assume that you are hoping to learn how to help a relative or friend who is in trouble. Of course, you could be a devotee of one of the organizations whose members this book is meant to help, or a former cult member, or maybe you just have an interest in Strategic Interaction therapy. Because of my desire to help people, I am writing this book for anyone who wants to learn. I am frustrated by the impossibility of personally giving information and counsel to all the desperate people who call me, each of whom is seeking to help a friend or loved one escape the grip of destructive mind control. It is my hope that this book will help.

My entire approach is based on my belief that growth is an essential part of the human experience and that when people are encouraged to grow, they will do so according to what they believe is best for them. In my travels around the world, I have interacted with people from many different belief systems and have concluded that there are basic, universal needs that transcend the requirements of the physical body. I have found that people want to have a positive sense of identity and a connection with others in a greater community. They want to feel and give love rather than hate and fear. They prefer to live with trust rather than mistrust. They would rather be told the truth than be told lies. They would rather be free than enslaved.

One of my chief motivations in exposing the destructive and deceptive practices of mind control cults is my high regard for religious freedom. I believe that everyone has the right to believe, and the right to *not* believe, whatever they choose. As a member of the Jewish faith, I believe in a God that created us with free will and the freedom to choose. I am also especially aware how often minority groups have been persecuted for their beliefs, or for merely being different. As a matter of principle, I am opposed to censorship or banning any group. Indeed, I celebrate diversity. I also believe that no legitimate group should fear an honest critique of its practices. In fact, I have found that my model for analyzing mind control practices has helped some individuals and groups to see that they were unknowingly perpetrating mind control and undermining basic human rights. In general, I believe the best way to prevent such abuse is to educate and warn people about the dangers of mind control.

The First Amendment of the U.S. Constitution grants freedom of religion as it pertains to belief. In essence, people have the right to believe whatever they like — even if those beliefs are demonstrably wrong, like "the earth is flat." However, the Constitution does not give people or institutions the right to engage in behavior that violates other people's rights or the laws of the land, even if they claim religious motivation. Many cult leaders believe that it is necessary for them to practice deceptive recruitment and mind control techniques for ideological reasons. But if the effect of their actions is to make the person dependent and subservient, then I believe it is hurtful and people's rights are being violated. The bottom line for evaluating any organization is the consequences of its behavior. It is also the easiest way to evaluate distinctions between legal and illegal, ethical and unethical conduct.

I honor and respect all religious forms that honor and respect a person's individuality and freedom. I am a civil libertarian who seeks to protect the right to believe whatever one wants to believe. That is why my work has had the broad support of religious leaders from a variety of denominations and spiritual paths, including Baptists, Buddhists, The Church of Christ, Episcopalians, Hindus, Jews, Lutherans, Methodists, Pagans and Neo-Pagans, Roman Catholics, The United Church of Christ, Unitarians, and many others. I support a person's right to choose his spiritual path and want religious institutions to prosper.

Much of my work has been with people involved with religious cults, although I have certainly seen my share of other types of groups. I have helped former trainers and participants of large group "awareness training" programs, people who have been involved in irresponsibly conducted drug rehabilitation programs, and former salespeople for large, pyramid-structured, multi-level commercial operations. In recent years, I have encountered a wide variety of less formal cult situations, such as people whose family dynamics were cult-like and women who experienced battered-wife syndrome under controlling husbands. Over time, I have come to realize the pattern that ties all of these situations together: they all involve mind control techniques that restrict a person's ability to think, feel, and act autonomously.

The public's need to recognize cults and their destructive influence has never been greater. The mass suicides of the Heaven's Gate members, along with those of the Solar Temple group in Canada and Switzerland, and the tragedy in Waco, Texas, have brought the dangers of cults to the forefront of the world's consciousness. Yet, cult activity has increased exponentially since Jim Jones decided that his 900 followers should no longer inhabit the earth. Conservative estimates report that there are more than 10,000 destructive cults operating in the world today, directly affecting tens of millions of lives.[4] Those numbers are growing rapidly.

Cults are increasing in number and size for many reasons. Among the most fundamental of these is the breakdown of families, communities, and the growing sense that Western society is in decay. Economic factors play a role. A large and growing segment of the world's population is poor, while a relatively small elite controls an ever-increasing share of the world's resources. As more people become disenchanted with their lot, they seek answers in fringe groups of all types, from fanatical religious sects to New Age groups offering enlightenment, to militia groups that plan political and social revolution.

Add to all of this the new Millennium, an event that is essential to understanding the recent escalation in cult activity. Prophecies that go back hundreds of years, and in some cases thousands, are being used today by visionaries and madmen as the lens through which current events are viewed and interpreted. Will the Messiah come to Earth in the next few years? Around the world, millions of Jews, Christians and Muslims certainly think so. Many believe that "false prophets" and the Antichrist are working to establish a one-world government under Satan. Fear of a holocaust called Armageddon is even more widespread. The apocalyptic prophecies of the 16th-century French mystic Nostradamus are believed by many to apply to the present day. Some people predict that extraterrestrial beings or other mysterious spiritual entities will either rescue or destroy the human race in the next few years. Curiously, the Mayan calendar runs out in the year 2000. The year 2000 and the third Millennium (which begins in 2001) represent magic round numbers of the kind that have always stirred the human imagination, so we can expect that many groups far larger than Heaven's Gate will be standing by, preparing to rise to another plane of existence.

Apocalyptic visions, even those shared by large groups, are not new phenomena. What is new is the means by which they can be promulgated. We have television, faxes and the Internet to spread inaccurate and alarmist ideas quickly. More ominous still, we have technologies that can give groups, and even individuals, the power to create apocalyptic disasters. On the other hand, many of the same technologies can also be used to disseminate valuable information and protect people's rights.

For these reasons, the coming years will be an especially fertile time period in which profound changes, both positive and negative, could take place. Throughout the world, millions of people are searching to find new purpose and meaning in their lives. Growing numbers of spiritual and political movements everywhere are offering people hope for the future. The Millennium thus brings fresh challenges, and with them fresh opportunities.

Living within a global community is an increasingly interdependent affair. We must cope with incredible stresses in a world that has never before been so interconnected by mass communication and transportation. In order to safeguard our personal and collective freedom, it is imperative that people learn more about how the mind can be positively and negatively influenced. People must learn to know themselves and take responsibility for their own beliefs, values and behavior. They must also develop and use a social support network to connect them to the resources of a greater community, and to help them to enjoy the fulfillment that can come with healthy, interdependent relationships.

In this book, I will establish criteria to distinguish between healthy and unhealthy groups and relationships. Cult leaders and their few establishment defenders love to compare their groups to benign mainstream organizations. I will focus attention on the critical differences. Chapter by chapter, we will analyze what practices and tactics constitute destructive mind control. By identifying common cult scenarios, you will see how families can work together to free their loved ones. You will gain practical knowledge by reviewing checklists of important concepts, filling out evaluation forms to design a customized approach, and rehearsing communication strategies and dialogues to prepare for interaction with your loved one. (In most scenarios and dialogues in this book, clients' names and identifiable characteristics have been changed to protect their privacy.)

I believe that real love is stronger than conditional love. The love that family members and close friends have for a person is much more powerful than any relationship within a mind control cult. Relationships in mind control groups are usually based on the conditions of obedience and membership. Once the member passes the "honeymoon" phase and these conditions are made evident, friends and family have the potential for increasing a positive influence over time. Time is on their side because mind control is never one hundred percent, because the human spirit wants to be free, and because, ultimately, cults do not deliver what they promise.

Chapter 1

We Have a Problem!

Too often, destructive cults go unnoticed until it is too late to help. On March 26, 1997, the bodies of thirty-nine men and women, all dressed alike and draped in purple shrouds, were found throughout a million-dollar mansion in San Diego, California. In the weeks that followed, we heard the disturbing story of the Heaven's Gate cult: how several members had castrated themselves as part of the group's purification process, how its leader, sixty-six year-old Marshall Applewhite, made his followers believe that the "willful exit of the body" would mark their "graduation" to a higher spiritual plane; and how all active members had committed suicide so that a UFO trailing the comet Hale-Bopp could transport the group to "distant space," or "the Kingdom of God."[1] The Heaven's Gate tragedy was one of the largest and most visible mass suicides on U.S. soil, and the event left most of us wondering, *How could this have happened? Why would anyone do such a thing?*

Some people looked to the group's belief system for answers. Many pointed to their widely publicized Internet web site, where members left a collective suicide note entitled "Exit Press Release."[2] According to the statement, members of Heaven's Gate were not causing their own premature deaths, but rather leaving behind their physical "containers" in order to reach the "Next Evolutionary Level."

1

While an investigation of such beliefs is certainly valuable, an understanding of the suicides is incomplete until we look at the group's behavior. The philosophical orientations of destructive cults vary widely, but their methods are strikingly similar. By examining the conduct of cults like Heaven's Gate, we can see how individuals are aggressively and deceptively recruited, indoctrinated with a new set of beliefs, and made dependent on the leader and the group through the use of mind control.

The story of Gail Maeder

Alice and Robert Maeder[3] did not recognize their daughter when they first saw the infamous Heaven's Gate farewell video, which was broadcast two days after the discovery of the mass suicide in Rancho Santa Fe. Like the other members of the cult, Gail had cropped her hair short and the bags under her vacant eyes made her look much older than her twenty-seven years. She had pretty much broken off contact with her family in 1994 when, shortly after a breakup with her boyfriend, she was recruited into a group.

Unlike many families, Gail's parents quickly realized that she was in a cult, and began researching cult tactics and mind control techniques. They learned that cults often attract people during transitional stages in their lives and use their vulnerability to manipulate them. They also learned that though Applewhite claimed to allow free choice in the group, the conduct of each member was controlled by an extensive list of "Major Offenses and Lesser Offenses," which included "Having likes or dislikes," "Breaking any instruction or procedure knowingly," "Taking any action without using my check partner," and "Trusting my own judgment—or using my own mind."[4] Ultimately, Gail trusted Applewhite's judgement, with devastating consequences.

After the tragedy, I met Alice and Robert at a cult awareness conference. They told me that reading my book, *Combatting Cult*

Mind Control, had been a "lifesaver" in that it helped them understand what happened to Gail. I winced. I wished that it had saved their daughter's life. It is my sincerest hope that this book will be a true "lifesaver" for other cult members.

As a spiritual searcher, Gail fit the profile of a typical cult recruit. Other members were less obvious targets. Many held steady jobs before making the decision to follow Applewhite. Among the thirty-nine dead were a bus driver, a computer trainer, an environmentalist, a car salesman, a nurse, a paralegal, a medical assistant, a homemaker, and a local TV personality. Although situational and psychological variables can make a person more vulnerable to cult recruiters, anyone who is unaware of mind control tactics can become a target of a destructive cult.

WHAT IS A DESTRUCTIVE CULT?

There are many different types of destructive cults, and the diversity of cult beliefs and practices sometimes makes it hard for family members and friends to decide whether their loved one is in trouble or not. Although there are still groups whose followers cut their hair short and wear identical clothing, like the members of Heaven's Gate, this is by no means the case with most modern-day cult groups. Today, for example, many cults require their members to wear business suits so that they blend in with their environment.

All cult members may not look alike, but I have found that destructive cults follow specific behavior patterns that set them apart from other groups. By learning to identify these patterns, you will be better qualified to determine if someone you care about is actually involved with a cult. A group should not be considered a "cult" merely because of its unorthodox beliefs or practices. Instead, destructive cults are distinguished by their use of deception and mind control techniques to undermine a person's free will and make him dependent on the group's leader.

Authoritarian leadership

In essence, a destructive cult is an authoritarian group that is headed by a person or group of people that has near-complete control. Charismatic cult leaders often make extreme claims of divine or "otherworldly" power to exercise influence over their members. Many legitimate religions have had powerful figures who have inspired enormous dedication in people. Being a powerful leader is not inherently wrong, though it carries a high potential for abuse. A group becomes destructive when its leader actively uses such power to deceive members and to rob them of their individuality and free will. For example, I was told to surrender my free will (viewed as Satanic) to God's representative, Moon, and his sub-leaders. Marshall Applewhite told followers that an alien entity was speaking through him, and used this message to justify his absolute control over their lives. Leaders of numerous groups—including the Twelve Tribes, International Churches of Christ, and Jehovah's Witnesses—claim it is God's will that members follow them.

Deception

Destructive cults also use deception to recruit new members. When I was first approached by Moonie recruiters, they told me they were part of the "One World Crusade," which I later learned was one of many front groups for the Unification Church. They claimed to be students who were involved with a small community of young people struggling to overcome cultural barriers. It was not until much later that I found out what the group was actually about, what its members really believed, and what would be expected of me. What makes this all so insidious is that members often speak and act with the greatest sincerity because they have been subjected to the same mind control techniques that they use to recruit others.

Destructive mind control

Finally, destructive cults use mind control techniques to keep members dependent and obedient. You will learn the specific criteria that define mind control in Chapter 2 but, generally speaking, cult mind control can be understood as a system of influence that is designed to disrupt a person's authentic identity and replace it with a new identity. By immersing people in a tightly controlled, high-pressure social environment, destructive cults gain control of their members' behavior, thoughts, emotions, and access to information. They take over their minds.

Mind control can be packaged in different forms and, today, groups in many areas of society are using various combinations of destructive mind control techniques. The four main types of cults are religious cults, political cults, therapy/large group awareness training cults, and commercial cults. Understanding how each type of cult operates will help you assess your own situation, and will provide a frame of reference for future discussions of other types of groups.

THE FOUR MAIN TYPES OF CULTS

Religious or spiritual groups

What ties these groups together is their focus on religious dogma or spiritual practices. In many Bible-oriented groups (Jewish, Christian, Muslim), leaders claim to be a Messiah, Prophet, or Apostle. In some, an elite group of several people, the "governing body," claim to know the real meaning of Scripture. In groups based on an eastern religion (Hindu, Buddhist, Sikh, Jain, Sufi), leaders claim to be "enlightened" avatars, gurus, rinpoches, Perfect Masters, or reincarnations of various enlightened masters from the past. For example, in the early 1980s, a man named Frederick Lenz started a "Buddhist" computer cult with a credo of money, status, fame, and greed—all of which are antithetical to Buddhist beliefs.[5] He called himself Atmananda, and later, Zen Master Rama, and finally, just Rama, proclaiming that he had been an enlightened master in many other lifetimes. In Pagan and neo-Pagan cults, leaders claim to be masters of the occult — witches and warlocks. Other cults use a hodgepodge of religious teaching. Some cult leaders claim that they can channel powerful entities from other dimensions. One housewife claimed to channel a 35,000-year-old spirit from the continent of Atlantis.

Many cults are the elaborate inventions of their leaders, like Roy Masters' Foundation for Human Understanding. A former stage hypnotist and diamond cutter, Roy Masters started a national radio show called *How Your Mind Can Keep You Well* and sold audio tapes which he claimed could teach people a new form of meditation. When I listened to these tapes, it became clear that Masters was actually using powerful hypnotic techniques to indoctrinate his listeners. Later, he began to tell his followers that he was a sinless messiah, and held seminars in which he would stage exorcisms by hypnotizing people to believe that demons were leaving their bodies.

Although most cult leaders claim to be of the "spiritual" realm, we can see their true colors when we examine how much emphasis leaders place on the material world—their luxurious lifestyles, millions of dollars of real estate, extensive business enterprises, and so on.

Political groups

These groups are often easily identified as dictatorships: brutal, repressive regimes that imprison or kill critics and dissidents. They control the press, prevent free assembly and elections, and lack the necessary checks and balances to prevent abuses of power. In retrospect, the former Soviet Union may best be understood as a political cult.

Other political cults include terrorist groups that resort to the killing of innocent citizens to promote their cause. Suicide bombers are often members of these extremist political groups. When you hear about a suicide bombing in the Middle East, for instance, you may wonder how someone could give his life in order to kill others. My research on mind control can easily explain the methods. Such fanatical acts are frequently the result of destructive mind control.

I have met and counseled members of smaller, political cults in the United States. These groups are typically small and operate numerous front organizations. They claim to champion human rights and social justice and yet their activities are on such a small scale that they have no chance of having any real social impact. One woman I met joined a social service agency at the suggestion of a college professor. She was not allowed to visit home for almost seventeen years. The group leader claimed to be a great revolutionary. After his death, his legacy was a cult of a few hundred people and a small stockpile of rifles and handguns.

Therapy/large group awareness training groups

Unethical therapists can become the leaders of cults when they make their patients dependent on them, rather than empowering them to become functional and independent. Such therapists who cross ethical boundaries often take advantage of clients, isolating them from friends and family, having them turn over bank accounts, perhaps even taking sexual advantage. Therapy cults can include a single therapist and his clients or a collection of therapists who not only run workshops and group therapy sessions, but also purchase property where members may live together.

Even well meaning therapists may impose their value system on patients in a way that is unethical. For example, some therapists believe that most, if not all, adult problems have been caused by childhood sexual abuse. In sessions, patients are encouraged, and may even be persuaded, to uncover memories of childhood sexual abuse, or even Satanic cult involvement, that never actually occurred. Some vulnerable patients have been led to believe that they were abused as children, and families have been shattered as a consequence.

These therapists are clearly acting below the ethical standard of care required of mental health professionals. While the statistics on child abuse are shockingly high, and while it is clear that childhood sexual abuse can have a devastating impact on individuals as they grow up, there is no evidence to suggest that all, or even the large majority, of adult problems have been caused by childhood sexual abuse. On the other hand, scientific evidence does show that memories of childhood abuse can be repressed in some people. Finding out whether this is the case requires a delicacy and skill on the part of the therapist that cannot exist when the therapist believes that "everyone is abused," and that the purpose of therapy is to find that abuse.[6]

Leaders of large group "awareness" training programs may not even hold a degree in psychology or counseling. Yet they conduct workshops and seminars and charge hundreds, and sometimes thousands, of dollars to provide psychological "insight" and "enlightenment," usually in a hotel meeting-room environment. These groups use many of the basic mind control techniques to create a "peak" experience for participants, not surprising since many business cult leaders were once members of other mind control cults.

Some customers are manipulated into signing up for more expensive, "advanced" courses where they become deeply enmeshed in the group. Once committed to the group, members are told to either recruit friends, relatives, and co-workers, or cut them off entirely if they are critical of the members' involvement. These groups have caused untold nervous breakdowns, broken marriages, and business failures, not to mention some well-documented suicides and deaths by reckless accidents. The people who run these groups often have questionable backgrounds and few or no credentials.

If you are ever pressured to attend a weekend workshop for several hundred dollars, ask the person to describe in detail what takes place. If the response is, "I can't tell you," or "I don't want to spoil the experience for you", then my advice is to respond with a determined, "No, thank you!"

Commercial groups

These cults play upon the fantasy of great wealth and power to lure people into an almost slavish devotion. Many are pyramid-shaped, "multi-level marketing" organizations in which members deceptively recruit people, who in turn recruit others, so they can supposedly make a percentage of the new recruits' income. These groups claim to raise self-esteem but former members have told me they felt worse the longer they were part of the organization. Top members pressured them to buy motivational audiocassettes and videotapes and to attend regular "pep rallies" which they promised would enhance performance. Some said that they spent so much money, and got so deep in debt, that they had to declare bankruptcy.

Well-known legitimate businesses have unwittingly hired "consultants" to train their employees. The result can be an infiltration into the company by a cult group. Believers within the company pressure other employees to attend cult programs. If they refuse, they are fired or demoted. Several companies, including a computer company, were taken over in this manner, and eventually went bankrupt.

Although most cults fall into one of these categories, there are countless other types of cults, from computer cults to science fiction and New Age cults. The approach of the Millennium has spawned many new space-related and UFO cults. Throughout the world, people are stressed out, sleep-deprived, and disillusioned with existing political, social, and religious institutions. They are hungry for hope. Charismatic cult leaders with delusions of grandeur or an appetite for power and money are eager to take advantage of this situation by recruiting and indoctrinating people into a form of mental slavery.

WHO IS IMPACTED BY CULTS?

Letters, telephone calls, e-mails, and faxes come to me from all over the world. Some are from former cult members of groups I have never heard of. Most are from desperate people who have read *Combatting Cult Mind Control* and want to know more about how to help a loved one leave a cult. Readers may assume the calls are usually from parents trying to rescue a child who is eighteen to twenty-four-years old. Many are, but most are concerned with cult members who are in their thirties to late fifties. Nor are the calls only from parents. I have heard from family members of all kinds — children trying to rescue parents, wives trying to rescue husbands, brothers trying to rescue sisters, boyfriends trying to rescue girlfriends, and vice versa. I have even worked with a boss trying to rescue an employee, a coach trying to rescue a team member, and a clergyman trying to rescue a member of his congregation.

What I have learned is that anyone, and any relationship, can be impacted by cult involvement. All of us are affected by cults. Think about the people in your life:

Mothers, fathers, children, brothers, sisters, grandmothers, grandfathers, aunts, uncles, nieces, nephews, cousins, stepmothers, stepfathers, stepsisters, stepbrothers, wives, husbands, girlfriends, boyfriends, lovers, friends, neighbors, employers, employees, co-workers, coaches, clergy, religious leaders, teachers, therapists, social workers, psychologists, psychiatrists, guidance counselors, doctors, lawyers, law enforcement officials, former members, politicians, government leaders, concerned citizens, taxpayers....

I wish I could tell you that everyone who comes to me follows through. The fact is, people may discover that their loved one is in a cult but feel reluctant, powerless, or even afraid to help. Many different issues block people from actively getting involved with helping someone leave a destructive cult, as we will discuss in Chapter 5. Reading this book and informing yourself about cults and mind control is the first step toward overcoming such barriers and freeing your loved one. As long as your loved one is alive, I encourage you to do everything within your power to try to rescue him now—because there is nothing we can do when it is too late.

COMMON CULT SCENARIOS

To give you an idea of how people begin to deal with the vast array of cult situations, I have included a sampling of the urgent and desperate stories families have recently shared with me. Again, names and identifying features of clients have been changed to protect their privacy.

I have italicized passages to emphasize the most important concepts in discussing mind control situations. We will return to these themes at the end of the chapter.

Case One: Son in Bible cult

MOTHER: Our eighteen-year-old son Jeffrey is a college freshman. A few months ago, he told us he was going to Bible studies. Naturally, we were very pleased. Now we are not so sure. He rails on and on how *all the other churches are dead* and unspiritual, except the one he joined, of course. He wants to quit school and work full time bringing people into his group. Jeff always wanted to be a doctor, ever since he was a child. We are so upset. We just don't know what to do.

SH: Tell me more. What's the name of the group he is involved with?

MOTHER: We don't know.

SH: Could be one of Kip McKean's International Churches of Christ. I get a lot of calls about that group. To make an assessment, we'll need to know the name of the group and the leader.

FATHER: I did ask him once who the leader was and he said "Jesus Christ."

SH: That's very common. Ask your son, "Who founded it as a legal entity?" and "Who is the local leader?" and "Who is the worldwide leader?" Did he give you any literature? That might give us some information.

FATHER: When he does talk to us, he's spouting memorized verses from the Bible. He says he wants to "save" us, but we've always considered ourselves to be good Christians.

MOTHER: *I don't recognize my own bright, warm, loving son.*

FATHER: He has turned into a fanatic! Steve, something is very wrong here. We talked with our minister. He said he heard you give a very informative lecture on "The Shepherding/Discipleship Movement." He thought you might be able to help us.

SH: These Bible groups distinguish themselves from more mainstream, orthodox churches *by demanding a one-over-one discipling relationship*. Each member is assigned to another member who controls and supervises all aspects of his life—studies, relationships, finances—everything!

MOTHER: What should we do?

SH: I'll send you my Background Information Form (see page 29 at the end of this chapter). Fill it out and we'll talk again soon.

Note: This international group should not be confused with the mainstream Church of Christ, or the United Church of Christ. McKean's group was started in 1979 in Lexington, Massachusetts.

Case Two: Brother in one-on-one destructive relationship

ALICE: Steve, I feel totally frustrated with my brother, Peter. We are both in our mid-twenties. Since we were little, we've always been very close, but not any more. Not since he got involved with Patty. I think his life has been in a downward spiral ever since.

SH: What makes you say that?

ALICE: *He has turned his back on all his friends.* He's about to lose his job as a mechanic because he has become unreliable at work. Some days he doesn't even show up. He refuses to talk to our parents.

SH: Why is that?

ALICE: He said he's tired of the family always complaining about his relationship with that woman.

SH: Tell me more about Patty.

ALICE: Patty is a divorcee ten years older than Peter. She runs his life. I know he has tried to get away from her, but then she threatens to kill herself. I think it's *psychological blackmail.* Recently, she has been threatening to kill him first, before she takes her own life. I'm at my wit's end. I've tried to get my parents to do something, but they take it all too personally. They feel hurt and rejected. All they manage to do is argue about Peter and Patty and whose fault it is.

I was driving home from work when I heard you being interviewed on the radio. On this program, you were talking about *one-on-one relationships that followed the same destructive mind control patterns as cults* that had hundreds of members.

SH: One-on-one relationships that are based on manipulation, deception, dependency and isolation can be very destructive.

ALICE: Is there any hope for my brother?

SH: The fact that you are willing to help and are seeking professional advice shows me there is reason to hope. We need to find the time to sit down so you can fill me in on all of the details. Then, we can formulate a plan.

Case Three: Father controlled by "mystic"

ERIC: I did a computer search under "cults" on the World Wide Web to see if I could find information. That's how I found your Web page. Steven, our mother died two years ago and it has affected our father tremendously. He's a devout Roman Catholic who has fallen under the spell of a forty-five year old "mystic." She goes by the name of Mandy, and claims to have the power of prophecy.

CAROL: My brother and I are very concerned. This Mandy is ruining our relationship with our father.

SH: Tell me more. Have you been able to find out any information about this woman?

ERIC: Yes. We hired a private investigator to dig up the truth about Mandy's past. The P.I. found a lot of damaging information. This woman was once arrested for prostitution. From interviews with people in her past, there's evidence that she's a pathological liar.

CAROL: When we presented this evidence to Dad, we thought it would certainly be enough to wake him up from this nightmare. But he refused to face the facts.

SH: What happened?

ERIC: Since then, Mandy has been giving *threatening prophecies* to him that Carol and I would die horrible deaths if we continue to interfere. She tells him that if he donates more money to her phony "charity," then God would be appeased.

SH: Has he given her any gifts or money?

CAROL: *He gives her large sums of money.* He is *spending more and more time with her* and her other followers.

SH: Have you been able to locate any others who were hurt by her?

ERIC: Yes. In fact, one man, Roger, used to be a close friend of Dad's before Mandy ever showed up. We spoke with him, and he's willing to help, although we don't think our father would speak with him right now.

SH: Since your father is a devout Catholic, have you tried to speak with your priest?

CAROL: Yes. But it seems the Church is reluctant to get involved.

SH: It sounds like Mandy has a lot of control over your father. How does the rest of your family feel about your father's involvement?

ERIC: Everyone is upset. We have a lot of resources in this family, but we just don't know what to do.

SH: Have everyone read my book and let's set up a time when we can meet.

Case Four: Fiancée in secret cult breaks engagement

REBECCA: I was reading an article in *The Boston Globe* about another cult group, and it set my mind to wondering. Your name was mentioned in that article, so I thought I would give you a call. My ex-fiancée George and I have been going together for five years. I love George. We are planning to get married — or at least we were.

SH: What happened?

REBECCA: George is always busy on Tuesday and Thursday nights. He also goes away one weekend a month. He won't tell me where he's going. He calls them "important classes," but they seem to be *secret meetings*. His secrecy is driving me crazy. How can I spend the rest of my life with a man who has this mysterious other life? I gave him an ultimatum: "Tell me where you are going and what you are doing, or else!"

SH: What did he say?

REBECCA: He didn't say anything. He broke off our relationship. *(Crying)* Was it my fault? What was I supposed to think? What could I do? Please excuse me — I'm very upset.

SH: Tuesday and Thursday night, eh? I think I counseled someone from that group last year. He was in the group for over ten years. I wonder if he knows George? I bet you he does.

REBECCA: I still love George. I want to help him.

SH: Would you want to help him even if he doesn't return to you?

REBECCA: Yes. I love him. It would feel good if at least I tried to wake him up.

SH: Well, I think I can help. I'll call the fellow I helped and see if he is willing to speak with you.

Case Five: Daughter in cult rejects family

FATHER: This whole mess started a month ago when our daughter Debbie was approached on the street and asked to do a "free" personality test.

MOTHER: Then they invited her inside to watch a free movie that starred her idol, John Travolta. Apparently, it was a recruitment film for Scientology. How can a person be such a successful actor while being in a cult?

SH: That's a good question. There are two distinct parts to this group. Wealthy people spend their money for all of the auditing, courses, and training. They only see the glamorous side. People who don't have hundreds of thousands of dollars may wind up going into massive debt or join "staff" and work for a pittance each month.

You know, *a cult member is like an actor* who has been given a role. But unlike actors, *cult members actually come to believe the "role" is reality.* With this particular group, they believe that people can develop godlike powers, like telepathy or telekinesis. Did you ever see the movie *Phenomenon?* Travolta's character can learn a new language in twenty minutes and move paper clips by pointing his finger. James Randi, the magician, has offered a one million dollar reward for anyone who can demonstrate that they have powers like these. No one has ever succeeded under the watchful eye of a professional magician.

MOTHER: When she told us what happened, I got hysterical! I said, "Don't you know this group is a cult?" She just stared back at me and said, "You're wrong! If John's in it, this group can't be bad!"

SH: Actors and actresses are human beings. Their lives may be very functional in certain areas and dysfunctional in others. *Everyone is vulnerable to cult mind control.*

MOTHER: She figured if this group had done so much for the movie star, she'd give it a try.

SH: *The leaders of destructive cults don't treat everyone the same way.* Celebrities typically have a very different experience from rank-and-file members. The rich and famous do not experience the same level of exploitation as the rank and file. They perform valuable public relations activities for their groups and typically give large sums of money.

FATHER: I tried the rational approach with Debbie. I told her the founder of this group was an aging science fiction writer with no religious or psychological credentials.

MOTHER: But all that matters to her is that her movie star hero is a member.

SH: Just because people are wealthy, famous, or successful in their work doesn't mean that they haven't been influenced by a destructive mind control cult.

MOTHER: *She has moved into the group's headquarters.* She doesn't want to see us. When we call and ask to speak with her, they say she isn't around. We're really frightened.

FATHER: She's an adult. I can't bear watching her withdraw money from her trust fund to pay for these so-called "courses." What should we do?

SH: I can promise you that *the group will extract as much money as they can* from her, so I'd advise contacting your attorney immediately. It's going to be a major project, but you can help Debbie. The sooner you learn about destructive mind control techniques, cults, goal oriented communication and Strategic Interaction Therapy, the faster you will be able to make a positive difference in her life.

Case Six: Former member wants to help those still in group

SUSAN: Last month I got out of a psychotherapy group that was very cultish. The leader was an unlicensed psychologist. I wound up spending fifteen years under his complete control. I moved into a group-owned apartment, and my husband had followed me into the group. *I also recruited two of my closest friends.* The "therapist" convinced me that my husband and I were incompatible, and we got divorced. This psychologist controlled *my behavior, my thoughts and my emotions.* I was completely under his influence. Eventually, *he wanted to have sex with me* as well as the other women in the group. When he offered me drugs, it was too much. I escaped, but my friends and my ex-husband are still in the group.

SH: Did the psychologist make people cut off family members if they refused to pay for their therapy?

SUSAN: Exactly. The therapist *told us that all of our problems were caused by our parents and family members.* We believed that if they really cared about us, they would take financial responsibility for our healing. When families refused to pay, he said it was "proof" that they didn't love us. Or so we thought.

SH: I've encountered these "blame-the-family-and-make-them-pay" groups before.

SUSAN: Of course, no one got healed. We just became more and more dependent on the group. Now, I can't go on with my life until I rescue my friends and ex-husband who are still trapped.

SH: It's quite natural for you to be concerned about those you leave behind. My first piece of advice is to first spend some time focusing on yourself! Learn about cults and mind control and get the proper counseling to help you become strong.

SUSAN: With all due respect, Mr. Hassan, I was abused by psychotherapy, and I think it's the last thing in the world that I need.

SH: You were abused by an unethical therapist in what sounds like a mind control cult that used "therapy" as its front. If you were in a religious cult, you might have the same aversion to anything religious. Ethical counseling respects a person's individuality and seeks to give tools and perspectives that empower a person. The goal is to help people to stand on their own two feet and function in their lives. *Cults want people to be isolated and dependent.* Help yourself first, and then you can be most effective helping the others.

SUSAN: I just can't deal with the idea of sitting down with any therapist right now. I want to rescue my friends.

SH: I understand your feelings. Have you read any books or seen any videotapes that helped explain cult mind control patterns?

SUSAN: I read your book. That's why I'm contacting you.

SH: Have you tried to contact your friends' families yet?

SUSAN: I'm sure I could get in touch with them. Should I give them a call? We haven't talked in a long time.

SH: I suggest taking things one step at a time. Are you open to meeting with some people who were once in a cult?

SUSAN: Why?

SH: Because I think it would be valuable for you to deepen your understanding about the universal patterns of mind control. It will also help give you emotional support by speaking with people who will more readily understand what you have been through. Also, they can share some videotapes about cult mind control issues. Get stronger first, and then help your friends.

Case Seven: Born in a cult

MATTHEW: Steve, I'm thirty-three years old. I ran away from home when I was fifteen. I couldn't stand my parents' oppressive religious demands. I wanted to live more like my school friends. I wanted to play games. I wanted to celebrate Christmas. I wanted somebody to make me a birthday party. Even more important, *I wanted the freedom to learn and read without threats and punishment.* I thought to myself, "If God is such a tyrant, I want no part of God."

SH: Sounds like you were raised in the Jehovah's Witnesses.

MATTHEW: Precisely. When I was old enough, I enlisted in the Marines. My parents were horrified, because it is expressly forbidden to be in the military if you are a Witness. Over the years, I've had very little contact with my family because the Watchtower Society labeled me an apostate. *My family members and friends were told they would be in sin if they talked with me.*

SH: Are you in contact with anyone in your family?

MATTHEW: Yes. In the past couple of years my sister, Ruth, has been willing to talk and meet with me—albeit secretly. I think she's on the fence. She knows there are major problems with the Witnesses, but she's afraid to do anything. She loves me, though, and I love her. I've read your book and I want your help to rescue my family.

SH: Spiritually, where are you now?

MATTHEW: I've come around to a belief in God and have spent some time reading the Bible.

SH: You may know that the group has its own version of the Bible, which isn't very accurate—the New World translation. Theologians have ridiculed it, saying it has hundreds of errors. Members, though, believe it's superior to all other translations — a big deception. Have you read Randy Watters' books? He's a former elder at JW headquarters, Bethel, in Brooklyn. The highest ranking defector is Ray Franz. He has written two books about the group. He was a former governing body leader and a member for sixty years.

MATTHEW: Really? Sixty years and he left!

SH: You have some reading to do. I want you to have a clear understanding of what the issues are: the history of the JWs, the contradictions within their own doctrine, the Biblical problems, as well as the mind control and cult issues.

MATTHEW: I'm willing to do all of that. Do you think there's hope?

SH: Yes. You might not be able to help everyone to leave the group, but you can set the process in motion. You said your sister Ruth would be most receptive, so let's plan some Strategic Interactions with her first. There are plenty of former members who will offer you support and help.

Case Eight: College student joins UFO cult and disappears

ADAM: Our twenty-seven-year-old son is involved with a UFO group. We have no idea where he is. We haven't heard from him in five years.

SH: Most cults don't want the member to maintain contact with family and friends, unless they can be recruited or solicited for money. In some cases, *the cult member refuses to respond to letters and phone calls.* In other cases, *the family doesn't even know where their loved one is.* You are not alone. There are many other families in your situation.

ADAM: I guess we are asking, "Can you get someone out of a cult when you have lost contact?"

SH: Yes. Of course, one of the necessary steps is to eventually re-establish contact. But *each case is unique, and a customized strategy should be put into place* in order to have success. It also depends on the resources within your grasp. One client, a District Attorney, had "loaned" his car to his son. The young man drove off with other cult members, leaving no forwarding address. The father filed a report that his car had been stolen. Police found the son in Texas. They also found marijuana in the car. He asked the police to hold his son until he could fly there. The father was able to speak with the Judge and arrange for his son to be released on bail to his custody. I was called in to counsel his son. It was a creative solution to the problem.

In the Rama (Frederick Lenz) computer cult, members were told to use post office boxes and voice mail and never to let their family know where they were living. Many cults move the members around the country, and the world, so family and friends lose track of them. There are things you can do even if you don't know where your loved one is. I say, "Do the best you can with the resources you have." Here are just a few things you can do now:

- Put out missing person flyers.
- Do a search on the Internet.
- Hire a reputable Private Investigator.
- Network with counter-cult organizations.
- Network with former members of the group.
- Network with the families of other members.

ADAM: How do you go about finding a former member?

SH: I will see if any of my sources can be of help. You can also make inquiries. We might also be able to get the media interested in doing a story. They have a lot of resources. If we can't locate a former member of this group, then we'll try to find a former member of a similar group. There are literally thousands of former members willing to reach out to help those still imprisoned in cults. Do you have access to a computer?

ADAM: Sure.

SH: First, set up an e-mail alias so your identity can be protected. Learn to use different Internet search engines. There are some sites that do meta-searches, like Metacrawler, Dogpile, or AskJeeves which automatically search multiple engines for you.[7] There are also many different newsgroups. I have a list of resource links on my Web page.

Your son's group may even have a web page. You know, Heaven's Gate, the group whose members committed suicide in March 1997, told their members to cut off contact from their families and friends. But they had a web page; they even had a web business. Members could have been located easily since they lived communally. I have been asked, "What could the family, relatives and friends have done to keep in contact with members of Heaven's Gate?" My first strategy would be to help locate ex-members, especially recent defectors of the group. I would recommend counseling those people first. The investment of time and money to do this really can make a difference. Some of them might be willing to help —give information and perhaps even contact their friends in the group. Families of cult members could pool their resources to do this.

Another strategy would be to locate and contact people at the businesses that employed the cult members and ask them to help. I'd start by spending a day or two training trustworthy people and suggesting ways that these colleagues could communicate effectively with the members of the cult on behalf of family and friends. Also, if the group does have a for-profit business, you could even set up a situation where someone is contacting the group to hire them—thereby gaining access. *Step by step—that's the approach.* The group your son is in publishes books and tapes because it wants to recruit new members, right?

ADAM: Yes.

SH: That's another avenue to explore. My Strategic Interaction Approach encourages *resourcefulness*. There is a great deal of *preparatory work* to do. We will plan how to *interact strategically.* You may be amazed to learn *how many ways there are to reconnect seemingly lost relationships. Flexibility and teamwork* will dramatically improve your chances of getting back in touch with your loved one.

Note: Be careful! For many years, the nonprofit Cult Awareness Network (CAN) was a grass roots organization which provided information and support to those in need. In 1996, the Cult Awareness Network (CAN) name, logo, and phone number was purchased by a member of the Church of Scientology in federal bankruptcy court. CAN is now operated by cult members or their defenders who do not believe that mind control cults even exist.

When an unsuspecting family member or friend calls CAN, they will not get the help they need. Unfortunately, CAN's confidential files were turned over to Scientology. The good news is that a new organization, the Leo J. Ryan Foundation, was established in February 1999, with its headquarters in Connecticut. The Foundation intends to fill the void left by the purchase of CAN. Meanwhile, the American Family Foundation continues its mission of helping to raise cult awareness through its own programs and publications. Their contact information can be found in the appendix of this book.

Case Nine: Employer recruiting for cult

I met Diane at a dinner party held by a mutual friend. When she found out I was an expert on deceptive mind control groups, she had a lot of questions to ask me.

DIANE: My employer and mentor, Mary, has told me it's vital that I spend the next two weekends at a "Transformational Seminar." Two beautiful fall weekends in a stuffy hotel ballroom. What could they possibly say that would hold my interest? Mary keeps repeating, "You're going to love it! I guarantee it will change your life for the better." What do you think, Steve?

SH: A "Transformational Seminar" may have certain characteristics of a destructive mind control business cult.

DIANE: I don't have the extra $500 to cover the fee, but I have no choice. I don't want to offend my boss. I can't afford to lose my job!

SH: Going unprepared to one of these workshops is unwise. I'm afraid that you are not *adequately prepared to resist the recruitment and indoctrination procedures* that would be directed against you.

I can share with you the tools and resources you need to educate yourself. There are a lot of good articles about this group on the Internet. I can put you in touch with some former members. Then we'll figure out your best options. Unfortunately, you might need to find another job.

Case Ten: Wife joins cult and takes children with her

DAN: I'm trying to get prepared for a bitter custody battle. I am determined; I don't want my children to be infected by the bizarre practices of this guru cult my wife got herself into. I've read your book, and I want to ask you if you would be an expert witness for me.

SH: How long have you been married?

DAN: Nineteen years.

SH: How many children do you have?

DAN: Three. Two girls, twelve and fourteen, and a seventeen-year-old son.

SH: Do you love your wife?

DAN: Interesting that you should ask. I do. I still love her very much. After reading your book, I now know she has been the target of destructive mind control.

SH: Then you should probably work to rescue her. Are you pressing for divorce, or is she?

DAN: She is. As far as I can figure out, *her guru wants to get his hands on our property and savings.*

SH: What does your wife's family think of the involvement?

DAN: I haven't talked with them for several months. At first, when she got involved with the guru, they were horrified. Then my wife started telling them lies about our marriage. She told them that I was abusive and controlling.

SH: Were you?

DAN: I have a strong personality, but I was never abusive. This whole thing is a nightmare.

SH: Long-term relationships are usually pretty complicated anyway. When you factor in a "guru" and mind control, then things get immeasurably more complicated and difficult. But I believe if you *take it step by step*, we will figure out how you will be able to *build greater rapport and trust* with your wife and children. Have you ever written her a love poem or a love letter? Maybe you can tell her that you've changed your mind and don't want a divorce, that you love her and you want to go with her to see a marriage counselor. In the meantime, I think you will definitely want to try to *approach her family and get them involved.* Ideally, they should be the ones to initiate a Strategic Intervention, sidestepping the marital issues. But don't do anything yet. I need a lot more details before we arrive at a workable, long-term strategy.

These ten cases are just a small sampling of the people I have assisted in the past years. At first, many of the people I've helped were not sure whether their loved one was actually in a destructive mind control situation. If you read carefully, however, you can see underlying themes which tie all of these stories together.

COMMON CHARACTERISTICS OF A MIND CONTROL ENVIRONMENT

Manipulation
- exclusivity/isolation
- manipulation, deception, dependency and isolation
- all the other churches are dead and unspiritual
- demanding a one-over-one discipling relationship
- has turned his back on all his friends
- spending more and more time with the group
- secret meetings
- moved into the group's headquarters
- the cult member refuses to respond to letters and phone calls
- the family doesn't even know where their loved one is

Abuse of power

- psychological blackmail
- threatening prophecies
- gives group large sums of money
- the group will extract as much money as it can
- member's guru wants to get his hands on family property and savings
- the guru wanted to have sex with me

Creation of the cult identity

- I don't recognize my own bright, warm, loving son.
- controlled my behavior, my thoughts and my emotions
- a cult member is like an actor/ they actually come to believe the "role" is reality

If more than one of these characteristics sound familiar, there is a good chance that the group in question is a destructive cult. The chapters that follow will give you more specific criteria for evaluating the destructive potential of a group.

Many people feel overwhelmed and hopeless when they first realize that their loved one is in a cult. But I have found that once friends and family understand the Strategic Interaction Approach, this sense of helplessness is often replaced by confidence and hope for the cult member's future.

IMPORTANT ASPECTS OF THE STRATEGIC INTERACTION APPROACH

Real love is stronger than conditional love

- The fact that you are willing to help and are seeking professional advice shows me there is reason to hope.
- I love him.

Preparatory work: learning to think and act strategically

- The sooner you learn about destructive mind control techniques, cults, goal-oriented communication and Strategic Interaction therapy, the faster you will be able to make a positive difference in her life.

- Learn about cults and mind control and get the proper counseling.

- Get a clear understanding of what the issues are.

Goal-oriented communication

- Build greater rapport and trust.

- Step by step—that's the approach.

Resourcefulness

- Flexibility and teamwork.

- Approach her family and get them involved.

- There are many ways to reconnect seemingly lost relationships; each case is unique, and a customized strategy should be put into place.

The task of helping someone leave a destructive cult is more manageable when concerned friends and family work as a team to prepare themselves and plan a workable strategy. This strategy will be based on love, respect, resourcefulness, and, most importantly, a clear understanding of destructive mind control.

The following information form can be used by friends and family to assess their own resources and plan a course of action. Taking the time to think about your situation and writing down all your thoughts and feelings can be a therapeutic experience, and will help you relate your experiences to the information in this book. The form is also available on the Internet at: http:// www. freedomofmind.com

BACKGROUND INFORMATION FORM

Name of cult group (or other negative influence):
When did the mind control situation begin?
Describe chronology of involvement. If there were several different mind control influences, please detail on additional pages.

Individual Background

Name:
Age/Sex:
Physical attributes (height, weight, attractiveness, disabilities):
Individual's authentic identity: Who was this person prior to meeting the group? How did he/she think and act (intelligent, creative, optimistic, pessimistic, idealistic, cynical, spacey, a leader, a follower)?
What did he/she believe?
Did he/she have a well-formed political or social value system?
Did he/she have clear-cut life goals?
If not, what was he/she thinking about doing?
Motivational style[8] (moving toward positives/away from negatives):
What were the things that motivated him/her?
Who were the people that motivated him/her?
Myers-Briggs Type (extrovert/introvert, intuitive/sensing, thinking/feeling, judging/perceiving):
Educational experience:
Work/job experience:
What were his/her interests (sports, music, art, computers)? Hobbies? Skills?
What was his/her life like? Did he/she have high or low self-esteem? Please explain.
What was his/her religious experience, education and affiliation?
Spiritual, mystical experiences? Belief in psychics, telepathy, or UFOs?

Was he/she interested in community (Scouts, chorus, sports)?
Where did he/she grow up (city/rural/foreign country)?
Did the family move often? Dates, locations, impact?
Who were his/her close friends? Are they still in contact? If not, why not?
Did he/she feel a part of the family or extended family?
Did he/she have good communication skills? Able to express his/her thoughts or feelings? A good listener?
Was he/she ever abused emotionally, physically, sexually or psychologically?
Did he/she suffer any specific traumas (accidents, deaths, rape, beatings, divorce, expulsion from family)?
Was he/she under stress (breakup of relationship friend or close relative dying; parents divorcing; difficult or frequent moves)?
Did he/she use drugs? What kind? When? How much? How often?
Sexual identity (preference/experience)? Was he/she promiscuous?
Had he/she even been in psychotherapy? On medication?
What was his view of counselors/therapists/educators/authority figures?
What was his/her state of mind just before entering the group?

Family Background
Parents:
Name of father:
Name of mother:
Married? Divorced? Deceased? Remarried?
What does father/stepfather do for a living?
What does mother/stepmother do for a living?
Names and ages of siblings:
Current status of siblings (occupation, location, frequency of contact):
How is relationship between siblings?

Roles, favored/disfavored, special needs?

Describe patterns of relationships or lack of relationships within family:

Any history within family of violence, abuse, alcoholism or drug addiction?

During childhood, were parents away often?

What are parents' inherent resources (good communication skills, analytical, spiritual, effective organizer, good at following through on plans)?

What role models have the mother and father been?

What type of discipline has been used? Physical? Verbal? Has it been fair? Has it been consistent?

Communication patterns (interrupting one another, speaking for one another, indirect communication/triangulation):

Conflict resolution style: respectful communication with fair and balanced decision-making? rigid and authoritarian? frequent fights and volatility? avoidance of conflict?

Are there any non-family members (clergy, coach, teacher, employer) who are special to your loved one?

NOTE: Additional questions covering Course of Action are located at the end of chapter 4. A workbook to accompany this book is being developed.

Chapter 2

What is Destructive Mind Control?

When I was in the Moon cult, my friends and family told me time and time again that I had been "brainwashed," or that I was under "mind control." At the time, I thought "mind control" meant being handcuffed, tortured, and interrogated under bright lights, and I knew that hadn't happened to me. So, when people called me a "brainwashed robot," I thought they were just persecuting me for my beliefs, and their negative comments wound up reinforcing my commitment to the group. Like any member of a destructive cult, I needed to learn what mind control really is, and how it is used, before I could understand that I had been subjected to it.

During my deprogramming, Robert Jay Lifton's 1961 book *Thought Reform and the Psychology of Totalism*[1] provided me with my first frame of reference for understanding mind control. I was able to leave the Moonies because mind control had been defined for me in a way I could easily understand. In Chapter 22 of his book, Lifton identified eight criteria that distinguish the use of "thought-reform," or mind control: milieu control, mystical manipulation, the demand for purity, the cult of confession, sacred science, loading the language, doctrine over person, and the dispensing of existence. Lifton wrote that while many groups will exhibit some of these points, a group that demonstrates *all eight* criteria is using destructive mind control.

LIFTON'S EIGHT CRITERIA

1. **Milieu control**
   Control of environment and communication within that environment. This includes not only what people communicate with each other, but how the group gets inside a person's head and controls his internal dialogue.

2. **Mystical manipulation**
   The contrived engineering of experiences to stage seemingly spontaneous and "supernatural" events. Everyone manipulates everyone else for the higher purpose.

3. **The demand for purity**
   Establishing impossible standards for performance, thereby creating an environment of guilt and shame. No matter how hard a person tries, he always falls short, feels badly, and works even harder.

4. **The cult of confession**
   The destruction of personal boundaries, and the expectation that every thought, feeling, or action—past or present—that does not conform to the group's rules be shared or confessed. This information is not forgotten or forgiven but, rather, used to control.

5. **Sacred science**
   The belief that the group's dogma is absolutely scientific and morally true, with no room for questions or alternative viewpoints.

6. **Loading the language**
   The use of vocabulary to constrict members' thinking into absolute, black-and-white, "thought-terminating clichés" understood only by insiders.

7. **Doctrine over person**
   The imposition of group beliefs over individual experience, conscience, and integrity

8. **Dispensing of existence**
   The belief that people in the group have the right to exist and all ex-members and critics or dissidents do not.

UNDERSTANDING SOCIAL INFLUENCE PROCESSES

After World War II, many wondered how so many people — German citizens who had led ordinary lives before Hitler's rise to power — could have participated in mass genocide. Social psychologists began to research the various ways that individual thoughts, feelings, and behaviors can be influenced by the actual, imagined, or implied presence of others. The focus of social psychology is the individual within the group; it looks at how social forces affect various components of our identities. Literally thousands of social psychology experiments have been conducted in the past fifty years, some of them yielding great insights into our behaviors, beliefs, and motivations.[2]

When I returned to college, my classes in social psychology gave me a clearer understanding of how cults use social influence processes, such as group pressure and obedience to authority, to control their members. In the 1930s, an early social psychologist named Kurt Lewin explained about his "field theory," which described how behavior is related to both a person's personality and his environment:

> "Each person, in this view, is surrounded by a "life space" or dynamic field of forces within which his or her needs and purposes interact with the influences of the environment. Social behavior can be schematized in terms of the tension and interplay of these forces and of the individual's tendency to maintain equilibrium among them or to restore equilibrium when it has been disturbed."[3]

A Jewish refugee from Nazi dictatorship, Lewin was a passionate admirer of American democracy. He spent his career exploring group cohesiveness, group decision-making, the differences between authoritarian and democratic leadership, and techniques of attitude change and conflict resolution. These topics have all become central to any discussion of cult mind control. Lewin was also interested in how a person's attitudes are changed by his being a member of a group that reaches a collective decision, and how such a person will tend to hold fast to that decision while ignoring later information that conflicts with it. This work might have inspired his student, Leon Festinger, to formulate his "cognitive dissonance" theory, which, as you will learn, influenced my conception of cult mind control.

The power of social influence processes has since been demonstrated in thousands of studies. In 1971, Dr. Philip Zimbardo conducted a now-famous experiment on the social psychology of imprisonment. He and his colleagues took pains to make the prison experience seem as realistic as possible. Twenty-one middle-class, emotionally stable, mature, law-abiding student volunteers were divided into guards and prisoners. The experiment was supposed to last two weeks, but had to be aborted after only six days. One of the guards reported:

> "I was surprised at myself...I made them call each other names and clean out the toilets with their bare hands. I practically considered the prisoners cattle, and I kept thinking I have to watch out for them in case they try something."[4]

Within a few days, the prisoners had organized a rebellion. They tore off their ID numbers and barricaded themselves inside their cells. The guards sprayed them with a fire extinguisher, burst into their cells, stripped them, took away their beds, and thoroughly intimidated them. By the fifth day, one guard had written in his diary:

> "I have singled him [one prisoner] out for special abuse both because he begs for it and because I simply don't like him.... The new prisoner refuses to eat his sausage. I decided to force feed him but he wouldn't eat. I let the food slide down his face. I didn't believe it was me doing it. I hated myself for making him eat but I hated him more for not eating."[5]

Meanwhile, the prisoners had become humiliated and obsessed with the unfairness of their treatment. Zimbardo and his colleagues had not expected such a rapid transformation:

> "What was most surprising about the outcome of this simulated prison experience was the ease with which sadistic behavior could be elicited from quite normal young men and the contagious spread of emotional pathology among those carefully selected precisely for their emotional stability."[6]

This experiment, which lasted less than a week, demonstrates in a frightening way how much a person's identity depends on what role he is playing, how others treat the person, what uniforms or clothing the person wears, and so on. One can only imagine what might have happened had powerful mind control techniques been added, and for a longer period of time, as occurs in a cult involvement. Zimbardo's experiment also points to the dilemma articulated in 1957 by Vance Packard in *The Hidden Persuaders*: "When you are manipulating people, where do you stop? Who is to fix the point at which manipulative attempts become socially undesirable?"[7]

Zimbardo has since become one of the leaders in the study of mind control. I have been a guest speaker in his course at Stanford University called "The Psychology of Mind Control." It covers the broad area of social influence and offers comprehensive coverage of the principles, paradigms, theories, research methods, experiments and practical applications of mind control. The goals of Zimbardo's course are similar to the goals in this chapter. He writes:

> "We will try to understand how cults recruit members, indoctrinate them and shape their lives for noble religious deeds or ignoble secular ones. We will learn that there are no tricks or special gimmicks, only the systematic application of many techniques we have seen used and developed in other arenas of social influence — only more intensively over extended periods."[8]

Zimbardo taught me the single most important and universal rule of social psychology, the "fundamental attribution error." People consistently attribute other people's behaviors to their dispositions rather than to the environmental pressures on them. Especially in the United States where individuality is prized, people tend to assume that they act because it was "their idea" rather than because they have been influenced by outside forces. Social Psychology has demonstrated that everybody is deeply influenced by their environment. It is human nature to adapt to what is perceived to be "correct" behavior.

WHAT IS MIND CONTROL?

At first, many people think of mind control as an ambiguous, mystical process that cannot be defined in concrete terms. In reality, mind control refers to a specific set of methods and techniques, such as hypnosis or thought stopping, that influence how a person thinks, feels, and acts. Like many bodies of knowledge, it is not inherently good or evil. If mind control techniques are used to empower an individual to have more choice, and authority for his life remains within himself, the effects can be beneficial. For example, benevolent mind control can be used to help people quit smoking without affecting any other behavior. Mind control becomes destructive when it is used to undermine a person's ability to think and act independently.

As employed by the most destructive cults, mind control seeks nothing less than to disrupt an individual's authentic identity — behavior, thoughts, emotions—and reconstruct it in the image of the cult leader. This is done by rigidly controlling the member's physical, intellectual, emotional, and spiritual life. A person's uniqueness and creativity are suppressed. Cult mind control is a social process that encourages obedience, dependence, and conformity. It discourages autonomy and individuality by immersing recruits in an environment that represses free choice. The group's dogma becomes the person's only concern. Anything or anyone that does not fit into his reshaped reality is irrelevant.

MIND CONTROL OR BRAINWASHING?

The term "brainwashing," coined in 1951 by journalist Edward Hunter, is often used as a synonym for mind control.[9] Hunter translated the word from the Chinese *hsi nao*, "wash brain", to describe the process by which Americans captured in the Korean War could suddenly reverse their allegiance and confess to fictional war crimes. How was it possible that, weeks after being captured, trained military personnel would confess to crimes they never committed, be content in their incarceration, and adopt entirely new belief systems? In the 1950s, military psychologists and psychiatrists Margaret Singer, Robert Lifton, Louis West and Edgar Schein were sent to research thought reform and devise ways to protect soldiers from it in the future.

Like Lifton, Edgar Schein turned to the brainwashing programs in China. His book *Coercive Persuasion*, which he based on interviews with former American prisoners, mirrored Lifton's thoughts that physical coercion seemed to be an important feature of "brainwashing."[10] However, Lifton later came to believe that thought reform could in fact be accomplished without physical coercion or violence.[11]

As senior psychologist at Walter Reed Army Hospital in the 1950s, Margaret Singer studied the effects of thought reform on Korean War Prisoners. Singer, who has gone on to do pioneering work in the field of cult mind control, summarizes fifty years of her work on thought reform processes in her book *Cults in Our Midst*.[12] She lays out six conditions for thought reform.

SINGER'S SIX CONDITIONS FOR THOUGHT REFORM

1. Gaining control over a person's time, especially his thinking time and physical environment.

2. Creating a sense of powerlessness, fear and dependency in the recruit, while providing models that demonstrate the new behavior that leadership wants to produce.

3. Manipulating rewards, punishments and experiences in order to suppress the recruit's former social behavior and attitudes, including the use of altered states of consciousness to manipulate experience.

4. Manipulating rewards, punishments and experiences in order to elicit the behavior and attitudes that leadership wants.

5. Creating a tightly controlled system with a closed system of logic, wherein those who dissent are made to feel as though their questioning indicates that there is something inherently wrong with them.

6. Keeping recruits unaware and uninformed that there is an agenda to control or change them. Leadership cannot carry out a thought-reform program with a person's full capacity and informed consent.

For me, some of the key differences between "brainwashing" and mind control, or thought reform, are as follows: The term "brainwashing" is often associated in people's minds with overtly coercive behaviors, exemplified by the image of a prisoner at the hands of abusive jailers. At the beginning of a "brainwashing" process, the subject looks at the "agents of influence" as the "enemy," and is forced to comply with them.

With mind control, the "agents of influence" are viewed as friends or mentors, which cause people to lower their defenses, making them more vulnerable to manipulation. The key to mind control's success lies in its subtlety, the way it promotes the "illusion of control." The individual believes he is "making his own choices," when in fact he has been socially influenced to disconnect his own critical mind and decision-making capacity. In other words, he believes that he has freely chosen to surrender his free will to God or to a leader or ideology. When one steps back and objectively evaluates the vast amount of social influence used to get him to "surrender," the degree of manipulation becomes very obvious.

COGNITIVE DISSONANCE THEORY AND THE EVOLUTION OF THE BITE MODEL

In 1950, psychologist Leon Festinger summarized the basic principle of his cognitive dissonance theory: "If you change a person's behavior, his thoughts and feelings will change to minimize the dissonance."[13] As Festinger described, "dissonance" is the psychological tension that arises when a person's behavior conflicts with his beliefs. Like hunger, this tension is an uncomfortable state that drives people to take measures to reduce it. People prefer that their behavior, thoughts, and emotions be mutually consistent, and can tolerate only a certain amount of discrepancy between these three components of their identities. Psychological research has shown that if any of the three components changes, the other two will shift to reduce the cognitive dissonance. This tendency can manifest itself in several different ways. For example:

- When people behave in ways they see as either stupid or

immoral, they change their attitudes in order to believe that their behavior is sensible and justified.

• People who hold opposing views are apt to interpret the same news reports or factual material about the disputed subject quite differently — each sees and remembers what supports his views, but glosses over and forgets what would create dissonance.

• When people who think of themselves as reasonably humane are in a situation where they hurt innocent people, they reduce the resulting dissonance by marginalizing or "putting down" their victims.

• There is a human inclination to reduce cognitive dissonance by rationalization.

In 1956, Festinger wrote *When Prophecy Fails*, a book about a Wisconsin "flying saucer" cult. The leader, Mrs. Keech, said she was receiving messages sent by a superior "Guardian" from the planet "Clarion." She reported to the press that on December 21, there would be a great flood and all except a chosen few would perish. Her followers sold their homes, gave away their money, and waited for the spaceships.

When morning came — with no saucers and no flood — one might think the followers would have become disillusioned. But when Mrs. Keech proclaimed that the alien had witnessed their faithful vigil and decided to spare the Earth, most members wound up feeling more committed to her in spite of the public humiliation. According to Festinger, the reason for this renewed commitment is that the cult members' feelings and thoughts had changed to reduce the dissonance created by their behavior.

Cognitive dissonance theory gave me a more formal, structured way of thinking about mind control. Of course, cognitive dissonance theory is a gross simplification of a highly complex phenomenon. I am sure that in the future, there will be even better scientific theories to help explain this phenomenon.

The Evolution of the BITE model

There are three components to Festinger's theory—control of behavior, control of thoughts, and control of emotions. Each component can be affected by the other two. It is by manipulating these three elements that cults gain control over a person's identity. Through my experience working with former cult members, I have identified a fourth component that is equally important—control of information. When you control the information that a person is allowed to receive, you limit his capacity for independent thought. These four factors, which can be more easily remembered as BITE[14] (Behavior, Information, Thoughts, and Emotions), will serve as the foundation for your understanding of mind control.

THE BITE MODEL

I. Behavior Control
1. Regulation of individual's physical reality
   a. Where, how, and with whom the member lives and associates
   b. What clothes, colors, hairstyles the person wears
   c. What food the person eats, drinks, adopts, and rejects
   d. How much sleep the person is able to have
   e. Financial dependence
   f. Little or no time spent on leisure, entertainment, vacations
2. Major time commitment required for indoctrination sessions and group rituals
3. Need to ask permission for major decisions
4. Need to report thoughts, feelings, and activities to superiors
5. Rewards and punishments (behavior modification techniques—positive and negative)
6. Individualism discouraged; "group think" prevails
7. Rigid rules and regulations

THE BITE MODEL (continued)

II. Information Control
    1. Use of deception
        a. Deliberately holding back information
        b. Distorting information to make it more "acceptable"
        c. Outright lying
    2. Access to non-cult sources of information minimized or discouraged
        a. Books, articles, newspapers, magazines, TV, radio
        b. Critical information
        c. Former members
        d. Keep members so busy they don't have time to think and check things out
    3. Compartmentalization of information; Outsider vs. Insider doctrines
        a. Information is not freely accessible
        b. Information varies at different levels and missions within pyramid.
    4. Spying on other members is encouraged
        a. Pairing up with "buddy" system to monitor and control
        b. Reporting deviant thoughts, feelings, and actions to leadership
        c. Individual behavior monitored by whole group.
        d. Leadership decides who "needs to know" what and when
    5. Extensive use of cult generated information and propaganda
        a. Newsletters, magazines, journals, audio tapes, video-tapes, and other media
        b. Misquotations, statements taken out of context from non-cult sources
    6. Unethical use of confession
        a. Information about "sins" used to abolish identity boundaries
        b. Past "sins" used to manipulate and control; no forgiveness or absolution
    7. Need for obedience and dependency

THE BITE MODEL (continued)

III. Thought Control
  1. Need to internalize the group's doctrine as "Truth"
    a. Adopting the group's map of reality as "Reality" (Map = Reality)
    b. Black-and-White thinking
    c. Good vs. Evil
    d. Us vs. Them (inside vs. outside)
  2. Use of "loaded" language (for example, "thought-terminating clichés"). Words are the tools we use to think with. These "special" words constrict rather than expand understanding and can even stop thoughts altogether. They function to reduce complexities of experience into trite, platitudinous "buzz words."
  3. Only "good" and "proper" thoughts are encouraged.
  4. Use of hypnotic techniques to induce altered mental states
  5. Manipulation of memories and implantation of false memories
  6. Use of thought-stopping techniques, which shut down "reality testing" by stopping "negative" thoughts and allowing only "good" thoughts
    a. Denial, rationalization, justification, wishful thinking
    b. Chanting
    c. Meditating
    d. Praying
    e. Speaking in "tongues"
    f. Singing or humming
  7. Rejection of rational analysis, critical thinking, constructive criticism. No critical questions about leader, doctrine, or policy seen as legitimate
  8. No alternative belief systems viewed as legitimate, good, or useful

THE BITE MODEL (continued)

IV. Emotional Control
  1. Manipulate and narrow the range of a person's feelings
  2. Make the person feel that if there are ever any problems, it is always his fault, never the leader's or the group's
  3. Excessive use of guilt
      a. Identity guilt
          1. Who you are (not living up to your potential)
          2. Your family
          3. Your past
          4. Your affiliations
          5. Your thoughts, feelings, actions
      b. Social guilt
      c. Historical guilt
  4. Excessive use of fear
      a. Fear of thinking independently
      b. Fear of the "outside" world
      c. Fear of enemies
      d. Fear of losing one's "salvation"
      e. Fear of leaving the group or being shunned by group
      f. Fear of disapproval
  5. Extremes of emotional highs and lows
  6. Ritual and often public confession of "sins"
  7. Phobia indoctrination: inculcating irrational fears about ever leaving the group or even questioning the leader's authority. The person under mind control cannot visualize a positive, fulfilled future without being in the group.
      a. No happiness or fulfillment outside of the group
      b. Terrible consequences will take place if you leave: hell, demon possession, incurable diseases, accidents, suicide, insanity, 10,000 reincarnations, etc.
      c. Shunning of leave takers; fear of being rejected by friends, peers, and family
      d. Never a legitimate reason to leave. From the group's perspective, people who leave are "weak," "undisciplined," "unspiritual," "worldly," "brainwashed by family or counselor," or "seduced by money, sex, rock and roll."

It is important to understand that destructive mind control can be determined when the overall effect of these four components promotes dependency and obedience to some leader or cause. It is not necessary for every single item on the list to be present. Mind-controlled cult members can live in their own apartments, have nine-to-five jobs, be married with children, and still be unable to think for themselves and act independently.

BEHAVIOR CONTROL

Behavior control is the incremental regulation of a person's physical reality, which includes both his environment (where he lives, who he associates with, what he eats, when he sleeps) and his conduct (tasks, rituals, and other activities). Behavior control comes in many forms, including sleep deprivation or manipulation, change of diet, invasion of privacy, separation from friends and other newcomers, and isolation for workshops or other indoctrination exercises.

Cults often impose an oppressive time schedule on their members' lives in order to control behavior. When members are not engaged in cult rituals and indoctrination activities, they are typically assigned specific goals that restrict their free time and behavior—anything to keep them busy. In a destructive cult, there is always work to be done.

Some extreme cults, like Heaven's Gate, control behavior by requiring members to rarely be alone, often having them together, eating, working, meeting, and sleeping, twenty-four hours a day. A former member of Heaven's Gate told me that Applewhite decided "how we lived, what we wore, how we cut our hair, what we ate, how we slept. We had all our funds in a group pot, all our time spent with the group."[15] The Bible-based cult, Twelve Tribes, employs all of the same tactics, only in the name of God.[16] To discourage individualism, members of some cults are assigned to a "buddy," discipling partner, or central figure who monitors their daily behavior. All of a cult's members are bound together by group rituals, which may include mannerisms such as speech, posture, or facial expression. In the Moonies, since Koreans were considered to be the master race, we were made to feel special when we sang Korean folk songs, ate kim chee (Korean pickled cabbage), bowed, or removed our shoes before entering a group center.

The pyramid-shaped structure of cults allows leaders to enforce a strict system of rewards and punishments for all behaviors. Obedience and good performance are rewarded with public praise, gifts, or promotions, while disobedience and poor performance are punished with criticism, demotions, or assignment of menial tasks like cleaning toilets.

One of the easiest ways to understand behavior control is to look at the difference between a legitimate church and a Bible cult. In a legitimate church, if your mother is sick or injured, you might go to the minister or pastor and say, "My mother is ill. I'm going to visit her in the hospital. Please say a prayer for her." In a Bible cult, you are expected to humbly approach the leader or sub-leader and ask, "Can I have permission to go visit my mother?" In the more destructive cults, the permission is often denied, or the person is told that their work in the group is more important. In the Moonies, whenever leaders didn't want members to get emotionally involved with their family, we were told to "Leave the dead to bury the dead." Of course, all outsiders were considered to be "spiritually" dead.

Other groups tell their members, "You can't choose your wife or husband; it has to be arranged," or "you have to get permission from the elders." If you fall in love with someone, it has to be a member of your group — and if you fall in love with someone who isn't in the group, then you will be expelled, excommunicated, or disfellowshipped. Cult members often have to ask permission to go to college, or to study a particular subject. In the case of the Jehovah's Witnesses, members are told not to celebrate birthdays or holidays, like Easter or Christmas, because if they do, they will be in sin. I know a woman who was excommunicated from the Jehovah's Witnesses because she sent a birthday card to a nonmember. Many cult members are not allowed to step foot inside a church because it's considered to be evil and a sin. When a cult tells members that they can't associate with former members, even with their best friends or members of their own families, it is using both behavior control and information control.

INFORMATION CONTROL

The human mind cannot function properly without information. By controlling both the flow of information and people's ability to process it, cults prevent them from making sound judgements about their own lives or the group's actions.

Information control begins during recruitment, when cults withhold or distort information to draw people in. People don't join cults—cults recruit people. People become involved with cults when they are:

- Approached by a friend or relative who is already a member.

- Approached by a stranger who befriends them (often a member of the opposite sex).

- Invited to a cult-sponsored event, such as a lecture, symposium, or movie.

- Enticed into buying a cult book advertised as a "best-seller."

- Invited to a seemingly harmless "Bible study" session.

- Curious about a personal or classified ad, flyer, or poster.

- Recruited when they take a job with a cult-owned business.

Very often, a person does not suspect he is being recruited. Perhaps a friend or relative has just had some incredible insights or experiences and wants to share them. If the recruiter is a stranger, more often than not the person believes he has made a new friend. But in reality, friendships don't form overnight; they take time to develop, with each person gradually sharing information in a balanced way. Cult recruiters are skilled at drawing information from people without revealing much about themselves or the group.

They don't tell people up front *who they are, what they believe, and what they want from them.*

By compartmentalizing information, cults keep members from seeing the big picture. People are given only the information they are deemed "ready for," or as much as they "need to know" to perform their jobs. Cult ideologies allow for many levels of "truth," including "outsider" and "insider" doctrines. The more moderate outsider material, which contains diluted versions of the group's beliefs, is given to the general public and new converts. Recruits who ask questions are often told that they are not yet mature enough to know the whole truth. Insider doctrines are reserved for people who are already thoroughly indoctrinated. In this way, assessments of cult doctrines are delayed until the recruit's ability to make them objectively is impaired.

A common form of information control involves blocking out any critical or negative points of view. Some cults simply forbid members to have access to any non-cult material — such as newspapers, magazines, television, radio, and the Internet — while others have more subtle ways of controlling information. For example, to restrict access on the Internet, Scientology provides software to members that automatically blocks access to sites by former members and critics.[17]

The control of information also includes the supervision of members' interactions with all other people. People are expected to spy on one another and report improper activities or comments, such as criticism of the leader, doctrine, or organization. This information, as well as anything divulged by a member during confession, is often used against people to manipulate them. Some cults have even wire-tapped telephones and intercepted letters to gain information that could be used to control former and present members.

Looking at a group's attitude towards information is the fastest way to evaluate whether it is using destructive mind control. A legitimate organization will allow people the freedom to think for themselves, read whatever they like, and talk to whomever they choose in order to arrive at their own decisions, whereas a destructive mind control group will want to do the thinking for people.

THOUGHT CONTROL

In a mind control cult, the group's doctrine is seen as absolute "Truth" and the only answer to people's problems. Cult doctrine teaches its members to think: "We are the way! We are the truth! You who are not in the group are lost. We know, and you do not know." It preaches black-and-white thinking, dividing the world into simplistic dichotomies—good versus evil, us versus them. The cult doctrine is reality. Believers have a hard time approaching the doctrine as a mere map or set of guidelines that are open to interpretation as well as alternatives.

Many cults have their own "loaded language" or coded symbols and expressions, including buzz words, clichés, and trite platitudes that are used to shut down the thought process. In the Moonies, whenever something went wrong, it was called "indemnity," which meant that you had to meet a spiritual condition to right a past wrong. If it rained while Moon was giving a lecture at Yankee Stadium, it was "indemnity" because America wasn't loving the Messiah enough. Words are the tools that we use for thinking. If you can control the words people use, you can control their thoughts.

In the majority of destructive cults, most of the techniques members learn are not taught directly or consciously, but rather through the process of behavioral modeling. They learn by watching older members, listening to the leader, and modeling themselves after their behavior. Eventually, they unconsciously pick up some of the leaders' behaviors, including speech patterns and gesticulations. When I was being taught how to lecture in the Moon group, I learned by attending countless lectures, observing, listening, and praying to God to let His spirit come into me so that I could be like the older brother who was teaching. Four years after I got out of the Moonies, I started learning more about hypnosis, and I realized I had been trained to use hypnotic processes without even knowing what hypnosis was. For example, I was taught that the eyes are the windows of the soul, and when you talk to people you should look at a point three inches behind their eyes. I later found out that this technique was actually a hypnotic induction pattern, called eye fixation, which can be used to produce an altered state of consciousness, or "trance," in other people. These unethical uses of hypnotic techniques can be used to confuse and disorient a person, thereby setting him up to become an obedient slave.

Although I am aware of several cult leaders specifically studying Neuro-Linguistic Programming (NLP), I suspect that most cult groups use informal hypnotic techniques to induce trance states.[18] They tend to use what are called "naturalistic" hypnotic techniques. Practicing meditation to shut down thinking, chanting a phrase repetitively for hours, or reciting affirmations are all powerful ways to promote spiritual growth. But they can also be used unethically, as methods for mind control indoctrination.

When a person enters a trance, the conscious, analytical mind is disengaged. The subconscious mind is engaged. Trance is not sleep, but focused attention. If you have the ability to focus your attention, then you can enter an altered state of consciousness. It is a gift to be able to shut out noise and distraction, but it can also be a liability if a cult recruiter is trying to influence you. When you're in a trance and someone with an ulterior motive or hidden agenda tries to indoctrinate you, you're that much more susceptible. In this very special state of relaxation, messages can easily take root in your subconscious. Some cults even use hypnosis to manipulate people's memories or implant false memories.

Cult members are taught that the leader is always correct, and are not allowed to doubt or question him or her. Thoughts that go along with the leader are good. Any other thoughts need to be pushed down by chanting, praying, or speaking in tongues. Any negative feelings are always blamed on the individual. Any disillusionment means the member is doing something wrong: "You are not really committing yourself to God," or "You are not meditating correctly." No room is left to say, "Maybe the leader is wrong," or "Maybe the doctrine misquotes the Bible." Consequently, the member's ability to reality-test is suppressed. If you can only think positively, you bury your bad thoughts and feelings. Meditation or prayer, used in an automatic way, can shut off critical thinking. Through a technique called "thought stopping," these ordinarily useful and valuable actions are programmed to become mechanical whenever the member feels doubt, anxiety, or uncertainty.

Thought stopping is a behavior modification technique that can be used ethically. It is currently being used successfully as a technique in behavior modification programs. People who are chronically depressed often have a running negative conversation with themselves: "I'm stupid." "Nobody cares about me." "Life stinks." Running over and over in their heads, these repetitious negative thoughts keep them locked in depression. When used in an ethical, therapeutic way, thought stopping substitutes positive thoughts for these negative ones: "I'm growing." "I'm getting better." In this case, there is no hidden agenda. The patient, not the therapist, is in control of the behavior modification.

In the Moonies, I was told thought stopping would help me grow spiritually, and allow me to remain centered and focused on God. I didn't know it was a mind control technique. I had been indoctrinated to believe that thinking negative thoughts would allow "evil spirits" to invade me. When someone would ask me, "Why does Moon have an M-16 gun factory?"[19] I would automatically start chanting in my head: "Glory to heaven, Peace on earth." Frequently, in many Bible-based cults, the "devil" or "satan" is the source of the member's doubts. Reciting scripture, speaking in tongues, and humming can be used to stop critical thinking.

From the point of view of a mind control cult, there is never a legitimate reason to leave. The only people who leave are weak, selfish, or cannot control their need for sex, drugs, or other addictive substances. In the mindset of the group, people who leave are incapable of sacrificing or transcending spiritually.

EMOTIONAL CONTROL

Nobody sets out to join a group with the intention of being deceived and manipulated. Most ex-members will tell you, "During the indoctrination process I had a voice inside of me saying, 'Be careful! Get the heck out of here!'" In order to achieve emotional control, the cult has to silence that voice.

Emotions tell us things we need to know. Emotional control diminishes that self-awareness by distorting and narrowing the range of a person's feelings. Cults gain control over members' emotions by keeping them off balance. On the one hand, most cults make people feel special by showering them with praise—a practice called "love bombing"—to encourage loyalty and devotion. On the other hand, they spend a lot of time and energy manipulating their members' sense of guilt and fear to make them dependent on the group. Anger, homesickness, and jealousy are called "selfish" feelings. Members are expected to always think of the group, and never feel for themselves.

Fear! Lots and lots of fear! Although the group's message starts out with love and idealism, once a person gets indoctrinated into the inner levels, his world becomes one of fear—fear that the planet is going to explode, fear of nuclear holocaust, fear that he will lose his spiritual connection, fear that he will be possessed by the devil. Cults instill fear to bind members to the group, to such an extent that members may become paranoid or phobic.

A phobia is an irrational fear reaction to someone or something. An intense phobic reaction can cause physical responses like racing heartbeat, dry mouth, sweating, and muscle tension. Although I will touch on the subject here, Chapter 10 describes in detail how cults practice systematic phobia indoctrination, and how you can unlock the phobias that prevent the member from believing he can ever be happy and successful outside the group.

Phobias often immobilize people and keep them from doing the things they truly want to do. Indeed, phobias can rob people of free choice, and in mind control cults, phobias are methodically implanted to keep members from feeling they can leave the group and be happy. For example, the Moonies tell members that ten generations of their ancestors are stuck in the spirit world and are depending on them for salvation. If they don't do what the leadership tells them, all of their relatives in the spirit world will accuse them throughout eternity of lacking faith and betraying the Messiah. In the Jehovah's Witnesses, a person can have a severe phobia against merely walking into a church building. I remember hearing about an incident involving a young Jehovah's Witness who refused to participate in an emergency evacuation from a public school into a church. The ten-year-old boy absolutely would not enter the building, and had to be carried in crying and screaming, because he thought the church was filled with "devils."[20]

I've encountered people whose pre-existing phobias were used against them in a cult. During her childhood, one woman had been locked in a closet with a rat. When she got involved with a cult group, she was told that if she ever betrayed the leader, she would be trapped in a room with 10,000 rats with no way out for eternity. I once met a former Hare Krishna member who was told that if he ever left the group, he would suffer 10,000 reincarnations as a roach or a flea. Since I was raised in a Jewish family, the Moonies told me that 6 million Jews had died in the Holocaust to pay for the indemnity of the "sin" of failing to accepting Jesus as their savior. These horrible deaths, they said, set the foundation for Moon, the Messiah, to come again — and if I didn't follow Moon, all of these people would be angry and accuse me for the rest of eternity.

Control of behavior, information, thoughts, and emotions—on their own, each has the potential to significantly alter a person's identity. When all forms of control are used, the effect is much more extreme. The BITE model is a guideline for identifying and understanding aspects of mind control. Most destructive groups do not use all of the criteria I mentioned. A group that changes names, insists on a dress code, lives on an isolated compound, and cuts off contact with all outsiders is likely to be more dangerous than a group that does not. But what matters most is the overall impact on a particular individual, on his free will and ability to think independently.

Keep in mind, the BITE model exists on a continuum and characteristics can range from slight to very intense among groups. Also, the degree of mind control can vary greatly within a particular group. Someone at the widest ends of the pyramid, and, especially, fringe members, will usually experience much less control than someone at the core. I look at the core membership of an organization, not its fringe members, in my evaluation. For example, the Transcendental Meditation (TM) organization fits the BITE model although most TMers are on the fringe—they pay their money, are initiated and receive their "private" mantra, practice the 15-minute TM technique twice a day, and go no further.[21] Those who go on to advanced courses meditate for hours each day, learn to "fly," go to Maharishi International University, and come to view their Master as the only enlightened being on Earth, surely fit the mind control model.

Although influence processes are evident in virtually all aspects of modern life, constructive influences can easily be differentiated from destructive ones. In a benevolent group, influence processes are positive and ethical and the locus of control remains within the individual. Influence is used only to promote independent thinking and decision-making, self-awareness, and self-control. Individuality, creativity, and free will are respected and promoted. People recognize and understand the influences around them. Access to diverse information sources is encouraged.

In a destructive cult, the locus of control shifts to the group or its leader. The new recruit abdicates his ability to make decisions. A pseudo-identity is created which suppresses the authentic self and surrenders control.[22] Individuality is submerged, and free will subverted. People are kept in the dark, and the very processes that influence them are made to seem mystical or spiritual. Access to any contravening information is cut off.

CREATION OF THE CULT IDENTITY

Cults consistently manipulate the elements that form an individual's identity, including important beliefs, values, and relationships. Cult mind control dissociates a person from his authentic identity, and makes his new cult identity dependent on the group. From a mental health perspective, cult mind control splits elements of an individual's psyche into another distinct personality. The cult member actually comes to exhibit symptoms of a "dissociative disorder," as defined in the diagnostic manual for the American Psychiatric Association (300.15) the DSM-IV.[23] His behavior can also resemble that of a person with a dependent personality disorder.

One of the universal concerns of family and friends is their loved one's radical personality change. In order to be a good cult member, your loved one is taught how to manipulate and suppress his old self. The make-over often includes a new name, new clothes, new hair style, new manner of speech, new mannerisms, a new "family," new "friends," new thoughts, new emotions, and a new relationship with God.

Cult involvement seems to pull much of the common ground out from under family members, friends and their loved one. When you are talking to someone in a mind control cult, it is especially difficult to talk on a rational level. They are operating according to a different set of criteria than what makes sense to you in your model of reality. The use of destructive mind control techniques calls into question the very nature of any shared reality. After I joined the Moonies, my family and friends really didn't understand how the cult dismantled, or "unfroze," my personality. It was perfectly obvious to them that something was changing me into a person they did not recognize. By the time I "refroze" into the cult identity, they could no longer communicate with me in the ways they had previously.

The most common method for shaping a cult identity is pairing a new member with an older member. The "spiritual child" is instructed to imitate the "spiritual parent" in all ways — even to the point of mimicking the tone of the leader's voice. The cult identity is, essentially, a clone of the cult leader. During my every waking moment — and especially under trance — I was being instructed to be a "small Sun Myung Moon." I wanted to think like him, act like him, feel like him, talk like him, and walk like him. The Bible cult, The International Church of Christ, encourages an intense imitation of one's leaders in its practice of "one-over-one discipling." This modeling technique serves several purposes. It keeps the "spiritual mentor" on his best behavior. It also whets the new member's appetite to become a respected model so he can train junior members of his own.

After I left the Moonies, I found Edgar Schein's book, *Coercive Persuasion*, extremely useful in understanding how cults impose a new identity on their members.[24] Schein described the mind control process by using Kurt Lewin's model of thought reform:

- Unfreezing: the process of breaking a person down
- Changing: the indoctrination process
- Refreezing: the process of reinforcing the new identity

I have adapted and expanded Kurt Lewin's three-stage model as described in *Coercive Persuasion*.

**THE THREE STAGES OF GAINING
CONTROL OF THE MIND**

I. Unfreezing
    a. Disorientation/confusion
    b. Sensory deprivation and/or sensory overload
    c. Physiological manipulation
        1. Sleep deprivation
        2. Privacy deprivation
        3. Change of diet
    d. Hypnosis
        1. Age regression
        2. Visualizations
        3. Storytelling and metaphors
        4. Linguistic double binds, use of suggestion
        5. Meditation, chanting, praying, singing
    e. Get the person to question self-identity
    f. Redefine individual's past (implant false memories, forget positive memories of the past)

THE THREE STAGES OF GAINING
CONTROL OF THE MIND (continued)

II. Changing
    a. Creation and imposition of new "identity," done step by step
        1. Formally within indoctrination sessions
        2. Informally by members, tapes, books, etc.
    b. Use of Behavior Modification techniques
        1. Rewards and punishments
        2. Use of thought stopping techniques
        3. Control of environment
    c. Mystical manipulation
    d. Use of hypnosis and other mind-altering techniques
        1. Repetition, monotony, rhythm
        2. Excessive chanting, praying, decreeing, visualizations
    e. Use of confession and testimonials, individual studies, group activities

III. Refreezing
    a. New identity reinforced, old identity surrendered
        1. Separate from the past; decrease contact or cut off friends and family
        2. Give up meaningful possessions and donate assets
        3. Start doing cult activities: recruit, fundraise, move in with members
    b. New name, new clothing, new hairstyle, new language, new "family"
    c. Pairing up with new role models, buddy system
    d. The indoctrination continues: workshops, retreats, seminars

---

As I looked back at my involvement with the Moonies, Lewin's three terms, unfreezing, changing, and refreezing, struck a chord in me. When I was first recruited, I experienced a meltdown of my personality. During indoctrination, I underwent a radical personality change. When my identity refroze, it was as if I had become a clone of our leader, Sun Myung Moon.

This aspect of cult indoctrination was scientifically demonstrated by Dr. Flavil Yeakley, a well-respected psychologist and a member of the mainline Church of Christ. He administered the Myers-Briggs Personality Type Inventory Test to 800 members of The Boston Church of Christ, a cult group led by Kip McKean. At that time, this cult was trying to recruit members of the mainline Church of Christ. I suppose the leaders agreed to participate because they may have thought they could gain credibility with the two-million-member mainline Church of Christ churches.

The Myers-Briggs Inventory describes sixteen basic personality types. Whatever your type, it should remain the same throughout your lifetime. The major categories are Introvert/Extrovert, Sensing/Intuitive, Feeling/Thinking, and Judging/Perceiving. A questionnaire is filled out that reveals a person's preferences and disposition. For example, Extroverts are outgoing and feel comfortable with others. Introverts prefer to be with books, computers, and by themselves. People who are more Sensing are more practical (realistic), while Intuitives can be described as more innovative (following hunches). Other categories are Thinking (making objective, impersonal judgments) and Feeling (emotional, personal). Those who are considered to be Perceiving tend to keep things open ended and wait until the last minute to make a decision, while those who are deemed Judging like to reach closure quickly by choosing as soon as possible.

Yeakley did something that was very creative. He had the members fill out the Personality Type Inventory Test three times. They were instructed to:

1. Answer each question the way they would have before they joined the group;

2. Fill it out as present members of the group; and

3. Fill it out projecting five years into the future.

When Yeakley correlated the data of the first test, he found that before members joined the group, they varied widely in their personality types.[25] In the second test, the members were all moving towards the same personality type. They were beginning to match the personality type of the cult leader of The Boston Church of Christ.[26] The third test showed an almost universal move toward the leader's personality type. As a comparison group, Yeakley administered this test to members of Roman Catholic, Baptist, Lutheran, Methodist and Presbyterian churches and mainline Churches of Christ. There was no personality change before, during, or after they joined their churches. Yeakley published the results of this study in his book *The Discipling Dilemma*, which is available free on the Internet. [27]

Everyone has an authentic self. Although a healthy individual will grow and mature over time, his personality type should never change. Changes in personality type often indicate unhealthy social pressure that forces a person to act as if he were someone else. The results of Yeakley's study showed that cults create this kind of pressure. It also verified the existence of a cult identity which binds and gags the authentic self like a strait jacket. In my opinion, Yeakley statistically demonstrated the effects of destructive mind control techniques.

When interacting with your loved one, it is essential that you recognize the differences between the pre-cult identity (before recruitment), the cult identity (during membership), and the person's authentic self, which stays with them forever. Even people who are born into cults have an authentic self that was suppressed at birth. It is the strength of the authentic self that makes it possible to rescue people from cults years, even decades, after becoming involved with the group. When informed family and friends begin working as a team to educate their loved one about mind control, the walls erected by the cult identity will begin to crumble.

Chapter 3

The Strategic Interaction Approach

Ever since destructive cults first came to the attention of the public in the late 1960s, families have looked for ways to rescue their loved ones. Early rescue methods, represented by the deprogramming model, were unsophisticated and sometimes illegal. Over the past thirty years, counseling techniques and research in social psychology have evolved to give us more specialized and effective tools to help break the chains of cult mind control.

It has been over twelve years since I first published *Combatting Cult Mind Control*. Over time, I have assessed which approaches were effective and which were ineffective. As new patterns have emerged, my counseling has become more refined. This book brings together all of my knowledge into a unified, detailed, and user-friendly method, the Strategic Interaction Approach (SIA).

One of the biggest lessons I have learned is that when a loved one enters a cult, the entire family system is impacted. Parents are often consumed with guilt, fear, anger, and frustration. Long term successful marriages can buckle under the strain. Siblings, too, find themselves deeply impacted. Siblings who had very good relationships may feel annoyed when pressured by their loved one to join the cult, and even angry and upset when they are labeled evil for refusing. If there were existing problems, such as jealousy, mistrust or control issues, or trouble with communication and intimacy, a real quagmire can result. At the very least, most siblings feel frustration and anger as they see the pain the cult member is causing their family. As the weeks, months, and years go by, family members often struggle to maintain any hope for a positive future.

The first step in the SIA is to promote change and encourage growth and learning in the family, as well as in the cult member. Only then is it possible to create the conditions that will motivate the cult member to step away from the group and to begin questioning his cult involvement. A crucial belief of the approach is that the individual experiencing mind control will eventually break free. Because the only variables are time and ease of exit, you should do everything you can to make the process fast and easy.

JIM M. AND RAMA

One case that best illustrates the Strategic Interaction Approach involves a young man named Jim M. (not his real name) who had joined a quasi-Buddhist computer cult founded by the late Frederick Lenz, or "Rama." Jim's mother contacted me to ask for help, and I spent time talking with her so that I could get to know the family better. I learned that Jim's parents were divorced, and that both had since remarried. I soon realized that Jim's father would be an important asset in reaching out to him. Initially, Jim's mother was reluctant to contact her ex-husband. After meeting with me, her new husband, and Jim's brother Doug, she agreed to allow Doug to speak with his father. Doug asked his father to read my book *Combatting Cult Mind Control* and set up a meeting with him and his new wife.

This case demonstrates the value of bringing together a broad array of resources. Coincidentally, the father's new wife was a practicing Buddhist and was finishing her doctorate at a university in Boston. With her personal knowledge of Buddhism, she was able to provide Jim with a frame of reference for comparing Lenz's philosophy with legitimate Buddhist teachings, such as the Four Noble Truths and the Eightfold Path. When I found out that Jim's brother Doug was taking drum lessons from a former long-term member of the Rama cult, I asked Doug to approach the drum teacher, find out why he had left the group, and ask for his help.

Since Jim had always enjoyed the outdoors, we encouraged several of his closest childhood friends to go camping with him, sing songs, reminisce, and begin to raise questions about why Jim wanted to drop out of college, move to New York, and study computers —a field that he wasn't interested in until he got involved with Lenz. Jim also agreed to join his father on a camping trip. The idea was to have everybody doing various tasks, having specific conversations, and interacting with Jim from different angles.

What followed was a series of interactions between Jim and all of the family members and friends. The culmination was a meeting between Jim and the drum teacher. The drum teacher told Jim about several disillusioning experiences he had with the Rama group, such as spending large amounts of money on Lenz's courses and learning that Lenz was having sex with many of his female followers, including one of the drummer's ex-girlfriends. Finally, on the morning of the proposed camping trip with his father, Jim was asked to meet with me and some former members. He readily agreed.

Because we had done so much preparation work and built rapport and trust during mini-interactions, it quickly became apparent that the core issue for Jim was his belief that he had "spiritual" experiences, such as seeing a golden light emanating from Lenz and filling the room. I explained that hallucinations like these are often the result of easily reproducible hypnotic processes that have very little to do with being spiritual. Jim said, "Prove it." So I was forced to demonstrate this hypnotic effect for him. I asked him to close his eyes and meditate, as he had been doing for months as a student of Lenz. Once I saw his facial muscles relax, I added, "You're going to meditate even deeper than you have ever done before, and I don't want you to open your eyes until you're ready to see an even brighter light emanating from me." We waited less than a minute, and when he opened his eyes, he looked at me and said, "Whoa! That's brighter than the light I saw coming from Lenz! That's it — I'm out!" Everyone in the room breathed a sigh of relief, and Jim immediately added, "There are a number of people I want to share this information with, so I can get them out of the group too."

As Jim's family learned, the SIA creates many options by drawing on the resources, skills, and knowledge of everyone involved. The SIA is a hands-on approach that encourages friends and family to make progress one step at a time through what I call "mini-interactions"—phone calls, letters, or face-to-face visits. This was not the case with deprogramming or exit-counseling, which relied too heavily on setting up a formal, three-day intervention. Although you will be using the Strategic Interaction Approach, I want you to understand these older rescue models so that you will know what types of behavior to avoid when interacting with your loved one.

WHAT IS DEPROGRAMMING?

In the early 1970s, Ted Patrick[1], a man with plenty of street smarts but at the time, no formal training in counseling, believed that members of his family were being brainwashed by Moses David Berg, the leader of a group called the Children of God, now known as "The Family."[2] Patrick was determined to take action. He reasoned that since cults use indoctrination methods that "program" beliefs through hypnosis, repetition, and behavior modification techniques, he would reverse the process. He called the new procedure "deprogramming." We have since learned that the deprogramming model is too simplistic. An individual's mind and psyche cannot be programmed or deprogrammed like a computer.

A human being is not a robot.

Deprogramming is essentially a content-oriented persuasion approach that sometimes involves abduction and typically involves forced detention.[3] The actual deprogramming takes place when it is deemed possible to "pick up" the cult member, and when it is convenient for the deprogrammer. Typically, the cult member is driven to a secret location where he is guarded twenty-four hours a day. He often has no privacy, even in the bathroom. Windows are sometimes nailed shut so the cult member cannot escape. The deprogramming continues for days, and sometimes weeks, until the cult member snaps out of the cult's mind control or until he successfully pretends to do so.

A deprogramming triggers the deepest fears of cult members. They have been taken against their will. Family and friends are not to be trusted. The trauma of being thrown into a van by unknown people, driven away, and imprisoned creates mistrust, anger, and resentment. Cult members are convinced that these people are the embodiment of evil.

Deprogramming has many drawbacks. I have met dozens of people who were successfully deprogrammed but, to this day, experience psychological trauma as a result of the method. These people were glad to be released from the grip of cult programming but were not happy about the method used to help them.[4]

Professional counselor Cathleen Mann underwent a horrifying experience in 1990, while doing graduate research in psychology, which she wrote about in a letter to me.[5] A trusted professor had suggested that she do a participant-observer research project on the leader of the Church Universal and Triumphant (CUT), Elizabeth Clare Prophet. Cathleen studied the teachings of the group for a year, and not once was it suggested that the group was a cult, or even that it was controversial. She applied for membership in the group's Keepers of the Flame fraternity, in an attempt to better understand the teachings and methodology of the group. She met personally with Prophet at the group's headquarters in Montana, and she was strongly influenced by the charismatic woman. Little did Cathleen know that she would be subjected to mind control methods that could dismantle her critical faculties and indoctrinate her into higher levels of commitment to the group. She abandoned her research project shortly after the first meeting with Mrs. Prophet. She even agreed to consider moving onto the cult ranch. Concerned about her welfare and her changed personality, friends intervened and she was deprogrammed. She writes:

"One bright, crisp day around noon, I was sitting in my CUT-owned and regulated residence, when the door burst open. A trusted friend aiding the deprogrammers grabbed my clothes, stuffing them into a bag, picked up all the books and video tapes (given to me by Mrs. Prophet) stacked five feet high, and placed them in a waiting car. I struggled and argued with him, but he was forceful and literally dragged me to the car, which then drove off CUT property and down Montana Highway 89. At the time, I did *not* want to leave this group. I had already made the decision to stay if I could manage it, sacrificing my original intention to just conduct interviews.

I remember fighting and screaming for him to stop and listen to me, but he didn't care what I said. Much of what happened next was a blur. We arrived at a friend's house first. I was taken to another location, and there were two more people there, one allegedly a psychologist. While riding in the car, I remember trying to sleep, but I was jolted awake with unfamiliar voices and sounds, unfamiliar surroundings—I kept seeing Mrs. Prophet's face on everyone— and I believed that she must have been watching all of this. I remember thinking that she was there—taking notes on what I felt and thought, as she had done diligently in the past. I was psychologically devastated, and tried to avoid talking. I was still enthralled (but confused) about the whole experience with the group, and I thought I should refuse to cooperate with this embarrassing and humiliating process. I did not realize what had happened to me. During my stay on the cult property, I was completely shocked by what I saw and experienced, even though I had attempted to prepare myself in advance.

These deprogrammers set off to work immediately. They pulled out a picture of Mrs. Prophet and told me she was a cult leader and that I needed to spit on the picture. I refused. They called her names. One time they called her a profane name, and then laughed amongst themselves. I was not laughing. They played videotaped interviews of ex-CUT members and forced me to agree with them. They told me I had been part of a "demonic, occult force" and that I needed to come to terms with the fact that I might have "permanent damage." The psychologist told me that I "probably had Multiple Personality Disorder induced by the cult."

This persisted for several hours. They insulted my intelligence, my integrity, and my ability to choose what was best for me. They took away my rights as a person, and utilized very intrusive techniques that disoriented me, just like I had experienced with CUT.

It didn't take long for them to convince me that CUT was a cult. I already knew at some level that the CUT teachings were "silly" and probably not true. I had *not* been allowed to make an informed choice with proper information from the moment I entered Mrs. Prophet's presence. I would have figured out the inconsistencies and abuse on my own if I had remained in CUT much longer—or I would have soon come at odds with Mrs. Prophet and would have been a kick-out anyway. But, this was not what mattered to me. What these deprogrammers did was attempt to change my mind through *information control*—just like the cult did. They did not deal with the CUT-implanted phobias, which remained with me for years — the fear of certain colors, the identification of certain types of music with CUT rituals, the fear of retaliation and probable death should I ever leave this group.

Steve, if your approach had been used instead, I could have retained my self-respect and come to the realization myself that I had been duped. For months, even years, I beat myself up — "How could I have let this happen?" I could have retained my own sense of intelligence and the ability to use rational thought. What these deprogrammers did not realize, nor show any concern about, was that I had significant doubts during my time in CUT — this was not acknowledged or even considered. I was the "victim" to them, and that's all they understood or acknowledged. Even though I was "out," I went back to the teachings on and off for another year after the deprogramming. Finally, I couldn't take the inconsistencies any more, and I made the final break, discarding most of my CUT material into the trash can.

How much I wish that I would have had only one trauma to overcome in counseling later; instead, I had two — both traumatic, both disrespectful, both damaging. In both experiences, *me* the person was ignored for the agendas of others."

In the 1970's, there was really no option but deprogramming. In the 1980's, and especially the early 1990's, fewer deprogrammings occurred and exit-counseling became the preferred approach. Deprogramming is currently illegal in the United States if the person is over the age of eighteen. Predictably, in the event of a failure, criminal charges can be pressed against the family and the deprogrammers. Legal bills can become astronomical. The toll of a deprogramming failure can be particularly catastrophic to the loved one. Cult doctrine is reinforced. Relationships with family members are typically strained and family and friends can be devastated.

Cathleen's deprogramming experience caused her unnecessary harm. In addition, a deprogramming is often emotionally traumatic not just for the cult member but for everyone involved, including the family and even former members who help. Power and control are placed in the hands of an external authority figure rather than within the cult member. The timing of the deprogramming is not based on the best interests of the cult member but, typically, at the convenience of family members and the deprogrammer. Deprogramming does not typically involve counseling with family members beforehand, so it doesn't address the damage done to them by the whole cult experience. Nor does it adequately prepare them for follow-up care for the ex-member.

WHAT IS EXIT-COUNSELING?

Most families of cult members don't want to break the law by forcibly kidnapping and detaining their adult son or daughter. They do not want to risk alienating their loved one. Unlike deprogramming, exit counseling is non-coercive and legal. When done well, it uses finesse and not force. It is respectful of the person's free will because participation is voluntary. This was the method of choice in the 1980s and the early 1990s.

Exit-counseling[6] is a huge improvement over deprogramming, but it also has the limited focus of getting the cult member out of the group. Exit-counseling, like deprogramming, is essentially a content-driven, informational approach. Most exit-counselors are former members who have no counseling training whatsoever. It is out of their area of expertise to do anything more than provide information about cults and mind control. As with deprogramming, the exit-counselor is considered an external authority figure who will fix the cult problem.

As you may know, I have been involved with several hundred successful counseling interventions. I received my Master's degree in counseling psychology from Cambridge College in 1985 and continue to get counseling training and supervision to improve my knowledge and skills. In 1988, I devoted three chapters of my first book, *Combatting Cult Mind Control*, to my method of exit-counseling. The process starts with a preparatory meeting between the exit-counselor and concerned family and friends. They begin to make efforts to build a better relationship with the cult member. When a visit from the cult member is expected, the exit-counseling team assembles and waits nearby. The goal is to get the cult member to agree to spend three days with family, friends, and the exit-counseling team, without contacting the cult or walking out.

When things go smoothly, the cult member has three days to converse with family, relatives, friends, the exit-counselor, former members, and other experts. He is shown videotapes relating to mind control and cult issues. The cult member is allowed to spend time alone and can choose when to take breaks. He has control over what is discussed and with whom. He is encouraged to ask questions. The cult member can change his mind at any time and get up and leave.

But even when successful, the results of exit-counseling are often less than optimal. Traditional exit-counseling relies too much on content and too little on process. The method doesn't take into account the individual and family problems that existed before the cult involvement and which may persist. It is unequipped to deal with current psychological issues in either the cult member or anyone in the family. Consequently, there is little room to really customize the approach and get to underlying issues. Exit-counseling attempts would sometimes fail because of lack of education, preparation, timing, and proper resources.

Few people understand that cult indoctrination superimposes a new cult identity that suppresses and controls the individual's authentic identity. Relatives and friends think they are having a conversation with the person they have always known when, in fact, they are probably addressing the cult identity. In most traditional exit-counseling and deprogramming cases, the cult identity is submerged but left intact. The pre-cult identity assumes control, but the cult identity is not fully absorbed and integrated into the new post-cult self. Specialized knowledge and training are required to effectively promote healing.

THE STRATEGIC INTERACTION APPROACH

The Strategic Interaction Approach differs from the approach described in *Combatting Cult Mind Control* in several important ways, the most critical of which is the introduction of the three-part phobia intervention. In Chapter 10, you will learn how to use this step-by-step approach to help your loved one understand and overcome cult-implanted phobias. Until this is done, I have learned, interactions with a cult member are especially difficult and sometimes even counterproductive.

The SIA also differs from exit counseling in its emphasis on the process of change, rather than pure content or information. The exit-counseling model was premised on the fact that the exit-counselor would have information that was difficult to obtain. All that has changed because, today, cult critics and former members of various cults are publishing information about cults and mind control on the World Wide Web. With the advent of the Internet, anyone with a computer and a modem can network with other families, obtain assistance from experts and former members, and locate information in a way that was not possible before.

Because information about cults has become so accessible, we can spend more time developing a thorough understanding of the cult member, the group he belongs to, and the friends and family who care about him. Additionally, in the Strategic Interaction Approach we learn how to identify factors that make people more vulnerable to mind control, such as learning disorders, unresolved sexual issues, or pre-existing phobias that cults can take advantage of. We create a model of the parts of our loved one's authentic self that were cultivated for recruitment into the cult identity. Understanding these subpersonalities helps us relate to the cult identity and also helps us identify, and encourage, aspects of the cult self that are worthy of keeping.

The focus of the SIA is on the growth of the entire family and support network, as well as on the cult member. Family members and friends work together as a Strategic Interaction Team. They are asked to participate in each step of the process, improving their communication skills and enhancing self-awareness along the way. Team members are given the tools to take care of their own emotional needs and overcome problems such as low self-esteem, phobias, or addiction. When each family member takes responsibility for growth and change, it takes a lot of pressure off the cult member. His perspective often changes from "I'm the victim, and everyone is here to help me," to "We're a family, and everyone is growing and learning." In this way, families are able to model healthy behavior that will inspire the cult member to change.

We will begin modeling that change by learning to adopt positive beliefs, productive attitudes, and more effective modes of communication.

GOAL-ORIENTED COMMUNICATION

In the business world, the most effective salespeople expend a great deal of time and effort to develop rapport and trust with a client or customer. In the normal course of our personal lives, though, we rarely take the time to learn and practice ways to develop rapport and trust with our loved ones. This effort can bring much more than money—love, acceptance, kindness and respect.

The SIA helps family and friends shift from an emotionally-based form of communication to a goal-oriented style. We will no longer be informal and casual about what we say and do. We will not take our relationships for granted. Our objective is to grow, change, and develop better communication strategies that build rapport and trust. When we get the desired result, we will move forward to the next goal.

Goal One: Build rapport and trust.

During the SIA, you build a relationship with your loved one that is supported by a foundation of trust and rapport.

Goal Two: Gather information.

Throughout the process, members of the Team gather information about the pre-cult and cult self, along with the authentic self (a term I will discuss shortly).

Goal Three: Give information and plant seeds of doubt.

Once Team members are adequately prepared, they can begin planting seeds of doubt in the cult member by imparting important information.

Goal Four: Use mini-interactions to promote reality-testing and freedom of mind.

As they continue to collect and deliver information, Team members engage the cult member in a series of mini-interactions that ensure the loved one has the motivation and ability to reality-test and re-evaluate their cult involvement.

Goal-oriented communication encourages high levels of awareness as well as constant feedback and assessment from experience. Members of the Team learn how to:

- Set realistic goals.
- Identify key issues and concerns.
- Assess beliefs and values.
- Clarify motivation and objectives.
- Listen and speak effectively.
- Observe and utilize nonverbal behavior.
- Utilize rapport and trust building strategies.

NECESSARY BELIEFS

- Mind control is never 100% because it cannot erase a person's authentic self.
- The mind-controlled individual will leave the group. It's only a matter of how soon and how easily.
- Real love is stronger than conditional love.
- People want to be free and know the truth.
- Everything in life can be used as a learning experience.
- Cult behavior is predictable.
- Cults don't deliver what they promise.
- Change and growth are inevitable.

NECESSARY ATTITUDES

- Be curious, yet concerned.
- Be a good listener. Act as if you don't already know everything.
- Act within your sphere of control. Don't waste your emotions on things you can't change.
- Strive for gradual, cumulative progress. Don't just go for the "knockout" punch.
- You can always improve your communication skills.
- Do the best you can with the resources you have.

Learning to understand others

Team members will learn to interact with each other in a creative and resourceful fashion. If one person says something hurtful to another, I encourage the individual who was hurt to suggest a more constructive response to the other person. Each interaction among family, relatives, friends and the cult member is an opportunity for team members to hone their skills and to assess what works and what does not work. For instance, you can gain a better understanding of friends and family by role-playing or stepping into someone else's shoes. In the following exchange, I asked a cult member's mother to pretend that she was her daughter:

SH *(to mother)*: If you heard your mother ask, "You're going out dressed like that?" how would you feel?

MOTHER: I guess I would think my mother was criticizing the way I looked.

SH: That's what you would think. How would you feel? Would the comment make you feel good about yourself or your mother?

MOTHER: No, of course not!

Learning to express your emotions

Process-oriented goals will move us from a rigid position to a flexible, creative state. We will take steps to find positive, constructive ways to express your concerns more effectively:

1. Acknowledge the presence of a feeling inside you.
2. Recognize what emotion you are feeling. Is it helplessness or fear? Anger or hostility? Sadness or depression?
3. Respect your emotions as a legitimate expression of who you are and what you value as a human being. Dwelling on your negative emotions creates conflict, tension and fear. Anger and frustration can turn into self-hatred and self-pity. It can contribute to such physical problems as headaches, muscle tension, ulcers, colitis, and high blood pressure, and can grow into anxiety, emotional tension or depression. Ultimately, it can affect your interpersonal relationships.
4. Learn how to express emotions that are triggered by cult involvement in a way that brings you closer to your goals of improving communication and building rapport and trust. In some situations, you will want to speak directly to the person:

- Parent to cult member
- Sibling to parent
- Friend to cult member
- Client to therapist

Focus on your goals. Sometimes, it is more helpful to verbalize your feelings to someone other than the specific person. For example, there may be things that would make you feel better but would cause great pain or even harm if said directly to the person. A Strategic Interaction Therapist can help you to unburden yourself and make positive suggestions about what to do. Sometimes, it is a matter of finding the most effective way to say something. Sometimes, it is a matter of choosing the right time and place to communicate to get the best response. Over time, you will develop confidence and know how to adapt your communication style to fit the situation.

Using feedback to create a strategy

The SIA creates wave after wave of feedback and analysis. Over time, family, relatives, and friends become comfortable with and consciously adopt this goal-oriented style of communication. After the initial preparation and training, I sometimes assign tasks to specific friends and family members:

• If a Team member is particularly religious, I might suggest that the next time he's on the phone with the cult member (of a religious cult), he could ask that they say a prayer together for God's love and guidance.

• I might suggest to the father of the cult member that he talk with his son about his own childhood and his relationship with his father.

• I might recommend that the grandmother bake cookies and mail them to the cult member.

After each action, we evaluate the impact based on the response made to the interaction. For example, if the telephone prayer request resulted in a double prayer, we ask for specifics. Was the prayer able to build a positive bridge with the cult member? Depending on the report, I may recommend a longer, deeper prayer the next time they speak. I might suggest the religious family member write a letter saying how much closer he has felt since the prayer.

What was the response when the father told his son about his childhood and the issues he had with his father? Tears? A hug? A deep closeness with the cult member? If not, what happened? Was the father standing up, looking out of a window while he was speaking about himself, or was he sitting at eye-level beside his son? If the interaction went well, I might suggest a follow-up where the father asks his son, "What could be done now to build a more intimate relationship with you? What words would need to be spoken? What behavior would need to be experienced?" The father might need to convince the son that he is a top priority in his father's life.

If the homemade cookies were gobbled up and shared with others in the group, and resulted in a thank-you telephone call, then I would suggest doing it every few weeks, or at least once a month. Why? Because each time the cult member receives the cookies, it makes him feel loved. The grandmother can invite members of the group over for a home-cooked meal. We want to build bridges.

With every interaction, you should think of ways to amplify the positives and minimize the negatives. You want to mobilize a set of positive, growth enhancing experiences for the cult member to have with family and friends. The Strategic Interaction Team develops a repertoire of flexible and creative solutions. Many small and medium-sized shared experiences have a cumulative empowering effect. We will work in the least intrusive and most effective way possible to keep family, relatives, friends, and the cult member motivated to move closer in small, realistic steps. This work carries us towards a formal Strategic Intervention, if that proves necessary.

The Strategic Interaction Approach takes time and hard work. It also takes inspiration, motivation, creativity, improvisation, flexibility, humor, passion, and commitment. I have file cabinets full of testimonies from family members and ex-cult members who say that participation in a Strategic Interaction gave them a sense of control over the guilt, anxiety, fear, helplessness, and hopelessness that usually tears a family apart when their loved one is swallowed up by a destructive cult. The SIA provides a safe environment where building rapport and trust is the greatest good. A high level of self-esteem is one of the most important ingredients to a successful Strategic Interaction.

FREQUENTLY-ASKED QUESTIONS ABOUT THE SIA

1. What is the goal?

The goal of the SIA is to help the loved one recover his full faculties; to restore the creative, interdependent adult who fully understands what has happened to him; who has digested and integrated the experience and is better and stronger from the experience.

2. Who is in control?

You are! In all ethical counseling, the locus of control remains within the client. Strategic Interaction models a non-authoritarian, flexible, and open process. When you engage a therapist, he is there to help as the expert on family systems. He is not there to assume control and make all the decisions. Likewise, a cult expert may provide information and advice, but will not give orders. Family and friends are empowered to understand the issues clearly. In this way, Strategic Interaction can be considered self-help. Each person contributes as best he can, creating a synergy that ensures the whole is much greater than the sum of the parts.

3. Who is the client?

In the SIA, each person has issues that should be addressed. The focus is on the growth and development of healthy relationships within the family. The safe and nurturing environment created by the SIA offers many opportunities to heal old wounds. As an integral part of the family system, the cult member is automatically included in the process.

4. When is the best time to act?

The best time to act is when the cult member is questioning his involvement, is disillusioned, or burned out — or simply wants to leave. Mini-interactions are designed to help the cult member question his situation, reality-test, and accept help from family and friends. The SIA is an ongoing process that makes each telephone call, letter, and visit more effective. Every time we interact with the cult member, questions are asked and answered, and information is gathered and delivered. Strategies are formulated, and opportunities to develop rapport and trust unfold. Positive experiences accumulate.

If there is a need for a formal three-day intervention, it is planned when we know the cult member is ready. The time is right when we know that we have established trust and rapport with the cult member. Many times, mini-interactions may even make an intervention unnecessary.

5. Will our loved one be treated as an individual?

The Strategic Interaction is a customized approach that encourages everyone to develop positive, constructive patterns of communication. Family members, relatives and friends learn techniques to remove blocks and phobias. The goal is to restore the creative, flexible, interdependent adult. We want the cult member to understand what happened to him by helping him fully digest and integrate the cult experience. As the Strategic Interaction moves into the recovery phase, we want everyone to be stronger from the experience.

6. Does this approach integrate our loved one's personality?

In *Combatting Cult Mind Control* I described only a "dual identity" model: the cult identity and the pre-cult identity. The Strategic Interaction Approach liberates and then integrates the parts of the pre-cult identity that were co-opted by the cult identity. In addition, we draw out the individual's "authentic," or higher, self and enlist its help to make new associations with the cult self. For example, we recognize that idealism is an integral part of our loved one's authentic identity. By pointing out discrepancies between cult doctrine and hypocritical cult policies, the idealistic component of the cult identity can be encouraged to begin the questioning process. Eventually, the cult member becomes disillusioned with the group and feels motivated to walk out or ask for help.

The Strategic Interaction Approach provides in-depth counseling which promotes healing. By honoring the authentic self, the pre-cult self, and the core of the cult self, we help your loved one to integrate valuable parts of his identity into a healthy post-cult self.

7. Does the method include flexible strategies?

By taking an oppositional, "I'm right, you're wrong" approach, deprogrammers and exit-counselors often create a win-lose mentality. Strategic Interaction encourages adaptability and creativity by widening one's experiential base, which results in a win-win environment. For instance, if family members have never meditated and their loved one is in a meditation cult, then I encourage them to experience meditation.

8. Is the method concerned with our loved one's spiritual life?

With both deprogramming and exit-counseling, content reigns supreme. This approach can have hidden dangers. The ideological or spiritual perspective of the deprogrammer or exit-counselor could be anything from atheist, to agnostic, to orthodox Christian or Jew. I urge you to scrutinize the beliefs and affiliations of people who offer to rescue your loved one from a destructive cult. Many of these people will seek to impose their own ideological perspective. The ethical approach is to avoid imposing any ideological or theological viewpoint on a mind control subject.

The SIA allows for a spiritual orientation, but does not promote a rigid ideological viewpoint. My starting point is always the individual's and family's spiritual "roots," if any. At the beginning of every Strategic Interaction, I have family members and friends fill out Background Information Forms (See page 29, Chapter 1). Often, I find that the cult member had a strong spiritual orientation before he was recruited into a religious cult. I encourage family and friends to support their loved one's full recovery, spiritual as well as psychological.

9. How will we learn the content issues?

The family members, relatives, and friends must understand the seriousness, scope and depth of the cult experience. I want them to become familiar enough with the material to be capable of articulating information about mind control, their loved one's group, and other cults. This may seem like a daunting task, but the step-by-step, goal-oriented approach we take will make the work more manageable. After they have been adequately prepared, family members and friends can begin to attend cult lectures and read cult literature. These activities demonstrate that participants are "open-minded," and help to encourage rapport and trust.

Before any discussions about the belief system, indoctrination, or the leader, we deal with the cult member's phobias about leaving the group. Otherwise, your loved one will be under a great deal of unnecessary emotional stress.

10. How does the SIA handle recovery issues?

Deprogramming is over as soon as the person is out of the group. Ex-members are often left without trained people to follow-up. Consequently, family and friends are typically not prepared to know how to act as a support system. After an exit-counseling, former members may try to provide some support. One might opt for a one-or-two-week stay at Wellspring, a rehabilitation facility in Ohio, or a several month stay at Meadow Haven in Massachusetts. This depends on the financial resources and the ex-member's willingness to voluntarily attend.

Cults use fear and guilt to program their members to believe that their lives are worthless outside of the group. It is hard to imagine the pain these buried psychic land mines cause when the person manages to leave. Cult experiences and indoctrination have to be worked through during an essential soul-searching recovery period, which usually takes months and sometimes years.

If the person participated in distasteful behavior—if he recruited people, was raped, became a prostitute, or stole money—it is helpful that he receive ongoing counseling. Otherwise, he will spend the rest of his life traumatized by what happened to him, or feeling guilty for what he did while a member of the group.

During the recovery period, your loved one needs to learn how to use recovery techniques in order to visualize and work with his cult identity to reclaim personal history, power, and integrity. He must acknowledge that he was doing the best he could at the time with the information that was available to him.

The SIA provides a long-term recovery process for both the cult member and members of the family. Everyone is traumatized by the cult involvement, even those who are not directly involved. Feelings get hurt. Belief systems are assaulted or shifted. People lose sleep. They get depressed. Anger, frustration, and resentment are repressed. Each person who has been involved in the traumatic experience of having a loved one in a destructive cult needs support on psychological and emotional levels.

The heightened sense of urgency that arises when a loved one joins a destructive cult provides the catalyst for truly remarkable growth, change and development. Family members, relatives, siblings and friends are willing to work hard on their own issues for the sake of their loved one. They are willing to make commitments that might seem impossible under less trying circumstances. Their rewards are the many positive changes that take place as a result of working together to bring back a family member or friend lost to a cult.

Even in those circumstances where an individual does not

immediately decide to leave the cult, there is basis for hope. Many key issues will have been communicated, especially those dealing with phobias, information control, and the broader issues of cult mind control. The gentleness of the repeated mini-interactions will help the relationship to become more honest, caring and compassionate—setting the foundation for future interactions.

11. How effective is the Strategic Interaction Approach?

The Strategic Interaction Approach has an excellent record of helping people leave destructive groups. Each case is different and presents new challenges. Every set of family resources is unique. The Strategic Interaction Approach draws its strength from love, commitment, and flexibility. It provides encouragement, momentum, and practical knowledge.

Even when your loved one participates for only three days and decides to return to the group (which rarely happens), the seeds have already been planted. In such cases, the cult member usually walks out at a later date. When a cult member wants to leave the group, he should know that his family and friends will open their arms with love and support.

12. What is the therapist's role?

A Strategic Interaction Therapist, by definition, is a cult expert and mental health professional. Over the years, I have shared my approach with several individuals, taking them with me on cases and training them in SIA. I hope to encourage more people to learn my approach and plan to offer more training seminars and subsequent supervision. Former cult members with counseling training make ideal candidates for SIA training. During the SIA, the role of a therapist is to facilitate communication between the cult member and the Team by encouraging growth within each person. Although it is possible to empower a cult member to leave without the help of a formally trained counselor, I recommend that you contact a professional counselor to discuss your situation and plan an approach. If a therapist with experience counseling cult members is not available, you should make sure that your counselor has read this book before you begin preparing for an Interaction with your loved one.

In the following chapters, we will prepare, rehearse, and then conduct mini-interactions with the cult member. While Team members hone their knowledge and skills, they are shaping creative and flexible strategies. Plan A, Plan B, Plan C—we keep our options open!

When the time is right, we learn how to ask the cult member to spend some time away from the group—time to conduct research and ask questions; time to reconnect with family and friends. The levels of rapport and trust will be so high that your loved one will agree to participate in the Strategic Interaction.

Chapter 4

Evaluating the Situation

Your loved one has told you he is committing his life to a new set of beliefs and behaviors. You worry that he might no longer be thinking for himself. Have you tried to sit down and really talk with your loved one about his experiences, and yours? Have you tried to build a better relationship with him? Have you visited the group, read their literature, and talked with leaders? Have you found your loved one unwilling to sit down and discuss your concerns? Even when it feels that you have run out of options, alternatives are available that will lead to improved communication and, most likely, a happier conclusion.

The Strategic Interaction Approach will show you how to chart a new course of action based on the circumstances you face. Because each cult group, cult member, and SIA Team is unique, we will customize our approach to fit the situation. Before you rush to take action, it is important that you spend some time considering the following fundamental questions:

1. How is the cult member doing? How did he get there in the first place, and how deeply is he involved?

2. What is the destructive potential of the cult?

3. What, exactly, are your concerns and objections to his cult involvement?

Of course, your concerns are related to how destructive the cult is—and how it is affecting your loved one. Taking a step-by-step approach, answering each question in turn, will help you to think clearly about your position which, in turn, will enable you to effectively articulate your concerns to your loved one.

UNDERSTANDING THE CULT MEMBER

Most people would like to believe that they are in complete control of their mind at all times. It is easier to assume that rational thinking makes us invulnerable than to admit that we are all susceptible to mind control. But it is precisely this belief in our own invulnerability that allows cults to entrap unsuspecting recruits.

There are three primary reasons why intelligent, educated people with stable backgrounds can be drawn into cults. First, there is a pervasive lack of awareness about cults and mind control. Even when cult issues are covered in the media, mind control is frequently ignored or at best misunderstood. I can't tell you how many times I've been on a talk show where the host asks a cult member, "Are you brainwashed?" The cult member replies, "No, of course not." As if the cult member would actually say, "Yes!" What the host fails to realize is that the mind-controlled member will not know that he has surrendered control until he is able to step away from the group and learn about cult recruitment and indoctrination.

Second, many situations make people more vulnerable to recruitment. For example, a person whose parents have recently separated or divorced will be more likely to listen to a recruiter who describes his group as "one big happy family." Someone whose romantic relationship or marriage has just ended will be more susceptible to come-ons by an attractive person. Other common situational variables include the death of a loved one, illness, loss of a job, graduation (from high school or college), and moving to a new location (city, state, country). Situational vulnerabilities occur in everyone's life. It is easy to see how people tend to be more vulnerable to an attractive recruiter offering community, love and meaning during such episodes.

Finally, some individuals have psychological profiles that make recruitment easier for cults. In general, people who have difficulty thinking critically will be easier targets. For example, people who think in terms of magical or predetermined events will be more easily swayed by a cult leaders' prophecies or events if they appear to be synchronistic. People-pleasers, who seek the approval of their peer group out of insecurity, and anyone with low self-esteem, will be more vulnerable to the peer pressure exerted by cult recruiters. Individuals with good concentration and with vivid imaginations are more susceptible to hypnotic suggestion. People who engage excessively in hypnosis, meditation, and other activities that can induce an "altered state of consciousness" (such as television-watching, book-reading, sports, music, video and computer games) are more susceptible. Individuals with learning disorders, drug or alcohol problems, unresolved sexual issues (sexual identity orientation or, possibly, past rape or molestation trauma), pre-existing phobias (fear of heights, drowning, AIDS, sharks, aliens, terrorists, crime), and other unresolved traumatic issues will also be easier targets. Cults seek out such vulnerabilities and use them against recruits, often making grandiose claims that their group will solve all of the person's problems. People who have not achieved a happy, secure sense of self can be more easily drawn in. On the other hand, cults tend to avoid individuals who are seriously ill or, in some way, physically or mentally challenged. They want people who will be an asset, not a liability.

Once you have looked at the factors that may have contributed to your loved one's vulnerability, you can begin to assess his current situation in the cult. Here, the two critical questions are:

- Where is your loved one living?
- How deeply is your loved one involved?

WHERE IS YOUR LOVED ONE LIVING?

One advantage to having a loved one who lives at home is that the family may plan on frequent interactions. Yet, the cult member's presence may make it more difficult to actually create and carry out those plans. Family members have to be more discreet— for example, it would not do to leave critical materials where they might be found by the cult member. Some cults actually tell members to look through their parents' checkbooks or go through telephone bills to see if any contact has been made with known cult critics. Secure telephone bills, as well as articles, books, and tapes, somewhere safe and sound.

Many cult members live away, in a house or apartment. If they share their living space, do they live with only other cult members? If so, have you befriended the other people? If they live in their own place, do they live alone? If so, this is a good sign because there is some measure of privacy. Do they live with a spouse and children who are not in the cult? This is also good. There is less environmental control by the cult. Another important question is whether the person works for a non-cult business and receives a paycheck. The more independent a person is financially and physically, the less controlled he is by the cult leader.

If your loved one happens to be living in an isolated, communal cult where most outside communication is cut off, seek alternate sources of contact with the group. Use the Internet to network with other families who have loved ones in the group, and with experts and critics who may have up-to-date information about the cult's activities. If you know where the cult is located, you might look for a local clergyman or police chief who can help. When dealing with extremist, insular cults, ex-members will be especially helpful. Seek them out, hold mini-interactions with them to help them understand mind control, and ask their help to strategize about how to gain entry to the cult. Former members of your loved one's cult may not always be seen as a "threat" by current members.

They might be seen as potential returnees, and might be able to act as agents of the family without arousing suspicion.

What do I do if I have no idea where my loved one is?

Knowing the group or leader your loved one is involved with is an important first step in locating him. Again, former members may render invaluable assistance. Network and seek them out. However, in your investigations, you might want to use a pseudonym, especially when dealing with groups that want to keep cult members away from family contact. If you fail to protect your identity and cult leaders learn you are trying to effect a rescue, they will make things difficult for you—for example, by hiding your loved one. If you don't feel comfortable using a pseudonym, perhaps friends or other relatives may be willing to do the front-line work. E-mail different counter-cult organizations listed at freedomof-mind.com, my Web site.

Use the police, FBI, or other authorities if there is any suspicion of illegal activity. Together, you may come up with creative strategies. For example, I had one client who reported his car as stolen after his son disappeared with it and a drug-dealing "shaman." Before the cult involvement, the son had permission to use the car, but it was registered in the father's name, and had been driven out of state without parental approval. The police found and arrested the son in another state. Soon after, the father, a former District Attorney, convinced a judge to release his son to his custody. He persuaded his son to meet with me. The counseling was successful, and, of course, the charges were dropped.

Another approach, if you have the financial resources, is to hire a private investigator to help track down your loved one, as well as to gain information about the cult leader, the group's background, and the property where they live. Today, many people can be located on the Internet or in listings by name, address, and telephone

number available for purchase on CD-ROM. Occasionally, investi-
gators may need to travel to another state or country to track someone down, which can become quite expensive.

Private detectives can be immensely helpful. They do not need
to reveal the identity of their client. They might allude to a significant trust fund or other financial windfall that could motivate a
cult leader to produce the cult member in order to get hold of the
assets. Be careful about this strategy, though. It could backfire by
making the leader more interested in holding onto the cult member.

If you are on a tight budget, and are prepared to do the work
yourself, buy Dennis King's book *Get the Facts on Anyone*.[1] This
book contains useful information about finding missing persons,
and reveals many of the techniques used by professionals. Another
good book to read is *Investigating Extremists: A Manual for Law
Enforcement*, by Larry Zilliox.[2]

If you know where the cult member is, but all contact is
refused, then try appealing to the cult leader (or sub-leader) for
help. Leaders who are trying to create positive publicity and seek
legitimacy may be particularly receptive to this strategy. Your letter
or phone call should appeal to the leader's desire to create a positive image of the group. You might write or say:

"I'm contacting you (the cult leader or sub-leader) to ask for your
help. I know that your group believes in God (the family, love and
goodness), but I am worried about my son/daughter. I know that
I've made a lot of mistakes. I know I have said and done hurtful
things. I am truly sorry about doing such things. I have been losing
sleep and feel like I am at my wit's end. Please, would you consider
talking to my son or daughter and imploring him/her to see us (talk
with us, visit with us)? I would be so grateful."

Sometimes, the leader will actually order the cult member to meet with you. Cult leaders want to believe that they are good people, and often enjoy the opportunity to help a family reunite, if it suits their ego. Of course, if they suspect you are merely trying to get your loved one to leave, they will not cooperate. If the cult member cuts off contact because of an unsuccessful intervention attempt, apologize, promise never to do it again and ask forgiveness. My recommendation is to ask the cult member, "What do I need to do to regain your trust and forgiveness?" By asking a question of the cult member, you make him think and, hopefully, offer a set of terms. If he discovers telephone numbers or mail from known cult critics at your house, the cult member may cut off contact. Again, the necessary first step is to regain rapport and trust.

HOW DEEPLY IS YOUR LOVED ONE INVOLVED?

A new cult member who is in the "honeymoon" phase of his cult involvement will typically be harder to convince to leave since he has mostly positive associations with the group. Try making contact with other members of the group. Meet the cult member's friends, taking notice of their names. Ask where they are from. Befriend them. Also pay special attention to older members who will often have valuable stories about the group's past. For example, an older member may privately tell you, "Oh yeah, I remember when Armageddon was supposed to happen ten years ago." You may be able to use this kind of information later to reality-test with your loved one.

Long-term members are actually easier in some ways to counsel, since they have already experienced many lies and let downs such as false prophecies, broken promises, and hypocritical behaviors of leaders. Also, most long-term members will know people who have left the group. You may decide to ask, "Do you think it's possible to leave for legitimate reasons? Do you know anyone who ever left the group? Do you know anyone who left for legitimate reasons? Did you ever talk with them about why they decided to leave? Would you be open to talking with them about why they left?"

If someone was born into a cult, it could take years for them to decide to interact with you—or leave the group. But remember, many disillusioning experiences take place inside cult groups that you might not know about. As long as the member knows that there are people on the outside who care about him, he will feel that he has a choice to leave one day. Create positive, loving experiences for him, with yourself and others who are not members of the group.

I have found that the key to approaching people who have spent their whole lives in a group is patiently offering them experiences of an alternative way of living. For example, when Jehovah's Witnesses see that people who leave still believe in God, study the Bible, and lead decent moral lives, it is very persuasive. If they have a business that has other Witnesses as clients, maybe you can help them to expand their business or explore other business options so that they won't be so financially dependent on the group.

Invite your loved one to important occasions at home. If he is in a group like the Witnesses, don't invite him to a birthday party, since birthdays celebrations are considered sinful. Just invite him to a party and downplay the birthday aspect. The more positive social contacts you can provide, the better. Send gifts that create positive feelings about you, and try to pick items that your loved one will use more than once—clothing, for example.

Make an effort to keep in regular contact. A picture postcard depicting an image with a positive association and saying, "I miss you." or "I love you. Please write back." is better than not doing anything. Even if you spend years mailing letters and cards to your loved one, each piece of mail will remind him that you still care.

With these factors in mind, you should begin to develop profiles of your loved one's pre-cult (and authentic) self and his cult identity. You can then use these profiles to find better ways of communicating with your loved one.

What is the profile of the individual's pre-cult self?

Write your thoughts down in chronological outline form if possible. To help your recollection, think about relationships your loved one has with different people (grandparents, uncles, aunts, cousins, friends) in addition to immediate family members. Also, think about places you used to live, frequent, and vacation. Perhaps the person used to like to fish in a particular spot or travel to a particular location that has personal meaning. While searching your memories for examples, it is useful to think about activities he enjoyed, like sports, music, exercise, reading, seeing movies, and so on. Making an effort to remember details like these will cultivate personal awareness in yourself. It will also enhance the resources that we will use later to make a connection with the cult member.

Consider your loved one's strengths and weaknesses. For example, on a scale of one to ten, how would you rate his self-esteem before cult involvement? Did he have interests, hobbies, athletic skills, art, music? Other important questions include: How old was he when he joined? A nineteen-year-old has more resources needed to help him leave than someone born into a group. A thirty-year old cult recruit will have more life skills and resources than a nineteen-year old. Did he have clear-cut goals? Did he have friends? Did he communicate well with others? If the individual had a lot of problems before getting into the cult, you may consider connecting with his authentic self and with the idealistic and dissatisfied aspects of his cult identity.

What is the profile of the cult identity?

Start by talking with present cult members and get a good picture of their beliefs, language, and behaviors. Talk next with former members to get an even deeper insight into the prototypical cult member's identity. Begin to assess the cult identity of your loved one. How long has he been involved? The longer people are in a group, the more disillusionment they typically have experienced— yet the harder it is for them to leave because of the investment they have made. What jobs has he performed? Make a list of the person's work history in the cult. If you don't know, ask: Is he primarily a recruiter, or does he merely work in one of the group's businesses. Is he rank-and-file after ten years? Was he once a leader, but has since been demoted? What kind of access does the person have to the top leader? Where has he been stationed? Was he at the headquarters or at a small satellite center?

Throughout the SIA, you will continue to refine these profiles. The better you understand your loved one's authentic self and cult identity, the easier it will be to help him to think and act independently.

EVALUATING THE DESTRUCTIVE POTENTIAL OF THE CULT

Now, let's turn our attention to the cult itself. By investigating the leadership, organization, and doctrine of the group, you can understand the ways in which it uses mind control, and how those techniques are affecting your loved one.

Leadership

A good place to start looking for information about the destructive potential of a group is at the top. You should ask:

- Who is the leader(s)? What is his personal history? Was he ever married? Has he been divorced? Does he have children?

- What are the leader's credentials? Does he have a past criminal history? A psychiatric history?

- What kind of education, training, or occupation did he have before starting the group? Was he ever in a destructive cult?

- Does the leader make claims of exclusive wisdom, power, and spirituality?

- Are there any checks and balances of power in place?

- What has the cult leader put in writing or said in speeches?

Comparing the leader of your loved one's group to another leader of a mainstream organization may give you a better idea of how dangerous the person is. For example, Moses David Berg, the now deceased leader of "The Family," claimed that he was an Apostle, and at one point encouraged women in his group to become "Happy Hookers for Jesus." Female members were told to "share God's love" in order to get money, new recruits, and political favors. This teaching extended to encouraging sex with children—not surprising, perhaps, when one learns that Berg fled the United States after being indicted for child molestation. Religious leaders like the Pope or Billy Graham would denounce such behavior as gross immorality.

Another example is self-proclaimed Buddhist enlightened master, Frederick Lenz, aka Rama, who told his followers that they should make a lot of money, drive expensive cars, cut off contact with their family and friends, and hide their own thoughts and feelings to keep others from draining them of their energies.[3] A stark contrast to Lenz is the Dalai Lama, the political and spiritual leader of Tibet, who lives a life that emphasizes love, compassion, service, and connection to other living things. The Dalai Lama is humble and inclusive in his approach, and appreciates all the different world religions. Lenz said that he was enlightened, and demanded money from people for the privilege of receiving his "energy and protection." Lenz looked down on other approaches to Buddhism.

You will want to find information about the leader from former members, critics, and media databases. You can also network with a family support group. Videotapes of past television shows can often yield important and useful insights. For example, on a Larry King show, Frederick Lenz denied being an enlightened being—yet to his followers, that is what he claimed to be. During a recent *Dateline* interview, he couldn't answer even basic questions about the computer business which he owned. As we will discuss in Chapter 7, the Internet should always be used to conduct searches for information about the leader as well as the group.

Organization

Looking at the structure of a group can often tell you about the flow of power within it. In general, destructive cults can be seen as having a pyramid shape with a charismatic leader at the pinnacle and cult underlings arrayed beneath him. Directly below him is a small core of advisors who typically manage the cult's businesses. Below them is a somewhat larger group of sub-leaders. Below them —at the wide base—is the general membership. In groups where the leader has been dead for years, a small cadre of devoted follow- ers may have rushed in to fill the void. In any case, when a leader with a questionable background organizes a group so that power is totally centralized, you can assume a destructive cult is being formed. World-renowned Christian apologist Norman Geisler puts it this way: " Whenever you have an individual who claims a direct pipeline with God and has no accountability, if you don't have a cult today, you will have one tomorrow."[4]

When evaluating the structure of a group, you should pay attention to the following:

- Who are the people in charge, and what kind of power do they have over your loved one?

- Is the group small or large (thousands, millions of people)?

- Where does it have its center? Is it cut off from the world or is it seeking legitimacy?

- How does the group get its money? From donations or fundraising? Is the group organized as a nonprofit? Does it have businesses?

- How does the group spend its money? Does it use money to mount public relations campaigns? Does it hire teams of lawyers to effectively mute its critics through legal harassment?

- In cases where a group claims to have open accounting records, does it actually provide public access? If people are afraid to ask, what does this say about the atmosphere of the group?

The structure of a group also involves the relative freedom of members to leave the group:

- Are members made to fear even the thought of leaving the group?

- Are members isolated? Have they been cut off from family members?

- Are members emotionally or financially dependent on the group?

Doctrine

In the Strategic Interaction Approach, we look at the way a group behaves, not what it believes. Even so, a group's doctrine should be taken into account in assessing its destructiveness. In general, the more extreme the claims, beliefs, and prophecies (Armageddon, flying saucers), the greater the potential for abuse. The most dangerous groups change doctrine at the whim of the leader. The more developed and codified a doctrine, usually the more stable the group.

In the past, some mainstream religious organizations have supported mind control cults in legal struggles because they appear to share similar beliefs. For example, if a Bible cult says, "Jesus is the Lord," or when Sun Myung Moon says that he is "for family values," mainstream religious leaders often assume that the organization is legitimate. Some cults use their deep pockets to help the ministries of other religious leaders, like Jerry Falwell, then use that person to help legitimatize them.[5] This creates a façade that the group is respectable, which can be quite convincing to cult members. Investigate the facts for yourself.

You may come across cult pamphlets and Web sites that make it seem as though religious scholars and mainstream religious organizations support them, often in the name of freedom of religion. Cult leaders make television appearances to talk about how the cult awareness movement is a witch hunt. It is in the interests of cults to raise a controversy over doctrine. Cults frequently claim they are being persecuted for their beliefs. But destructive groups change the truth to fit the needs of the situation. There are many cult publications in circulation that raise doubts about legitimate criticism. Legitimate groups do not need to alter their doctrine to deceive the public. Other important questions to ask include:

- Is there an "insider" doctrine and an "outsider" doctrine— that is, a doctrine for the "elect" in the group and a doctrine for public consumption?

- Does truth change at different levels within the group hierarchy?

Any group's beliefs should be freely disclosed to people who want to join. During the recruitment process, destructive cults use deception, which includes outright lying as well as holding back or distorting vital information. There is no informed consent.

IDENTIFYING YOUR CONCERNS

Now that your loved one's involvement and the destructiveness of the group in question have been evaluated, it is time to prepare yourself for interaction with your loved one. This will include looking outward, at the cult and your loved one, as well looking inward. One of the most critical things you can do is to take time to observe and better understand your own thoughts, feelings, and behavior. Some of your concerns about your loved one's cult involvement may appear to take on a life of their own, generating tremendous stress and anxiety. I will discuss ways to alleviate such draining emotions in Chapter 6. Try to keep a clear head. Only then will you be able to communicate in such a way that you will be heard by your loved one.

What are your concerns about cult involvement?

As I have said, it is both common and natural for emotions—particularly fear, anger and frustration—to muddle family members' thinking. To help someone in a cult, it is essential that each family member and friend take the time to clarify concerns about the loved one and objections to his involvement by writing them down. Some families spend years avoiding the acknowledgment that their loved one is in a cult. The act of writing overcomes any remnants of denial.

I suggest planning at least one family meeting with the express purpose of writing down such a list of concerns. During this meeting, each family member should take notes. Audio or video tape recording can be used to document the meeting, unless someone objects. Taping is a good way of including people not physically present at a meeting. This meeting should be kept confidential and private. At some later point, the cult member will be told about the meeting, but be careful not to jeopardize your efforts early on by someone being too talkative.

By seeing and hearing themselves speak, family and friends can gain insight into their own emotions and modes of communication. I remember one meeting where I asked a cult member's mother, "What do you say to her when she asks what you think of her involvement with the cult?" She answered, "Well, I tell her that everything is fine, that she's an adult and can do whatever she wants to do." What the woman didn't realize was that, as she was speaking, she was emphatically shaking her head from left to right, indicating a subconscious "No!" I pointed this out to her, and encouraged her to stand in front of a mirror and pretend that her daughter was on the other side of the mirror. Recognizing nonverbal cues like these, whether in a mirror or on videotape, can help us understand and express ourselves more effectively. Usually, the family will prefer to destroy audiocassettes or videotapes once they are no longer needed.

Your list of concerns should encompass both broad and specific behaviors. An example of a broad concern would be: "My daughter doesn't seem to be able to think or act for herself." An example of a specific behavior would be: "She can never come home by herself. She always insists on bringing another cult member." You may include examples of how your loved one lied to you, either by omission, distortion, or outright falsehood.

Negative changes in behavior

Families often claim their loved one seems like a different person. If this is your concern, be sure to state clearly and precisely the specific behavior that is uncharacteristic. Depending on the person, uncharacteristic behavior may include lying, breaking a promise to come home for a visit, not coming home for visits at all, not answering letters or phone calls, or not initiating contact. If the individual has been involved for a long time, there could be hundreds of examples of uncharacteristic behaviors such as giving up a healthy diet in favor of one of junk food, going into dangerous neighborhoods to canvas for money, or not paying bills and taxes.

Cult members may abandon life goals, cut themselves off from family and close friends, no longer read books, newspapers, or see movies, or stop eating or sleeping properly. Many also work long hours for little or no pay, with no retirement fund or health care, and no time off or vacations. Often, they are not allowed to choose their own relationships or even where they live.

Positive changes in behavior

Not all cult behavior is negative. Make note of any positive changes since group involvement. For example, it is common for most religious cult groups to discourage the use of alcohol or drugs. If the person stopped smoking cigarettes because of their membership, this should be acknowledged as a positive life change. If the person used to be slovenly, and is now very neat, be prepared to compliment him. If he never exercised and now is very fit, make sure you make note of it. If the person had no spiritual life and now feels very spiritual, count that as a positive development. Expressing such observations will be important later when communicating with the individual because it will show your objectivity and fairness. It will also help you build rapport and trust.

Decide what concerns will be most effective to discuss

You should also divide your concerns and objections into categories of "likely to be effective" and "probably not effective." For example, if one of your objections is that your son has stopped attending Roman Catholic services because he has joined a Bible cult, you will need to decide whether such a concern would matter to him. When it comes time to discuss your concerns, we only want to express those that will be effective in influencing the person. However, all concerns, whether effective or ineffective, should be listed.

Use the Evaluation Checklist below to help jog your memory and identify all potential areas of concern. It is important that you know your concerns well enough to express them to others, because in the following chapter, we will be sharing your concerns with other friends and family and asking them for help.

EVALUATION CHECKLIST

Health

1. Is he eating properly?

2. Is he getting enough sleep?

3. Does he have health insurance?

4. Would he receive good medical care if sick or injured?

Prior Commitments

1. Education.

"He had one term to complete to get his college diploma and he walked away. We can't believe it! No amount of rational argument will convince him to finish."

2. Career / Goals

"She was planning to become a doctor. Now she stands on street corners recruiting new members."

3. Significant relationships

"They were going to be married and he broke off the engagement."

Finances

1. Surrendering Assets

"She gave all her money to the group—and her stereo and her car!

"He is using his life savings on cult sponsored classes and events."

2. Dependency Issues

"He has to ask the group for car fare. He has no money of his own—even though he works twenty hours a day."

Radical Personality Change

1. Physical appearance

Change in clothes, hair, weight, diet
Spaced-out expression, glassy stare

2. Personality

Change in speech patterns, facial expressions, or mannerisms
Decreased sense of humor
Secretive, evasive, or defensive behavior
Judgmental attitude towards family members
Fanatical—always proselytizing
Change from extrovert to introvert or vice versa
Change from analytical to magical-thinking
Change from lazy to industrious
Change in level of honesty
Lack of interest in former hobbies

3. Personal habits

Change from irresponsible to responsible
Change from sloppy to clean
Change from tardy to punctual

4. Communication style

Evasiveness, defensiveness, difficulty in communication
Use of "buzzwords," canned speeches

5. Relationships

Change in key relationships
Family and friends preached to as though they need to be saved
Pressure for money for personal reasons or group donations
Loss of contact with family and friends (in person, via telephone, mail)
Decreased physical contact—fewer or no hugs and kisses
Self-imposed isolation
Family events (unattended or unacknowledged births, birthdays, baptisms, confirmations, bar/bas mitzvahs, engagements, weddings, anniversaries, illnesses, deaths)
Majority of time spent with new group or organization

6. Philosophy

Change in political beliefs
Change in religious beliefs
Change in current education (changed from full to part time, changed major, dropped out of school)

7. Career

Abruptly ends career
Gives away money
Spends large sums of money
Radical change of goals

8. Medical

Ignores symptoms
Doesn't go to doctor
Ignores advice of doctors
Goes to free clinics

9. Change in living conditions

Move to new residence (group house, commune)
Move to new location
Move in with "strangers"

To Do

- Write what you don't like about your loved one's involvement with this group.
- On general principle, what bothers you about it?
- What specific behavior is objectionable?
- Make a chronological list of concerns. Are they escalating as time goes by?
- Prioritize your list. Which three concerns are most important?
- Make a list of uncharacteristic behaviors.
- Assess whether communicating your concern will be effective or ineffective.

Chapter 5

Building the Team

Friends and family members who are motivated by love will find their resources become limitless when they work together. Of course, it is natural to feel intimidated if you are alone when trying to help a cult member, particularly when that person is an adult and insists he is happy. It may seem that the cult has a great advantage in terms of money and manpower. It does. But unless your loved one is of special importance to the cult leaders, they will not care about the person like you do. Individual members usually get very little attention from the top leaders, who typically have "more important" matters to focus on. If you involve as many friends and relatives as possible to build an effective team, you will have the advantage over time.

A Strategic Interaction Approach Team is a support network, not only for the cult member but also for everyone affected by his involvement. The Team will be there to talk with the cult member, help you with mini-interactions and interventions and, ultimately, assist in your loved one's recovery from the effects of mind control. Each case presents a unique set of challenges and every person involved makes a significant contribution to the healing process. With flexibility and imagination, accidental or remarkable occurrences can work to the family's advantage. When they work together and support each other, Team members are given the opportunity to reorganize the family system in ways that can make each person's life better.

A family affair

I'm often surprised at how quickly an SIA Team, once set in motion, can evolve in unique and useful ways. A few years ago, after giving a lecture at a New Age program center in the Boston area, I was approached by a woman in her twenties who asked me what I thought of a particular female guru-led group.[1] I said that I had grave concerns about the group, and told her about a Web page that had been created by a former seventeen-year member. She told me how, ten years earlier, she had been introduced to the group as a young child by her mother. She had even spent a couple of years in India, where during the second visit she had a disillusioning set of experiences that led to her decision to leave the group. She was still having problems, though, and also felt conflicted about her mother, who was a respected American leader in the organization. The young woman took my telephone number and later called and asked me to do counseling. We proceeded to do so, and she later asked me to work with her mother.

Because she and her mother had always been very close, she felt she had enough rapport to approach her mother directly and ask for a three-day meeting. But while we were preparing for the intervention, she hesitantly asked me whether or not she should contact her brother. Of course I suggested that she contact him—especially since she told me that in the past, he had been very critical of their involvement with the group. She and her brother had become more distant and were having more trouble getting along than they had in the past. I told her, "Your mother is still involved with this group and we know your brother has criticized it. Tell him what you're up to and see if he's willing to participate in the intervention." Fortunately, he was very willing.

A few days after the intervention, her brother telephoned me. He sounded confused and shaken, faltering and stumbling over each word. After a prolonged silence, I asked him what it was that he wanted to say. He proceeded to tell me how he was in total shock because he realized that a group he had been involved with for years was a very secretive mind control cult. He begged me not to say anything, especially to his sister or mother—which, of course, I agreed to do. This was a small group of about one hundred men and women, he said, and no outsiders knew that it existed. Even his fiancée, who had lived with him for a number of years, did not know that he was involved. When she asked about his frequent meetings, he told her that he was attending a special class that involved acting, and that he couldn't really discuss it. It turned out that, in fact, his involvement was a major source of friction in their relationship because she felt there was a part of him that was not available to her.

I asked him to tell me more about this group, whose leaders claimed to be following the teachings of Gurdjieff and Ouspensky.[2] Previously, I had spoken with people who had been involved with a different cult group supposedly based on the same philosophy. The brother asked to have some sessions with me and sort through his experience. (He later married his fiancée, and they now have two lovely children.)

So, while doing an intervention with the woman's mother in a guru cult, we found out that her brother was involved with another destructive group. Of course, I encouraged him to talk with his sister and mother as well as his father, who was a respected Buddhist teacher, about his cult involvement. The mother eventually chose to leave the group, and the family grew closer than ever. She has continued to follow a spiritual path and has assisted others in leaving the cult. She even helped me counsel a woman involved in Aum Shinrikyo, the so-called "Buddhist" cult responsible for sarin nerve gas attacks in Japan in 1994 and 1995.

About a year later, I received a phone call from a woman who saw my name in a story in *The Boston Globe* about Scientology and the Internet.[3] Her fiancée had just broken off an engagement because he refused to tell her about his secret meetings. She thought he was having an affair or was previously married, but when she read the article, something clicked for her. She contacted me. A light went on in my head and I realized that it reminded me of this previous situation. I called the brother and it turned out that he knew her fiancée from the organization. I coached her and the two men spoke with each other by telephone. She and I later met with her fiancée and did some counseling together. He too chose to leave the group and the two of them are still together.

Cults are well-coordinated social influence systems that succeed because they organize their members to exert pressure and trap recruits in an all-encompassing web of control. But the uniformity of a cult is also one of its weaknesses because it makes the group extremely predictable in its actions. An SIA Team, on the other hand, can be creative, flexible and unpredictable. The more people you can find who want to help, the more options you will have.

When you begin to approach potential Team members, you may find that some people are reluctant to participate, or are even opposed to the goals of the Strategic Interaction Approach. Some people are completely in denial about the existence of a problem. Denial protects a cult member's family and friends from the uncomfortable realization that there is something wrong and that something should be done. The psychological mechanism of denial can operate with other major problems, too, like alcoholism, drug abuse, or compulsive gambling. An effective way to start working through denial is by gathering information. Talk about their experiences with former cult members, experts, other families with cult problems, as well as concerned family and friends.

Ask the person who is in denial: "What proof would you need

to be convinced that there is a problem?" Once the criteria are verbalized, then you can take the necessary steps to provide the needed information or experience.

Many potential Team members will know little or nothing about destructive cults when you first approach them. It may be that family members and friends are not in denial but, rather, have erroneous beliefs that block the path to any meaningful dialogue or fruitful action. Some of your loved one's friends may have been alienated by the cult identity. Relatives may say that they "don't want to interfere," others may not believe that mind control is possible. But with education and encouragement, many of these individuals will become effective members of the Team.

REFUTING ERRANT BELIEFS

You will need to know how to address other people's misconceptions and, eventually, you will have to articulate these issues to the cult member as well. To help prepare you, I have identified ten of the most common fallacies about mind control cults.

Errant Belief #1

"THERE'S NO SUCH THING AS MIND CONTROL."

People who reject out of hand the existence of mind control usually have distorted conceptions about mind control techniques. "Nobody can erase your personality and turn you into a brainwashed zombie," is one common belief. Yet, as we have seen, mind control does not erase a person's authentic self but rather creates a dominant cult self that suppresses free will. In speaking to a person who has doubts about mind control, you might discuss how the cult identity is not supposed to think, feel, or behave outside of the parameters of the cult doctrine. Understanding cult mind control

depends on making this critical distinction between the cult identity and the authentic identity.

By studying Chapter 2 of this book, "What is Destructive Mind
Control?" you have three powerful models to explain what we
mean by the term "mind control." It is also useful to cite the reading material for Dr. Philip Zimbardo's Stanford University
Psychology course entitled "The Psychology of Mind Control." As
mentioned earlier, the diagnostic manual for the American
Psychiatric Association actually has a category, Atypical
Dissociative Disorder 300.15, that uses the words "cults" and
"brainwashing."

It is also true that mind control does not affect all people at all
times with equal force. Individuals involved in the same cult can
experience vastly different levels of mind control. Some cult members may look glassy-eyed and zombie-like, but these are extreme
cases and are often the result of sleep deprivation or malnutrition.
More often, the member's cult identity seems well-developed, but
is actually co-opting the talents and skills of the authentic self. The
result is that, to the untrained eye, cult members can appear completely normal. Asking questions that can test a person's thoughts
and free will is the only way to evaluate the extent of mind control.[4]

Some may argue that people leave cult groups and, therefore,
mind control does not exist. But the truth may be that they have
become ill, become disillusioned, or been kicked out. The fact that
people walk out of cults does not mean that mind control doesn't
exist—it just means that mind control is not absolute. Since mind
control does not erase a person's authentic self or spirit, it is always
possible for people to escape to freedom.

Mind control is often misunderstood because relatively few
people have had experience with cults, although most of us can
relate to mind control in one way or another. If a potential Team
member has trouble understanding mind control, the following
questions might help them identify other influence processes that
they may have encountered:

- "Have you ever trusted or fallen in love with someone who lied, manipulated and took advantage of you?"

- "Did you ever stay in a relationship in which you felt controlled and disrespected?"

- "Have you ever been hypnotized or watched other people being hypnotized?"

- "Did you ever do something you didn't want to do because someone pressured you to do it (donate money, have sex, smoke cigarettes, use drugs)?"

- "Have you ever bought a product you didn't need or want and then realized how many advertisements for that item you had seen or heard?"

By asking some of these questions, you might stimulate the person to start equating some of these experiences to the issue of cult mind control. Since influence processes can be seen as varying in degree of impact, it might make it easier to see how the extreme conditions which cults use can produce extreme results.

Errant Belief #2

"EVERYTHING IS MIND CONTROL."

Mind control is everywhere, the reasoning goes—in psychotherapy, advertising, education, and the military, for example—so it must be acceptable. When we generalize and say that everything is mind control, all distinctions are lost. No insight is gained. A more productive model is to think in terms of a continuum of influence: at one end, respectful, ethical, growth-enhancing influence that recognizes the value of individuality, human rights, and creativity; at the other end, conformity, dependency, and slavery, where the value lies in the leader and the group.

Everything is not mind control, although destructive mind control can be used by almost any institution or person. Institutions and systematic social influence programs should be evaluated on a case-by-case basis. Some are positive; some are benign; some are hurtful. While influence processes exist in all areas of human endeavor, cult mind control is a distinct phenomenon found at the destructive extreme of the continuum.

Psychotherapy

Ethical mental health professionals use their knowledge of the mind to influence their clients in a process of growth and change. The locus of control throughout treatment should remain with the client, and not the therapist. It is true that there are many people affected by mental illness who want and need structure and an authority to help them make decisions. Others may never have individuated in their personal development; in other words, they are still acting like children, not like adults. If a person has been severely affected by mental illness, or some major psychological problem, he may need to depend on authority figures until he can become strong. There are also poorly-trained and unethical therapists who foster dependency for self-serving reasons.

Advertising

Advertising has a profound economic, cultural, and social impact on our lives. Advertisers use sophisticated psychological methods to manipulate our desires, thoughts, and behaviors. The goal is often to create a need where none previously existed, or to amplify a need, and influence people about how they should fulfill it. As we have learned from the promotional tactics of the cigarette industry, some forms of advertising can be harmful and deceptive. Of course, there are also good advertisements that are meant to inform, persuade, and motivate people to be responsible about their own lives and the lives of their fellow citizens. Becoming conscious of the power of advertising, or simply changing the station—or turning off the television or radio altogether—are the most efficient ways to minimize negative effects.

Education

There is no doubt that some educational systems are designed to indoctrinate rather than educate. They demand conformity and obedience. But there are other educational systems that encourage students to think for themselves, be creative, and respect themselves and others. Educational systems that use fear and guilt — and that focus on competition and conformity — produce ready candidates for destructive cults. Students should be taught critical thinking skills and be encouraged to oppose blind conformity. Education should also encourage students to think from different perspectives to further their understanding.

Military

The military is an example of a highly structured, pyramid-shaped organization. There is a strict hierarchy. Soldiers are assigned numbers, given haircuts and uniforms, instructed in ways of talking, walking, marching and fighting. It is a career where personal choice is much more restricted than in society at large. In boot camp training, particularly in the Marines, the SEALs and other Special Forces, the use of mind control techniques is considered essential to create the identity of an elite soldier.[5]

But unlike a destructive cult, the military is accepted and valued by society. Military leaders answer to other branches of the government in a democracy. The military is also governed by ethical codes and structural checks and balances. People join the military for a specified length of time, and receive pay and benefits. With a few unfortunate exceptions, the military does not use deception in recruitment. When people join the military, they know what will be expected of them. Soldiers are encouraged to maintain contact with their family and friends, and vacation time is given annually.

When people endure rigorous training such as medical school, law school, the military, or seminary, they are making a conscious choice to become a doctor, a lawyer, a soldier, or a priest. This training enhances their sense of identity, offers knowledge and skills and affords a variety of benefits. When a person is deceptively recruited into a destructive cult, the leaders immediately begin a process of tearing down, rejecting, and reprogramming the person's authentic identity. The person loses his free will. He does not receive many personal benefits, and there is no institutional way to exit with honor.

Errant Belief #3

"WHY SHOULD I DO ANYTHING? HE SAYS HE'S HAPPY!"

Members of the Heaven's Gate cult took turns making videotaped farewell statements that explained why they had decided to leave their "vehicles" behind and commit suicide. All of them claimed that they were exercising their own free will, and that they were happy to perform this radical act of dying.

It is wishful thinking to accept at face value a cult member's words that he is "happy." In a cult, happiness is often redefined as sacrifice or suffering. Happiness in Heaven's Gate was defined as overcoming "individuality" and "humanness," and suicide was redefined as advancing to the next level of existence. Ingesting the fatal pills with applesauce and vodka, and placing plastic bags over their heads was seen as a necessary stage of the metamorphosis. The cult identity was "happy" to die. To the members of Heaven's Gate, not agreeing to die was suicide because it meant not going to the higher level.

But as we have learned, this cult identity is created by sophisticated mind control techniques. It does not represent the whole individual. You might tell those who are taken in by the cult identity to look behind the smiling mask. Remember, members are taught to suppress negative personal thoughts and emotions. They are trained to speak only positively of their involvement. When the cult member says he is "happy," it is usually the cult identity that is talking. The cult self is doing what it has been instructed to do.

When I was in the cult, I told everyone that I was happier than I had ever been in my life. But when you are a Moonie, being close to God makes you happy, and God is defined as a suffering parent. Therefore, the more you can feel God's suffering heart and sacrifice, the happier you will be. By this Orwellian logic, happiness is suffering. As Moonies, we were also taught to suppress all negative feelings and thoughts, so we had to feel happy. We weren't allowed to feel anything else. If those feelings crept in, we were chastised and sent for retraining.

People must not accept such statements without examining the deeper issues. This is a time for reality-testing. If potential Team members have doubts because the cult member says he's perfectly happy, you should encourage them to pursue such blanket statements with follow-up questions:

- "What do you mean when you say you are happy?"
- "If you were unhappy, would you be able to admit it to yourself?"
- "Would you tell us if you were unhappy?"
- "What would need to happen for you to feel unhappy enough to walk away from your involvement?"

Errant Belief #4

"HE'S AN ADULT. WE HAVE NO RIGHT TO INTERFERE."

It is normal for people to resist interfering in the lives of their adult relatives or friends. In fact, the law states that once people reach the age of majority (usually eighteen, but in some countries twenty-one), they are responsible for their actions. However, cult mind control impairs an individual's capacity for mature decision-making. Especially at the beginning of the cult involvement, family members and friends know that something is wrong. But they often back off when the adult cult member says, "Don't tell me what to do. I am an adult. Don't try to control my life." People don't realize that this is a tactic to neutralize objections and induce passive acceptance. Cult members often threaten to cut off all contact if they are not "treated as an adult."

The fact that a person is of legal age does not mean that he is functioning as a responsible adult. For example, under hypnosis a person can be age-regressed to childhood. The individual thinks, feels, and acts like a child. That becomes his "reality." It is common for cult leaders to ask members to become like "children of God." In fact, an essential aspect of the cult identity is to possess the naïveté of a child. A child's idolization of the parent figure is precisely what a cult leader needs to be in total control. By taking advantage of the desire for childlike innocence, cult mind control undermines the normal resources of a mature mind.

If a concerned friend or family member is questioning his own right to interfere, remind him that his love gives him the right to be concerned. If a loved one is under the influence of destructive mind control, relatives and friends have the right and the obligation to take steps to undo the mind control process so that the person can think independently. Once the cult member has an opportunity to learn about mind control, recognize the features of destructive cults, and meet with former members and critics, he will be in a position to make an informed choice.

Errant Belief #5

"HE HAS THE RIGHT TO BELIEVE WHAT HE WANTS TO BELIEVE."

If a person wants to believe that David Koresh is the Christ, that is his right. If people want to believe that Sun Myung Moon and Hak Ja Han are the perfect True Parents, they are entitled. In a free society, people are free to believe whatever they like, but at the same time, they should be protected from undue influence processes that *make them believe* something and *prevent them from re-evaluating their beliefs.*

As we have seen, cult mind control makes it seem as though members are exercising their own free will, but this is only the illusion of choice. When people in a controlled environment are subjected to psycho-social influences—like group conformity or behavior modification techniques—they can be manipulated and indoctrinated into accepting a completely different belief system. Social psychologists have conducted experiments that graphically demonstrated how a person's beliefs can become extremely pliable under the right set of social circumstances. Because cult mind control techniques are more sophisticated and invasive than the methods used in these studies, cult indoctrination is even more effective in suppressing a person's free will.

If a person insists that he has freely chosen his beliefs, especially if they are contradictory to his previous beliefs, then he should be willing to engage in an in-depth questioning, to demonstrate that he was making his own decision when he adopted his new beliefs. For anyone born into a belief system, religious, political or otherwise, there always comes a time in that person's maturation into adulthood when he should challenge and test his assumptions. This is more than just a one-time process. It should be done by all of us, as we mature into responsible people.

Errant Belief #6

"HE'S TOO INTELLIGENT TO JOIN A CULT."

This was my mother's response in 1974, when I dropped out of college, quit my job, donated my bank account, and moved into the Moon Center in Queens, New York. She was trying to reconcile how her son, an honors student, could be foolish enough to be taken in by a cult and accept such stupid beliefs. She thought that I would see through it quickly and on my own. I only wish that she had been right.

Many people have a hard time believing that bright, talented people—often from good homes and with higher education—could fall under the control of a cult. What they fail to realize is that cults intentionally recruit "valuable" people—they go after those who are intelligent, caring, and motivated. Most cults do not want to be burdened by unintelligent people with serious emotional or physical problems. They want members who will work hard with little or no sleep. Most of the former cult members I have met are exceptionally bright and educated. They have an active imagination and a creative mind. They have a capacity to focus their attention and enter deep states of concentration. Most are idealistic and socially conscious. They want to make the most of themselves—and to make a positive contribution to the world.

Cult mind control groups thrive to the extent that they can recruit such intelligent, dynamic people. It is essential for all members of the Team to realize that cults target these people for recruitment. The more creative a mind a person has, the more his imagination can be used to control him. Indeed, bright people sometimes have even more sophisticated fantasies about the group and its doctrine than does the cult leader. The bright member usually follows his own fantasy construction of the group's belief system.

Errant Belief #7

"HE MUST BE WEAK, OR LOOKING FOR EASY ANSWERS. HE NEEDS SOMEONE TO TELL HIM WHAT TO DO."

This is a very commonly held, but fallacious generalization about cult members. People often try to find fault with people who experience tragedy by *blaming the victim*. Laying blame gives people a false sense of control over their own lives by distancing them from the victim. However, the idea that people knowingly join destructive cults is patently wrong. Most people are recruited at a vulnerable moment, without understanding the forces that are brought to bear on them. Sometimes a cult manipulates a recruit's strength. For example, by playing to my high degree of self-confidence, the Moonies managed to get me, and keep me, at their three-day workshop.

There is no doubt that many people in cults have emotional baggage and other assorted problems—everyone does. But focusing the blame for cult membership on the individual is a mistake. If a friend or family member blames the cult member, ask him to consider the following:

- Why would over 900 men, women, and children follow Jim Jones' order to drink Kool-Aid laced with cyanide?
- Why would members allow David Koresh to have sex with every woman in the group (including minors), while other men were not allowed to have sex at all, even with their wives? Why did most members die in flames rather than surrender to the authorities?
- Why would seven male followers of Marshall Applewhite castrate themselves?
- Why did the members of Heaven's Gate ingest vodka and pills and allow plastic bags to be placed over their heads to smother them?
- Why do the Jehovah's Witnesses want their members to die rather than accept a blood transfusion?

In my twenty-plus years of working with cult-related issues, I can categorically state that most cult members are not "weak" people, looking for someone to tell them what to do. I strongly urge you to meet a few dozen former members and come to your own conclusions.

Errant Belief #8

"SHE'S BETTER OFF WHERE SHE IS."

Sometimes family, friends, and even mental health professionals will think that a person is better off in the cult than where they were before their recruitment. It may be tempting to agree, particularly when a person has stopped abusing drugs or alcohol, or when a person is no longer being physically or sexually abused—although some cults practice physical and sexual abuse.

A cult may provide temporary relief from traumatic circumstances, but cult involvement doesn't cure anyone's problems. It substitutes unethical mind control practices for legitimate help. Destructive mind control is itself a form of psychological abuse. In the hands of a cult leader, mind control techniques can be devastating to an individual's psyche. By inducing a dissociative state and creating a dominant cult identity, cult mind control represses the real issues of the pre-cult and authentic identity. The cult member's past problems with family members and friends are used to break contact, rather than to resolve past hurt. When people leave a cult, all of these pre-cult issues resurface, along with the problems caused by membership in a destructive cult.

If a person's pre-cult life was unhealthy and traumatic, then ethical psychotherapy can set them on a path towards healing by facilitating the process of:

- Positive growth and change.
- Building self-esteem.
- Learning how to trust themselves and others.
- Developing better strategies for coping with life's issues.

When used by a reputable mental health professional, mind control techniques can be enormously effective, provided the client's autonomy is always respected. For example, there are ethical programs that can help a person overcome a drug or alcohol addiction. These structured environments are healthier and safer than destructive cults, because they encourage clients to:

- Think for themselves.

- Get in touch with their own feelings and needs.

- Be part of a meaningful community (without indoctrination).

There is no doubt that people deserve a chance to control their own lives. I know countless former cult members who have become teachers, lawyers, doctors, computer experts, and parents.

Errant Belief #9

"HE'LL WALK OUT ON HIS OWN WHEN HE IS READY."

This attitude presumes that the cult member has the resources and free choice to leave. He does not! If he did have free choice, I can say from my own experience, he would have left the group long ago. As we shall see, one vital step of the Strategic Interaction Approach is to remove the phobias that keep the cult member imprisoned. It is important to do what you can to speed up the reality-testing process, because the longer the person stays in a cult, the greater the damage done to the fabric of his life. The more healthy contact that cult members can have with family, friends, and non-members, the better their chance to leave sooner.

Former members often express anguish over damage done to their psyche and to their valued relationships. They feel sorry about lost educational and career opportunities. Even worse, they feel guilty about the people they recruited, the money they collected, and the unethical behavior they committed as members. The longer they were in, the deeper the regrets when they get out. Cults have shown us that a passive, hands-off, wait-and-see approach can have tragic consequences. Few people suspected that a UFO cult like Heaven's Gate would end in a mass suicide.

However, there are some families who realized that their loved one was under mind control. I first met Bob and Alice Maeder at a Cult Information Service meeting in New Jersey one year after their daughter Gail's death. Even though Gail had cut off contact with them, they had made repeated and often ingenious attempts to find and communicate with her. The Maeders are good people and loving parents. Even though they lost their daughter to Heaven's Gate, they still come to cult awareness meetings, appear on television, and participate in interviews in the hope that other parents will be spared their suffering. They want to tell you: "Do everything you can to rescue your loved one. Don't sit back and passively wait for her to leave."

Errant Belief #10

"WE'VE LOST HOPE."

Giving up hope is a dysfunctional coping mechanism. If family members and friends no longer believe that the person will leave the group, then at least they will no longer be sad and disappointed. Some people have actually told me that they have grieved their loved one as if he had already died. I say, "If the person is still breathing, then they are still alive!"

Negative beliefs can often become self-fulfilling prophecies. People become depressed when they think they have tried everything: they tried to talk with the person and it has done no good; maybe there was a failed rescue attempt; maybe the cult member married within the group and had children. Hopelessness occurs when families project the negative past into the present and future. Family members think that there is nothing else they can do. They feel totally resourceless.

Family and friends must find a way to adopt a new belief: that their loved one will inevitably leave the cult. Hope will sustain and motivate you through the many ups and downs of the rescue process. Build a support system and make sure to include others who have successfully helped their loved ones after long-term cult involvement.

I have encountered innumerable people who have left destructive cults after decades of involvement. Ray Franz ceased his association with the Jehovah's Witnesses after sixty years. Before you give up hope, I urge you to find long-term ex-cult members to speak with. Despite the many problems they have when they finally get out, they are always glad to be free. As long as the cult member is alive, there is reason for hope.

To determine the first logical step, review the facts:

- How long ago did you talk to your loved one?
- What were the circumstances?
- Were you practicing goal-oriented communication?
- Did you have information about destructive mind control?
- Did you have the resources of former members?

Even if you do not know where your friend or loved one is living right now, you can be a part of the solution by participating in SIA work. Every person in a cult is someone's relative or friend. You can make time to interact positively in the lives of other cult members—individuals in the same group as your loved one, as well as people in other groups—even if you have lost contact with your loved one. The person you help today may help you later, when you have found your loved one.

WHO SHOULD BE PART OF THE TEAM?

The first step in assembling a Team is to determine who is willing and who is not willing to help. You can start by making an exhaustive list of all the potential Team members you can think of. From this list, we will contact and educate those people who are most likely to make effective Team members.

Making the list

The core of the Team will usually consist of immediate family members and close friends. The family may be intact, divorced, or blended, and the cult member may not be in contact with his biological parents. People from broken families sometimes worry that, by contacting a family member, they might open old wounds. But years of experience have shown me that family members can usually find a way to overcome past differences by focusing on the needs of the cult member. I've seen families who were split by divorce, mothers and fathers who hadn't spoken politely to one another in ten years, coming together and sitting in the same room, helping one another, listening to one another, and working toward a common goal.

In any case, you should use as many of the family's inherent resources as possible. Next, add to your list:

- Friends and other significant relatives.
- Significant figures in your loved one's pre-cult life.
- Other families with loved ones in the cult.
- Ex-members of your loved one's group and of other cults.
- Anyone who cares about the cult member and who you can trust.

I have found that the work of fighting cults brings together the most unlikely assortment of people from many different socio-economic backgrounds and with diverse religious and political views. I have had an automobile mechanic who was very "hands-on" in his approach, working beside a philosophy professor who thought in terms of abstract concepts and ideas. I've seen the Orthodox Jew, the Evangelical Christian, the atheist, the agnostic, the humanist, the Muslim, the Buddhist, grandparents and young children, police, therapists, politicians, and media people—people from all over the world, collaborating and helping one another.

Criteria for choosing team members

The family will need to decide on each person who would be an effective team member. Potential Team members should be honest with you and agree not to reveal your efforts while the person in still affiliated with the cult. They should be willing to make a commitment to help the cult member. They should have, or be able to develop, a high degree of rapport and trust with the cult member and with other Team members.

Team members should also be motivated by love and concern for the cult member, not by self-interest. People who show genuine interest in your loved one—for example, a sister who wants to help her brother stand on his own feet—will be the most sincere and effective Team members. People who dwell on their own needs—for example, a girlfriend who wants him back for selfish reasons, or relatives who are embarrassed by his involvement—will be less effective, and could even make the rescue process more difficult. You will need to confront and educate such people about the importance of concern for the cult member's well-being in a Strategic Interaction. Only those who are willing to put the needs of the cult member first should become part of the Team.

Although no two Team members will look at the person's cult involvement in the same way, you will begin to see patterns of positive and negative thinking as you begin the process of building the Team. Some people's attitudes will bring you closer to your goals, while others will work against your efforts.

Approaching potential team members

The most appropriate family member should interview each potential team member before inviting them to join the effort. Sometimes this means one of the parents, but often it is one of the siblings who will get the best results. Take the interview one step at a time, beginning with a brief statement of your concern for your loved one: "I'm worried about John. What do you think?" Do not reveal too much too soon. Listen to what the person has to say. If the person seems in any way concerned, ask for a promise of confidentiality: "Would you be willing to promise that the rest of this conversation will be kept between us? Specifically, I don't want anything said to John (the cult member) or to *anyone* who might undermine our efforts. If you think you might want to tell someone, please check with me first."

A common mistake is to overwhelm the person with information: "We think John is in a cult. Would you read this information and be prepared to talk to someone who is more knowledgeable?" This approach could scare some people away. It could also cause the individual to overreact and contact the cult member. This can inadvertently drive the cult member deeper into the cult by causing distrust of the family. Each Team member must be made aware that if the cult member finds out about the family's efforts, the cult will spend more time indoctrinating the member.

To help people prepare themselves by thinking ahead, you can ask a hypothetical question: "If John asks whether you have been in touch with us, what do you think you would say?" Then rehearse a logical response with the person: "Yes, I spoke with them briefly on the phone. They wondered if I had heard from you. They expressed their love for you." This answer is better than denying that a telephone call was made, which is dishonest. You should not say anything that will make the situation worse.

Don't rule out important resources just because a person is busy or seems disinterested. Seek out pre-cult friends of your loved one, even if they haven't talked in years. If a friend is alienated now from the cult member, but had a good relationship at an earlier time, the Team should educate him about destructive mind control. Remind him that it is the person's cult identity, not his authentic self, which has created the rift between him and his friend. I have handled several cases where such a long-term old friend was willing to be trained and to visit the member for days at the cult, thereby demonstrating "open-mindedness" and a commitment to the friendship. Such people can be tremendously effective if they know what they are doing and work as part of the Team.

When evaluating potential team members, some of the important issues to keep in mind are:

- Who does the cult member trust?

- Who is most respected?

- Who communicates best?

- Who is closest in age and interests?

Not every potential Team member you approach will agree to help. If the person says, "I feel I have a divided allegiance," or "I don't want to do or say anything behind his back," you should respect his point of view. You might respond, "We understand. Think about it. If you ever change your mind and want to talk, please give us a call." Even when the person is not comfortable making a commitment, the rest of the conversation should be spent gathering information and building rapport and trust. For example, you might ask:

- "What do you know of our loved one's involvement?"

- "What are your special concerns?"

- "What kinds of things have you tried to say?"

- "I admire your friendship. I'm glad you have that connection."

- "Please stay in touch with us. We really want to help him.

You are a link to that."

On the other hand, if the person says, "Oh, he has really changed, and I'm upset about it." or "I've heard all of these terrible things about the group," then you are ready to move to the next level. Once the friend, relative or co-worker has made a commitment, you can begin the information-gathering process by giving him information about the cult and mind control techniques. Your next goal will be to help Team members educate themselves and look at all the issues, as you have done, so they will be prepared to interact with the cult member in a balanced, informed manner.

Attitudes that Enhance Success

- Belief that the individual experiencing mind control will leave the group in time.
- Belief in the person's integrity, intelligence, creativity.
- Belief in your and others' commitment to help and in your resourcefulness.
- Belief in God, or some greater force that gives you strength, solace and hope.
- Patience, flexibility, and determination.

Attitudes that Undermine Success

- Rigidity, stubbornness, arrogance, embarrassment.
- Hopelessness, panic, hysteria.
- Criticism and judgement—"I'm right, you're wrong".
- Anti-spirituality.

Chapter 6

Empowering Members of the Team

During my many years of counseling work, I have seen a wide range of family situations, from the most loving and close-knit, to the most unhealthy and destructive—torn apart by violence, alcoholism and emotional abuse. But by far most of my clients are families that fall in the most caring and functional end of the spectrum, which makes sense. Families with overwhelming problems usually do not have the resources to make the effort to help, though individual family members may. I have been amazed by the creativity and determination of such individuals. For example, I was once contacted by a sister of a cult member only to learn that her other siblings were also troubled: one was in jail, another a raging drunk, another had a debilitating nerve disease. Despite all of these other problems, she still wanted to help the person in the cult.

I have yet to see a "perfect" family. Every family has some type of emotional baggage, or skeleton in its history. It comes with being "human." Dad or mom may have spent too much time working. Mom was too involved and intrusive, dad was too distracted and distant, or vice versa. Maybe there was some illness, divorce, premature death, or trauma, or an abrupt move to another geographical location. No matter what the problems were in the past, family members who care and want to help can help. I am always very hopeful when there are loving, concerned people willing to make

131

such efforts. I know that they will be successful at assisting their loved one.

A cult involvement usually has a dramatic impact on everyone, not just the person in the group. Family members and friends can lose sleep, get angry and frustrated, and feel worry, shame, and even guilt. Often, everyone feels helpless. The Strategic Interaction Approach assumes a "family systems" approach. Even though the cult member is the "reason" the family goes for counseling (what family therapists call the "identified client"), what we discover is that everyone has issues to resolve. In a blended family, there is often anger and resentment between ex-wives and ex-husbands and their children. Issues such as these will play an important role in the events to come.

Cult involvement can last for months, even years. If families do not get the necessary support and help, they can be torn apart when unresolved problems come to the surface. Parents, siblings, relatives, and friends are often unprepared to cope with the intensity of their feelings and needs. People can become depressed and despondent and, consequently, may work against the family's hope and optimism. Sometimes a Team member may be suffering from low self-esteem, some sort of addiction, or a past trauma. In the SIA, it is essential to help each person take care of his own issues and concerns first. Why is this so important? It might sound trite, but it is true: We can not really help others until we learn to help ourselves. Family and friends see the cult member as someone who is "stuck" but often don't realize that, in some ways, they too might be "stuck."

There are innumerable instances of families that have unwittingly contributed to the loved one's susceptibility to cult manipulation. The classic example is that of a very rigid, controlling parental figure, usually a father, but not always. Such a person typifies the style of a prototypical cult leader, dictatorial and arrogant; black versus white and us versus them in their thinking; controlling, using guilt and fear to promote dependency. Ironically, at first the child may be attracted to the cult leader because the leader seems to be so "different" from the parents, when in fact the leader has similar patterns and is, in fact, much worse.

Sometimes there is a significant event or series of events that precedes the cult recruitment. I remember one Moonie case that was quite complicated. I found out that several months prior to the young woman's recruitment into the cult, her mother had suffered a nervous breakdown. Her father was completely overwhelmed by the stress of what happened to his wife and the burden of taking care of three children by himself. One night, the young woman was raped. She went to her father for help, but his lack of personal resources caused him to react poorly. He got angry at his daughter, denied the rape had occurred, and accused his daughter of making it up to get his attention. Unfortunately, she had, in fact, been raped. That trauma, her mother's nervous breakdown, and her father's rejection of her plea for help made her incredibly vulnerable to cult recruiters. Although this is an extreme example, it demonstrates the need to understand and resolve underlying issues first. There was no way I could discuss with her what is wrong with the Moon cult until the underlying pain of her pre-cult self could be unearthed and verbalized. Her father needed to acknowledge what happened and ask her for forgiveness. Only then could we deal with cult mind control issues.

When interacting with cult members, you may find that they become defensive. They may attack you or point to your shortcomings, or those of another Team member. The cult member might ask a parent, "Why should I talk with a therapist? You've never dealt with your drinking problem." Or a cult member may point to a sibling who is in an abusive marriage, but is doing nothing to stop the abuse. In such situations, family members would do well to admit that there are problems and try to overcome them. This not only builds rapport, but also shows the cult members that it is possible to change. In fact, modeling of changes is a key feature of the SIA.

I encourage each person to think about times in his life when he was stuck: in a relationship, a job, a belief system. Remember how you tried to improve your situation? Once you acquired the information, resources, and support, perhaps you did.

The feeling of being in a rut is a universal experience, but it does not have to be permanent. During his thirties, Harry Truman was bankrupt; in his sixties, he was the President of the United States. Donald Trump, one of the most successful businessmen in American history, rebuilt his fortune after near bankruptcy and bounced back, eventually writing a best-seller called *The Art of the Comeback*.[1]

It is inspiring to study such examples because they reveal an important underlying pattern:

- At first, the person may not even realize there is a problem.

- At a later point, they realize that they are stuck.

- They go on a search for additional resources and information.

- They gain a new perspective.

- They become "unstuck" by receiving help and following a new course of action.

As I have said before, mind control techniques are not inherently good or evil. In a cult, they are used to manipulate and exploit. They take the "locus of control" away from the individual and refocus it on an external authority figure. In the Strategic Interaction Approach, as we shall see, techniques such as thought stopping may be used to enhance self-esteem, calm panic and anxiety, and build self-confidence and self-trust. The techniques are identified and the "locus of control" is always within the individual.

Ethical, qualified counselors can teach, guide and nurture.

Their goal is to help you live a fulfilled, fruitful life. They do not try to keep you in therapy forever. In fact, they help you to identify your therapeutic goals and push you to achieve them. In some cases, I recommend marriage counseling with a specialized marriage counselor. In others, I recommend support programs or individualized psychotherapy. Most important is that each person moves forward to feel healthier during the Strategic Interaction. The SIA offers all persons who get involved many opportunities to learn more about:

- Their relationships with others.
- Their childhood development.
- What they think about themselves.
- How they compare themselves with others.
- How they treat others.
- How others treat them.

There are countless issues that can stand in the way of progress during a Strategic Interaction. When each Team member addresses his own problems, he empowers himself and the Team, and sets an example for the cult member to follow. Remember, our overall goal is growth and change for everyone, not just the cult member.

DEALING WITH UNDERLYING ISSUES

Self-esteem

Sometimes, even highly-accomplished people are unable to feel good about themselves. Their self-esteem is torn to shreds by negative inner voices that attack and judge them. In some people, these negative thoughts can cause panic and anxiety attacks. As a result, mere ideas can stimulate an intense physical reaction. It is essential to examine such negative, learned thought patterns. They are poisonous to your psychological health!

It's a positive step to find out that responses to stress have been unhealthy. We are then in the position to correct these responses. Issues that stem from the low self-esteem or the chronic depression of any Team member must be addressed while we are dealing with the cult situation. The condition of each person's self-esteem in the Strategic Interaction process is an important concern.

The Strategic Interaction Approach seeks to enhance each individual's feelings of self-worth. I try to help my clients build rapport and trust with the parts of themselves that are critical and judgmental. Blame or self-recrimination drains people's resources. We experiment with new actions and behavior that can help build self-esteem. We assess what works and what does not work. Every interaction with a Team member or the cult member is an opportunity for growth and change.

Each person will have higher self-esteem in certain areas and lower self-esteem in others. There is often a split between personal and professional resources. For example, a mother who had high self-esteem as a doctor and professor complained that she felt that she could help everyone's children but her own. I asked her, "What advice would you give if you looked at your daughter as if she were your neighbor's child?" She had never thought about it that way. Taking this new perspective, her resources as a doctor and scholar were available to her as a mother. Likewise, a father who has high self-esteem as a successful businessman can learn to transfer some of his professional skills to his personal life.

Once we have removed family system roadblocks, members of the Team will be able to play their strongest suit. We tap into those skills and talents that help them feel good about themselves. We explore new methods that are less punishing and more effective. We learn how to set reasonable, satisfying goals.

Making a self assessment chart

On a sheet of paper, list your strengths in each of the following categories. Use accurate descriptive language, and be specific rather than general. Describe carefully how these strengths will help you reach your goals during the Strategic Interaction.

- Physical appearance
- Personality traits
- How other people see you
- How you relate to others
- Work performance
- Personal performance
- Mental functioning
- Sexuality

Once you have done this, identify how you can enhance your self image further. Identify characteristics that are blocking you, or qualities that are missing that you will need to move forward. Visualize yourself in the future, feeling and being exactly the way you want to be.

Personality differences

Human beings tend to take their "maps of reality" and project them onto everyone else. We assume that others think, feel, and respond the same way that we do. Obviously, this is not true. There are fundamental personality differences from one individual to another that influence our perceptions.

One way to cultivate self-awareness and self-knowledge about personality differences among family members is by utilizing personality tests. When families participate in such evaluations, they can gain greater knowledge not only of themselves, but of their brothers, sisters, parents, children, spouses, lovers, and friends.

This can help them understand why they behave the way they do.

One book I often use is David W. Keirsey's *Please Understand Me II: Temperament, Character, Intelligence*.[2] It uses the widely-respected Myers-Briggs Personality Inventory Test as a model. Family members can use the test as one way of gathering information. If you have access to the Internet, the Keirsey Character Sorter and Keirsey Temperament Sorter II are personality tests that can be completed and scored free of charge on the Keirsey Temperament and Character Web Site.[3]

One of the benefits of personality tests is that the resulting self-awareness may be used to create a bridge between the cult member and the family. You might say to him, "Dad is this type, and Mom is that type. We're curious to see what type you are." When the time comes, families can ask their loved one to complete the test not just once, but twice: first, as they would before they got involved with the cult and, second, the way they presently feel. Of course, results will vary depending on the cult member's frame of mind while taking the test but, in general, it may reveal the cult member's personality type has changed. The more you understand about your loved one's view of his pre-cult identity, the better you will be able to recognize the cult identity—and the more easily you can engage his authentic identity.

This strategy worked particularly well in a case concerning a woman who was involved with a Bible cult. When her husband first called me, he was at his wit's end. Although he considered himself to be a Christian, his wife was frightening and alienating their children by telling them things like, "Daddy's going to hell." As a way of building bridges, I encouraged him to prepare for an intervention by getting in touch with his wife's family who, it turned out, knew very little about the group.

I learned that the cult member's brother, a devout Christian who knew the Bible well, had tried to debate theological issues with his sister but had gotten nowhere. Another of her brothers, I learned, was a psychologist, so I recommended that he read Yeakley's *The Discipling Dilemma*, which used the Myers-Briggs Test to measure radical personality change in members of another Bible cult. In addition, I asked him to read Keirsey's first book, *Please Understand Me*, and have each member of the family read the book and complete a personality test.[4] He also sent a copy of the book to his sister who was in the cult and asked her to do a personality test as part of the family counseling—so that family members could discuss the results and, hopefully, understand one another better.

Using the family's experience with *Please Understand Me*, he then introduced Yeakley's book to his sister, and began a dialogue with her about how dramatic changes in personality are considered to be unhealthy. The brother who was well-versed in Christian doctrine was able to point out differences between legitimate groups and other Bible cults. This laid the foundation for a meeting between the cult member and a former member of her group. In the end, she chose to leave the cult and return to her family. She has since been willing to appear on national television to speak out about her experience.

Values and beliefs

People's values and beliefs often have little or nothing to do with scientific fact or physical reality. Instead, they are usually influenced by parental, cultural, and peer expectations, and by personality type, as well as the need to feel loved, protected and accepted by those around us. The values and beliefs we adopt change rapidly in response to changes in our role or status. For example, union workers who rise to the level of management tend to shift to new patterns of belief because they have a need to belong to their new peer group. Similarly, your loved one has adopted cult-generated values and beliefs—perhaps about reincarnation or extraterrestrials that inhabit his body—as a way of gaining acceptance by the group. This concept will be important to remember when you communicate with him.

It is particularly important that members of the Team be aware of, and ultimately resist, the temptation to think in terms of "should" and "should not." A "should" is an absolute moral imperative, for example, "I should have been a better parent." If we do not live up to what we believe we "should" or "should not" be doing, we may judge ourselves to be bad, or unworthy as human beings. "Shoulds" are built on generalizations and absolutes, and tend to promote simplistic, oppositional thinking. They pollute language and communication. For every value-laden word like generous, diligent, intelligent, strong, or honest, there is a negative opposite: selfish, lazy, stupid, weak, deceitful. People often assume that they are either one or the other: "If you do this you will be good, otherwise you will be bad." This is far from the truth.

By carefully discovering or reviewing your "shoulds," you will gain greater insight into your values and beliefs. You will be able to express more effectively your concerns (which are based on your values and beliefs) to your loved one in the cult. If you can stop telling yourself you should be this or you should do that, you may avoid telling your loved one what he should or should not do.

To Do

- Have Interaction Team members complete a personality test.
- Discuss the results with each other.
- When deemed appropriate, you may show and discuss results with your loved one in the cult and ask him to participate.

Values and beliefs assessment

- Are your beliefs open to change?

- Do you allow for exceptions when circumstances warrant them?

- How do you feel when you make a mistake?

- Where do your values come from (parents, education, culture)?

- Do your values fit your own unique circumstances, personality, and needs?

- Do you test and evaluate your values and beliefs?

- Do you accept what others tell you at face value?

- Do your values lead you to positive action and behavior?

- Are your values realistic?

- Are your values life-enhancing, nourishing, and supportive?

- Do you ever find your values are life-restricting?

- Do you acknowledge your needs and feelings?

- What happens when you notice areas of guilt, conflict, obligation, or avoidance?

Sibling issues

Siblings are in a difficult position when their brother or sister joins a cult. Often they become jealous and resentful of the attention given the cult member. They might ask a parent, "How come you only think about John? He is in the cult giving away his trust fund. I'm working really hard, doing everything right, and you only pay attention to me when you want to hear about John!" Although this is an extreme example, these thoughts and feelings may arise. In the long run, parents should not put so much emphasis on the cult member that other relationships are neglected.

Sometimes, rather than communicating directly, people use a

third party to get a message across. This is called *triangulation*, and
it is a very dysfunctional way to communicate. Parents sometimes
put one of their children in the role of "switchboard" to communicate with each other or to get messages to other family members.
For example:

YOUNGER SISTER: My parents are always arguing over what they
should do about John. They put me in the middle. Do I agree with
Mom or do I agree with Dad? They want me to say whose fault it
is. They also put me in the middle, asking me to talk with my
brother. Sometimes I'm very angry. Most of the time I feel frustrated and depressed. It's bad enough that my relationship with my
brother is messed up. I don't need my parents always on my case
about it.

This type of indirect communication is usually ineffective, and
can be downright harmful. The solution is for the person in the
middle to refuse to convey messages. They should say, "Tell him
yourself, don't put me in the middle!"

Another issue comes when one of the siblings has himself left a
cult involvement. If the sibling was in the same group then, no
doubt, he is looked upon as a "traitor" by the cult member. It is
imperative that the ex-member obtain good cult counseling first,
and really sort out his issues. He needs to answer some of the key
questions, "Who am I? What do I believe? What do I value? How
do I want to live my life?" He needs to understand, and be able to
articulate, the key issues involved in cult mind control. This ex-
member will probably become a key person in the rescue effort. If
the sibling was in a different cult group, he usually has more flexibility and freedom to talk openly to the cult member about his
experience, since he isn't seen as an "apostate." There will be many
opportunities to explain mind control as it was used in their group.

To Do

- Have Interaction Team members fill out the Values and Beliefs Assessment.
- Discuss the results with each other.
- Seek professional advice on how to use the results directly with the cult member.

Addictions

One of the most difficult tasks facing some family members is being open and forthright about admitting to drug abuse or addiction. Indeed, there are drug and alcohol interventions now being done that are similar to cult interventions. If a potential Team member has a problem with drugs or alcohol, the family can have a mini-interaction with that person. There will be many benefits:

- The person will be healthier, less self-destructive.

- The person will become a model for positive change.

- The family system will be strengthened by the process of growth and change.

You might try involving the cult member in the process of change. For example, one family I worked with had a daughter in a New Age guru cult. During the two-day preparation meeting, it came to light that the father was an alcoholic. Fortunately, he admitted that he needed professional help. He said he loved his daughter very much, and wished he could change his behavior and help her. I suggested that the mother ask the daughter to come home for an "alcoholism intervention," the aim of which would be to get him into a treatment center.

I arranged to have a local family therapist set up the intervention. The daughter came home and participated in a preparatory meeting with the therapist. Family members, who were coached beforehand on what to say to the father, pointed out specific things that he had or had not done, such as breaking a promise to spend time with the family on Easter, or losing days of work and forcing the mother to cover for him. The cult member loved her father and really made an effort to participate. The father agreed to go for treatment, and the powerful emotional bonding between family members helped her to feel valued and needed.

A couple of months later, when her father was out of the facility and sober, we did a successful intervention with her. This time, the father took the lead. He was able to be a role model for change. He told his daughter, "You confronted me with my problem behaviors and with your love. I listened and I went for therapy. Thank you for giving me so much support. Now I need to let you know some of my concerns with your current situation. Please hear me and the other family members out." This created a context for powerful reciprocity, and made it easier to approach the cult member with his concerns.

Religious issues

Most people don't want to believe that they are closed-minded—and that will be true of your loved one. If you are a parent who is concerned that your son or daughter isn't thinking independently, it will be essential to cultivate and demonstrate open-mindedness as a way of encouraging reciprocity. This may be especially difficult when it comes to religious issues. For example, if you are a conservative Christian and your loved one is in a cult that teaches against the concept of the Trinity, you may run into a major stumbling block. Each side may try to force its view on the other. It is difficult to feel anything but defensive when one of your central religious beliefs is being attacked.

It is also important to understand that in most Bible-based cults, although the member is aggressively taught doctrine, it is not the doctrine that holds him in the group. It is the sense that the group is God's true people, a feeling cultivated by techniques of mind control. Thus, to engage the cult member in a Biblical argument or discussion is often futile. He perceives that you are being led by Satan (at worst) or that you are outside of God's Will (at best). Therefore, it is usually non-productive, creates barriers, and closes down communication.[5]

When people get stuck in a particular point of view, I recommend a powerful communication technique called "counter-attitudinal argumentation." Essentially, each side is given a structured amount of time, say ten minutes, to defend the other person's point of view as if it were his own. For example, the loved one who doesn't believe in the Trinity argues why he believes in the Trinity. The parent who believes in the Trinity presents all of the arguments against the Trinity, as if he believes that point of view.

Typically, neither side is able to verbalize all of the points properly or convincingly when this exercise is first performed. After all, individuals don't really understand, let alone believe, the opposing point of view. The beauty of the technique is that it is up to each person to teach the other how to think like he does. If this exercise is done by both parties with mutual respect and a strong desire to improve the relationship, the results can be truly amazing. The goal here is not to make the other person actually accept your point of view. It is to be able to step into another person's model of reality and look at things from that view. In order to have a free mind, you must be able to step out of your own perspective and into the shoes of others. If you think the cult member is rigid and stuck, then make sure that you aren't acting like him.

Team members who may be humanistic, agnostic, or even atheistic in their philosophical orientation will have particular difficulty if their loved one is in a religious group. Problems inevitably result when a cult member tries to recruit them with any religious dogma. Atheists often wind up putting down all religion, and usually dig themselves into a communications "black hole."

I recommend that atheists, agnostics, and humanists adopt a more resourceful philosophical posture. For example, they might say, "If I did believe in a God, it would be a God of truth and not a God of lies. God would need to be an honest God; otherwise, how could you trust Him?" Rapport is built and a foundation is established for future discussions pertaining to deception and lies. Although most cult members would agree that they believe in a God of truth, some cults attempt to use passages from the Bible to prove that God deceives or approves of deception. In such cases, you would do well to study these verses to understand the context in which they appear in the Bible. You might contact a pastor or rabbi for help.

Another example of a resourceful approach is, "If I did believe in the Bible as the inerrant 'Word of God,' as you do, then I would want to learn everything about it, and not rely on rote memorization of selected passages. I would want to understand things in context. I would want to study with 'believing' scholars who have devoted their lives to God and the Bible." By taking this posture, you are encouraging them to study more, and not rely solely on cult sources of information.

Team members might consider taking the stance that if there is a God, then He (She) would be a God of love—a Being who has love for all people, even those who don't believe in Him. And those who believe in such a God would display such love. A powerful description of unconditional love in people can be found in the New Testament, in 1 Corithinians 13:1-13:

> If I speak in the tongues of men and of angels, but have not love, I am a noisy gong or a clanging cymbal. And if I have prophetic powers, and understand all mysteries and all knowledge, and if I have all faith, so as to remove mountains, but have not love, I am nothing. If I give away all I have, and I deliver my body to be burned, but have not love, I gain nothing.
>
> Love is patient and kind; love is not jealous or boastful; it is not arrogant or rude. Love does not insist on its own way; it is not irritable or resentful; it does not rejoice at wrong, but rejoices in the right.

Love bears all things, believes all things, hopes all things, endures all things.

Love never ends; as for prophecies, they will pass away; as for tongues, they will cease; as for knowledge, it will pass away. When I was a child, I spoke like a child, I thought like a child, I reasoned like a child; when I became a man, I gave up my childish ways. For now we see in a mirror dimly, but then face to face. Now I know in part; then I shall understand fully, even as I have been fully understood. So faith, hope, love abide, these three; but the greatest of these is love."[6]

If a Team member has trouble relating to specific religious affiliations, he might take the time to learn more basics about a variety of faiths. A good starting place is Jeffrey Moses's book, *Oneness: Great Principles Shared By All Religions*,[7] which shows the similarities among all religions by pointing to common beliefs such as "Love Thy Neighbor," "Speak Truth," and "The Golden Rule." Another good book and audio tape series is Huston Smith's *The World's Religions*.[8]

Stress, panic, and anxiety management

Some family members actually develop a form of Post Traumatic Stress Disorder (PTSD) in response to their loved one's cult involvement. Parents visualize their child committing suicide, even when the cult has no history of that kind of behavior. When people have intrusive thoughts and negative feelings ("My God, is he going to kill himself?"), they can become immobilized. They spend hours, day and night, thinking their loved ones will kill themselves. Cult situations produce doubt, uncertainty, and fear of the unknown. Knowledge and information are your greatest assets.

MOTHER: I watch television and see images of bodies at the People's Temple, or Waco, or Heaven's Gate. I can still see the lifeless bodies under those creepy purple shrouds. When you watch the farewell videos, you know those young men and women were somebody's sons and daughters. My son is into meditation and computers, too. I haven't been able to sleep. I'm paralyzed with fear and worry.

To help this mother, I would say, "Let's find out what needs to change in order for you to sleep—before we talk about what you can do to help your son."

Images and thoughts—as well as actual experiences—stimulate panic in cult situations. In a panic or anxiety mode, people feel restricted and uncreative. The brain selects the emergency ("fight-or-flight") response because it does not have enough information or it has been misinformed. The perception of danger activates the autonomic nervous system, which has two branches: the sympathetic and the parasympathetic nervous system. The sympathetic nervous system prepares the body for action by releasing adrenaline and noradrenaline into the bloodstream. The parasympathetic nervous system is responsible for restoring the body to relaxation. When a person perceives or anticipates danger, the brain:

- Receives a stimulus
- Interprets the meaning of that stimulus
- Selects a response
- Signals the body to cooperate as needed

Being able to slowly and objectively size up a situation is a crucial skill. We observe. We take a curious yet concerned posture. We gather information in a relaxed, thoughtful manner, but we do not rush in to fix the problem. Using this information, we can determine what action to take next. Some fears are valid, but none should be blown out of proportion. The best response to fear is to have a plan, or multiple plans, to prepare for any unforeseen contingencies. There are also many techniques that can help you gain control over your life experience.

THERAPEUTIC CONTROL TECHNIQUES

Cults use unethical, deceptive mind control techniques to create damaged, dependent personalities with low self-esteem. On the other hand, the SIA teaches ethical, therapeutic mind control techniques that encourage autonomy and high self-esteem. Team members can prevent panic attacks by interrupting the panic cycle at the point where their brain interprets the stimulus, thereby preventing the sympathetic nervous system from triggering a fight-or-flight response. The following exercises can be used to break unhealthy thought patterns and curb anxiety by intervening before the sympathetic nervous system is activated.

Overcoming distorted thought patterns

A powerful therapeutic technique called cognitive-behavioral therapy offers concrete tools for identifying and correcting dysfunctional thought patterns. David Burns' book, *Feeling Good: The New Mood Therapy*, is a great resource for identifying and challenging problematic thought patterns.[9] Recognizing such thought patterns in yourself will also give you insight into your loved one's psychological state, since cults actively instill distorted thinking in their members. In fact, one of your aims will be to get the cult member to reality-test and to correct such destructive habits. Here are some examples of common patterns to overcome:

Overemphasis on the past: ignores the possibility that things can ever change in the present or future.
FATHER: He never listened to my advice when he was young. It won't work now, either.

Overgeneralization: making a universal rule from one isolated event.
BROTHER: Last week, we had a fight on the telephone. He hates me. He's always hated me.

Global labeling/toxic put-downs.
Friend to Cult Member: You sound like a brainwashed robot.
Aunt to Cult Member: How could you be so stupid as to believe this nonsense?

Self-blame: inappropriate or exaggerated guilt over past events.
Father: The divorce was pretty rough. I know I didn't handle it well. It's all my fault that he's in the cult.

Denial: complete avoidance of the existence of a problem.
Mother: He's not really under mind control. He's just confused.

Rationalization: creating excuses for why things are the way they are.
Sister: She's better off where she is. If she weren't in the cult, she'd be out on the street doing drugs.

Filtering: selectively paying attention to the negative and disregarding the positive.
Mother: I spent all day with him and had a wonderful time, but he went back to the cult. I feel like a complete failure.

Polarized thinking: black-and-white categories, with no middle ground.
Father: It's too bad that he's wasting his life in that cult, working so hard with nothing to show for it.

Personalization: assuming everything has something to do with you.
Mother: I left three messages for him this morning and he hasn't called back. He must know I'm in touch with a cult expert.

Mind-reading: making presumptions about what others are thinking without asking first.
SISTER: I know you're upset with me for not telling you first.

Control fallacies: assuming that you either have total control or you are a total victim.
FATHER: I just want to go in and snatch him, sit him down, and snap him out of it.
MOTHER: Nothing I do has any effect at all.

Emotional reasoning: assuming things are the way you feel.
BROTHER: I feel that anyone willing to believe that crap is just weak.

In his book, Burns makes sugggestions that can produce real changes in the way you think and feel. Here are some of the methods I use with my clients.

Thought stopping

1. Identify automatic negative thinking; write down on a piece of paper your ten most recurring negative thoughts.
For example: *"He will never get out of the cult."*
2. Ask yourself: "What thoughts would I like to have instead?" Write them down next to the negative thoughts. Example: *"He will get out of the cult! It is only a matter of how fast and how easy it will be for him to leave."*
3. Think about the most common circumstances that trigger a negative thought. Write them down. Example: *"When I go into his room, or look at his picture."*
4. Visualize being in one of those circumstances, but this time, interrupt the negative thought and replace it with the positive thought.

5. Rehearse saying the new, *constructive thought again and again.*
*Repeat over and over: "He will get out of the cult! It is only a matter of
how fast and how easy it will be for him to leave."*

Positive messages

Another method that can help encourage you to have positive
thoughts and feelings is to write messages to yourself on post-it
notes and put them on your refrigerator, on your bathroom mirror,
or in your car.
Some examples are:

- Blessed are we who can laugh at ourselves, for we shall
  never cease to be amused.

- The Serenity Prayer: *God grant me the serenity to accept the
  things I cannot change, the courage to change the things I can,
  and the wisdom to know the difference.*

- Life is a journey, not a destination.

- Be more compassionate towards myself.

- Friendship is founded on trust and love. Trust that I am
  loved.

- Gratitude is a great attitude!

- Energy follows thought.

- Think good thoughts.

- It's never too late to have a happy childhood.

Visualization

There are many visualization techniques mentioned throughout this book. Try this simple one to help you feel more confident
and successful.

Step 1: See yourself from an outside perspective, as if you were on television—happy, confident, standing tall, doing whatever tasks need to be done.

Step 2: Now, visualize yourself stepping into that picture, becoming that happy, confident, productive person. See your loved one out of the cult, happy and fulfilled. Visualize in color, in focus, and with as much detail as you can imagine.

Self-hypnosis

Dr. Brian Alman has written a good book called *Self-Hypnosis: The Complete Manual for Health and Self-Change*.[10] I first learned self-hypnosis in 1980 in order to improve my free throws in basketball. I learned to focus my mind, ignore the outside environment and negative thoughts about missing the shot, and focus on being in my body and seeing the ball go through the hoop. I later learned how to use self-hypnosis to help quiet my mind when I needed to fall asleep, and began to use it as a creativity strategy when I needed to write.

If you experience difficulty learning self-hypnosis from reading a book, make sure you go to a certified hypnotherapist. Don't go to just anyone who advertises their services. I am a member of The American Society for Clinical Hypnosis (ASCH) as well as The International Society of Hypnosis (ISH). These organizations require that their members have professional credentials and make sure they have proper training and operate within ethical guidelines. I have been teaching workshops for both organizations for many years and find their members are able to quickly understand cult mind control due to their training.

Deep muscle relaxation

Muscle tension is a major component of anxiety and panic attacks. You should learn to pay attention to muscle tension in specific areas of your body and consciously release that tension. This is called progressive muscle relaxation. Start by tensing the muscles in your feet, and then relaxing them. Repeat this over and over until your feet feel completely relaxed—then move on to your ankles, calves, thighs, and so on until your whole body is relaxed. Of course, nothing beats a deep, relaxing, professional massage. You can also combine two techniques. For example, you can try a visualization technique, in addition to progressive muscle work, to attain deep muscle relaxation. Close your eyes and imagine a beam of sunlight shining on the tense area and focus on relaxing those muscles.

Deep breathing techniques

Breathing is one of those activities that we take for granted. I advocate that, several times a day, you take a series of long, deep breaths. It brings much-needed oxygen into your body and expels waste products like carbon monoxide. Exhale slowly, deeply, and deliberately, and make sure your exhalation lasts longer than your inhalation. Sometimes it helps to vocalize your exhalation, as if you were letting out a sigh of relief. Once you have completely emptied your lungs, they will naturally refill themselves, making the inhalation easier and more therapeutic.

Meditation

When used as a form of relaxation training, meditation focuses our minds and allows us to step out of the stresses in our lives. It quiets and disciplines the mind by focusing on a single item at a specific point in time. Reflective meditation gives a person the opportunity to learn about his fears, problems, and concerns, instead of being consumed by them. There are hundreds of different ways to meditate.[11] I personally like to just sit and focus on my breathing. When I am very agitated, I find it helpful to count in my head—inhale, "one, two, three, four," exhale, "one, two three, four."

In a basic meditation session, I suggest that you:

• Focus on being aware.

• If you have a thought, let it come in and go out.

• Realize that you are more than your thoughts, more than your feelings, more than your body.

• Feel connected to all living things, and God, if you are a believer.

Another form of meditation for families with deep Biblical convictions is to focus upon a particular passage of Scripture, and reflect thoughtfully on its meaning and application for one's life of faith. Some examples are: Joshua 1:8; Psalm 119:11, 15, 48, 97-99; Psalm 143:5; I Timothy 4:13-15.

Prayer

If you believe in God, prayer is one of the most powerful tools for empowerment. Team members who have deep religious convictions often draw great strength from regular prayer. Some clients have even asked their entire congregation, church, temple, or community to pray for their loved one. My mother told me she prayed for a year, asking God to let me have an accident and break my leg so they could rescue me from the Moonies. In fact, I had a van accident due to sleep exhaustion, and broke my leg, which led to an intervention!

I personally recommend positive, open-ended prayers which petition God to give strength, wisdom and resources to all those in need. Don't just think about your own needs. Pray for everyone!

MODELING POSITIVE CHANGE

The most powerful way to influence a person is to be an effective role model. If you want to encourage someone to grow and change, become a model of growth and change.

When parents have an unhealthy, abusive relationship with one another, the cult member might challenge them: "Look at your life. How dare you say that my leader is abusive!" If these parents want to influence their son or daughter, they should start making changes in their relationship. They must model those changes first. Then, they will have greater leverage to be taken seriously.

If the mother has problems speaking her mind to her controlling, domineering husband, she should learn to assert herself, particularly in front of the cult member. By doing so, she will be modeling the concept of standing up to an authority figure. The cult member will see that Mom can change. She can stand up for herself. That is a behavior we want to encourage in the cult member.

Members of the Strategic Interaction Team must all be role models. Particularly during interactions with the cult member, Team members should ask themselves, "Am I demonstrating that I am interested in improving my life? Making the world a better place? Am I showing that I am open and want to learn?"

If you want your loved one to believe the world is not such an evil place, and that there are plenty of constructive, worthwhile, and exciting things to do, then do some of those things yourself! Tell your loved one about your experiences. Remember, living fully and well is its own reward. Find things to do that energize you and make you feel good and resourceful. Approach each night of sleep with gratitude for the opportunity to be alive and look forward to a new day.

Chapter 7

Understanding Cult Beliefs and Tactics

To truly connect with a cult member, you must really understand his group, both in terms of its doctrine, *what* it leads members to believe; and its tactics, *how* it makes them believe. In this chapter, you will learn the many ways you can locate, evaluate, and utilize information about your loved one's group. Like a detective, you will conduct research, look for clues, ask questions, and follow leads until you know your subject inside and out. The more you learn, the more effective and confident you will be.

Deborah Reichmann and the Twelve Tribes[1]

When Marjorie and Michael Reichmann were told by their twenty-two year old daughter, Deborah, that she intended to join a group called the Twelve Tribes Messianic Communities, in Harrisonburg, Virginia, they recall having the same concerns that any parent might have: they knew nothing about the group and were generally unfamiliar with the nature of destructive groups. If the group was destructive, they naïvely believed, their college educated daughter would see that and leave.

Though they felt powerless to stop her from going, the Reichmanns immediately began educating themselves about the Twelve Tribes. In 1995, little could be learned on the Internet.

They gained their first insight into the group through discussions with several pastors in the Harrisonburg area. These meetings and others with residents in the area, led them, ultimately, to my first book and to Bob Pardon and Judy Barba.

Bob Pardon is a minister and friend who, with Judy, runs the New England Institute of Religious Research near Cape Cod. I have worked with Bob for many years on numerous cases, and have the greatest respect for his integrity, compassion, and deep commitment. Bob has a great deal of Biblical knowledge and has even studied Greek, which has proved invaluable in counseling members of Bible-based groups. Having spent two years investigating the Twelve Tribes—interviewing members and observing the group's behavior—Bob and Judy had amassed a tremendous amount of information about the group. They had written an extensive paper on the Twelve Tribes, which can be found on their NEIRR.org web site.

Bob and Judy helped the Reichmanns to understand the group's beliefs, for example, why the group taught that women should not wear makeup. They also shared critical details about its deceptive practices, such as the fact that, despite its claim to be led by "elders," the cult is actually run by a single person named Elbert Eugene Spriggs, a former personnel manager for the Dixie Yarn Company, who now calls himself "Yoneq."[2] They described how the group members were led to believe that they were following the one true Christian calling. Bob and Judy also put the Reichmanns in communication with former members who had been involved for many years in the group's top leadership. When it became clear to them that the group was a destructive mind control cult, the Reichmanns decided to meet with me for the purposes of planning an intervention.

During a two-day preparation session, we discovered that Deborah's sister and brother-in-law had been approached by neighbors, who were members of Kip McKean's International Churches of Christ (ICC). The family had knocked on their door and invited them to a "Bring Your Neighbor Day" event and home Bible Study. The brother-in-law remembered being impressed by their enthusiasm, though the sister had been skeptical because they seemed so pushy. It had never struck either one of them, until our meeting, that this apparently "typical suburban family" was part of a group under the influence of mind control. They watched videotapes of the ICC, and Bob, Judy and I spent some time teaching them about the cult. We encouraged them to share with Deborah what they learned about ICC—for example, how McKean claims that his group is the one and only Christian group on earth, and the only one whose Baptism is accepted by God—and hopefully help her to see parallels to the Twelve Tribes.

The Reichmanns had been encouraged by Bob and Judy, and later myself, to maintain good communication with their daughter, and to avoid doing anything that might be viewed as "negative." They learned, and put to great use, most of the communication strategies and techniques that have been integrated into this book. During his visits to the group's commune, Michael joined members in preparing meals, washing dishes, and singing and dancing. Through such activities he earned the cult members' trust, and he was able to get a firsthand understanding of the group's beliefs and practices. He and Marjorie even invited members of the cult to visit them in their home in the Midwest, which they did, further convincing the group leaders that the family was "safe." Because of all their preparatory work, it was much easier for Deborah to be given permission to return home for a visit and, ultimately, for our meeting.

Once Deborah came home, the Reichmanns told her that they had met some people who were knowledgeable about the Twelve Tribes, and who had shared some things about the group that she might be unaware of. They asked whether she would be willing to meet with us and consider another point of view. Deborah was so confident that the group was "of God," and so eager to allay her family's concerns, that she agreed. Present, besides Bob, Judy and myself, was a former twenty-year Twelve Tribes member, JoEllen Griffin, who had almost died while in the group due to lack of medical care.[3] The family asked Deborah to meet with us for a few days of uninterrupted time so that she could have the opportunity to make a fully informed decision regarding her commitment to the group. They told her that if, at the end of that time, she still felt compelled to return to the Twelve Tribes, they would not to stand in her way. After several days, Deborah decided to walk out of the group.

GATHERING INFORMATION

In order to communicate with the cult member and earn his trust, Team members must develop a working model of the cult's belief system and behavior. Learn as much as you can about the group's doctrine, and compare its beliefs to those of other groups, both healthy and destructive. Try to identify specific ways that it deceives members and keeps them dependent—whether it is by distorting the truth, misinterpreting religious texts, or deliberately spreading lies about its critics.

The Internet

Begin by searching the Internet. It is an excellent source of current information about cults. The Internet is changing the entire cult scene. If you don't have Internet access at home, a local library or school may allow public access, or perhaps a trustworthy friend will be able to help. Go to my Web site (www.freedomofmind.com) and make an effort to investigate and familiarize yourself with the resources listed. Contact other cult awareness resource organizations if the Freedom of Mind Resource Center doesn't have the information available that you need. Try using meta-search engines to seek out additional information about the group in question.

Given the democratic nature of the Internet, you'll probably find sites that defend your loved one's cult as well as sites that criticize the group. There are always two or more sides to an issue, so don't accept any information at face value. Instead, be willing to work and search all sides. You should take time to explore both pro and counter-cult sites. Learn both sides of the debate and develop your own opinions based on the best information available.

Don't take your privacy on the Internet for granted. You might want to protect your identity, particularly when sending e-mail or posting to a cult-related newsgroup. Keep in mind that some cult members are active, savvy Internet users who monitor Web sites, newsgroups, and mailing lists. At first, it's easy to feel intimidated by electronic communication, but if you inform yourself and take simple security precautions, such as establishing an e-mail alias, you can access the world of information on the Net without compromising your privacy.[4]

If your loved one visits you at home, you should protect the files, e-mail, and Internet bookmarks (or "favorites") on your own computer, particularly if the person is computer-literate. I recently met with a family who ran into trouble because the cult member searched his father's computer (without permission) and found an obscure file that contained a history of e-mails with me, tipping him off to a planned intervention. Each time you use your computer, be sure to remove all traces of cult-related information. Delete any e-mail that might arouse suspicion, and keep critical documents on a floppy or zip disk that you can store in a safe place. Security passwords and even encryption programs can be installed to prevent unauthorized access to your computer.

Cult literature

Find out if the group has a written code of ethics, and if so, whether it holds its leaders to those principles. Does the cult's behavior contradict its teachings? Do leaders give orders to lie, despite dictates that uphold truth and forbid lying? By reading cult literature, you will develop a reference point for identifying and understanding the group's deception.

For example, if your loved one is in a Bible cult, read the Bible to determine whether the leaders are misquoting or misrepresenting passages to delude their followers. If you're not comfortable or familiar with how to understand passages in context, then get professional help. Seek out cult-generated literature to understand the group's interpretation of the Bible. Visit the cult Web site and read their online literature. Download and print the files, and store them in a safe place. Although there are similarities among Bible cults, each group will have its own set of beliefs that you will need to understand. Team members should know the difference between mainstream groups like the Church of Christ (founded in the late 1800s) and cults like the International Churches of Christ (founded in 1979). While many benevolent religious groups provide guidance through one-on-one discipleship, most Bible cults impose a one-over-one, authoritarian discipleship in which a superior for all intents and purposes makes major decisions for the rank and file members.

If the person is in a Buddhist cult, I suggest that you read a book like *The Path With Heart: A Guide Through the Perils and Promises of Spiritual Life*, by Jack Kornfield.[5] Ask your loved one if he would be willing to read and discuss it. He might say, "Okay, if you read one of my books." As a rapport and trust-building step, you can offer to read his book first. To an outsider, cult books often seem bizarre, dense, or convoluted, making them difficult to read. Typically, the parents, relatives or friends can't get past the first chapter. If you have trouble, read one chapter. If you can't get through a chapter, read a section. Discuss what you read with your loved one as soon as you finish it.

Whenever you agree to read each other's material, the crucial part of that contract is that you will discuss what you've read. Instead of "Here, read this!" you can say, "Let's read this and discuss it together." This creates another opportunity for positive interaction. If you have questions about the material, write them down. Make notes for yourself. Discuss your thoughts with your loved one. Make sure to follow-up.

Always include a time frame when you ask for a promise: "When will you read this next chapter? Will you have it ready by next weekend when I call?" At the agreed-upon date, you can follow up by asking, "Did you enjoy the chapter?" If he says he still didn't have time to read it, express your disappointment and ask for another commitment: "When do you think you will have it read?" He might answer, "I need another week." Then you can say, "OK, let's make an agreement to discuss it next week." Even if he continues to postpone the discussion, you will still be planting seeds of dissonance. Eventually, he might ask, "Why can't I do what I want to do? I seem to be blocked at every turn." He has discovered something about himself and his environment. His broken promises bring you closer to your goal.

Parents, siblings, relatives, friends, and co-workers may also have problems keeping promises. When you break a promise made to a cult member, you lose rapport and trust. Demonstrate that you are making an effort. Show that you care, that you are willing to do something for your loved one, even though it may be unpleasant for you. Make sure to set goals and follow up. Don't allow yourself to get sidetracked. Stick with it!

Former members

Talking with former cult members is one of the best ways to understand cult beliefs and learn how mind control techniques actually affect people.[6] Ex-members will often be the most reliable sources of information available and, in some cases, may even want to help you plan and carry out the Strategic Interaction. I suggest that you meet and interview at least a dozen former members: some from your loved one's cult and some from other groups. Pay special attention to those who have received counseling and have digested and integrated their cult experience. Ask them hypothetical questions: "What would happen if we took this approach? What about another strategy?" They will often know the variables that tell you which approach is most effective.

Network with other families

Find other families whose loved ones are in the same cult. Agree to protect each other's confidential information. I've seen some really great friendships develop this way. By creating a network of concerned families, you not only offer each other emotional support, but also share news about groups' workings. You may even commit to helping others rescue their loved ones, once yours is free.

Learn the loaded language

By talking with former members and other families, you will also have the opportunity to learn the loaded language—the clichés, doublespeak and coded jargon—which the group uses to shut down critical thought processes. Each group has its own buzz words and trite platitudes. For example, Jehovah's Witnesses are specifically instructed to avoid using the word "God." If you want to build rapport and trust and gather information with a Jehovah's

Witness, you should use the term "Jehovah." In the Twelve Tribes, the word "Christian" is a great evil; to build rapport, use the term "believer." For me, the term "Moon" would automatically trigger a picture of Sun Myung Moon, instead of the celestial body that orbits the earth. Scientology has a dictionary of L. Ron Hubbard's definitions of words. When a Scientologist doesn't understand or agree with a passage in a book or article, he is supposed to look up its words in the cult's dictionary. Members can use a regular dictionary only to look up basic words like "the," "a," and "what." The point is that they are being retrained to take Hubbard's definitions for reality as their own. Members of some cults are trained so thoroughly that a word can elicit an automatic psychological or physiological response.[7]

If you don't know the loaded language or the triggers, you will need to observe carefully. When you use a term, watch how your loved one responds. Watch his face and body language. For example, if you say something and he changes physically and behaviorally—becoming glassy-eyed, distant, rigid—right before your eyes, ask yourself, "What did I say? What did I trigger? How can I reactivate the authentic identity?" Remember, cult jargon can often elicit the cult identity. You may want to learn the jargon, but don't use it if you're trying to interact with the pre-cult self. Remember, the cult armor is geared to fend off attack. If you approach with warmth and respect, your loved one will open up and talk with you. Also, pay attention to how your loved one and other cult members talk to one another. This information will help you understand the cult identity and communicate more effectively during Interactions.

Keep in mind that families also can have their own code words. Buzz words, like the term "respect," should be discussed and if necessary rephrased. Each member of The Strategic Interaction Team should make a list of buzz words. What are some trigger words in the family system? Families have their own armor that keeps them from being flexible and creative. It is good to ask ourselves every now and then, "Where are we stuck?"

To Do

- Research the cult beliefs and practices.
- Make a list of probable cult triggers.
- Check your list with former members.
- Make a list of loaded words and phrases.

Attend cult activities

Team members should not attend cult sessions or visit cult property without adequate preparation. If the cult member invites you before you feel ready, at first you might say, "I'd rather not talk to a stranger. I'd prefer to talk to you alone. If you don't know the doctrine well enough to explain it to me, do you know it well enough to make a commitment to it? Perhaps we could step back and look at the teachings of the group and how you came to accept them." Generally, the cult member will be open to talk to people who make the effort to listen. Remember: our first goal is to build rapport and trust, not to argue and prove points.

Once you've familiarized yourself with the group and its tactics, I sometimes recommend that someone on the Team ask to attend a cult gathering or lecture. That individual can tell the person that they want to learn more, and that they'd like to have firsthand experience with the group. This will allow you to build rapport and trust while you learn about the cult's behavior through observation. Getting a few people to go together to a cult program can also be effective, but they will need to work as a team.

I don't recommend that family members or friends attend extended workshops or indoctrination sessions. It's just too risky. Despite the best of intentions, people have been known to get recruited, even when they are prepared for such events. An alternative strategy would be to ask the leader or sub-leader to meet you at a restaurant for lunch. This will go a long way toward building rapport and trust, and it's also a good way to gather information. Understand that they, too, will have an agenda—to check you out and possibly recruit you. Most cults want good public relations. They believe that what they are doing is good. They want to recruit more people. As long as family members say, "At first, we overreacted when we called it a cult." or "We were influenced by anti-cult media." they will not be perceived as a threat. Spend time getting to know cult members who are close to your loved one. Talk with them and learn as much as you can—their names, where they are from, their interests. The more you learn about their experiences, the more tools you will have in dealing with your loved one.

Most importantly, talk to your loved one and to other members of the group, and ask them what you can do to earn their trust. When the cult member makes a reasonable request that will help develop rapport, like "Read the book," or "Come to a lecture," you should always try to do what he asks. If the task seems overwhelming, break it into smaller pieces.

DISTINGUISH INFORMATION FROM DISINFORMATION

To find the truth, you have to be able to distinguish between reliable information and misleading disinformation. This skill is especially important when seeking information about destructive cults, because one way a cult defends itself is by spreading lies and blurring the line between fact and fiction. By the late 1970s, the question of cult mind control was intertwined in the public eye with the issue of forcible deprogramming. This was partly due to a multi-million dollar public relations campaign financed by the major cults in an attempt to smear critics and divert the debate from the cults themselves. This was also due to the fact that deprogrammers were, in many cases, acting like vigilantes. In the propaganda campaign, cults have labeled deprogramming "the greatest threat to religious liberty." In cult lectures, booklets, and pamphlets, and on cult Web sites, deprogrammers are portrayed as money-hungry thugs who tie their victims to chairs, beating and raping them until they recant their religious beliefs.[8]

The Cult Awareness Network changes hands

The Cult Awareness Network (CAN), the largest grassroots organization for families with loved ones in cults, was falsely portrayed by the cults as a group of fascists who wanted to deprive people of religious freedom. In 1994, CAN lost one of scores of harassment law suits filed by cult members across the country, and the $1.875 million jury verdict sent the organization into bankruptcy court. Ultimately, CAN's trade name, post office box number, help line phone number, and service mark were sold at auction for $20,000 to Steven Hayes, a member of the Church of Scientology.[9]

CAN is now part of the problem. The wolf is wearing Grandma's clothes. If you call the CAN number today, most likely a cult member will answer, although that person will not reveal his cult affiliation. Any information offered by family members could be used against them in their efforts to liberate their loved one. The CAN Web site (cultawarenessnetwork.org) says it is operated by the Foundation for Religious Freedom and denies that mind control exists. The CAN site offers up a confusing mix of truths, half-truths and lies and attempts to equate "anti-cult" with "anti-religious." When a cult member visits the CAN site, cult-instilled phobias of anti-religious deprogrammers are reinforced. There are many other web sites being created to bolster cult groups' agendas to recruit and indoctrinate people around the world.

One of the most common disinformation tactics used by cults is a logical fallacy known as the "straw man," where a person weakens his opponent's position by misrepresenting his arguments and attacking an indefensible "straw man," rather than addressing the real issues. For example, cults frequently create a false image of mind control as a mystical force that can overpower any person in any situation. Naturally, this all-or-nothing straw man is easier to knock over than the actual positions taken by informed, experienced professionals—namely, that mind control techniques vary widely in application and effectiveness, and that while mind control is never absolute, it can nevertheless have devastating consequences.

I question the motives of any individual or group that takes the extreme position that under no circumstances can people be manipulated into adopting new beliefs. Whose interests are advanced by the notion that mind control is entirely implausible? If mind control is nothing but a hoax, why does professor and former Western Psychological Association President Philip Zimbardo teach a course at Stanford University called "The Psychology of Mind Control"?[10]

Cult propagandists love to try to convince members that "mind control is not recognized by mental health professionals." One simple retort is to cite the DSM-IV, American Psychiatric Association's diagnostic manual[11] that specifically mentions cults and brainwashing under 300.15, "Dissociative Disorder NOS." Of course, you can also cite the favorable reviews of *Combatting Cult Mind Control* in *The Lancet* and *The American Journal of Psychiatry* in 1990.[12]

Another tactic cult public relations people like is to misquote legal decisions involving cults. When talking with your loved ones, ask them for the case, citation, and even better, the official ruling.

When it comes to legal decisions, it is best to ask a lawyer familiar with cult-related litigation to help you get the documents to show and explain to the cult member.

Cult Defenders

In addition to cult propaganda, disinformation is being spread by cult members themselves, as well as by cult defenders—cult researchers who cite religious freedom as a justification for the existence of mind control groups. Some high-profile researchers have accepted funds or other perks from the cults they were studying. For instance, *The Washington Post* reported that Aum Shinrikyo paid the airfare, lodging, and other "basic expenses" of four Americans who came to the defense of the cult when Japanese police began investigating a 1994 poison gas attack on the Tokyo subways.[13] One of these Americans was J. Gordon Melton who writes books and articles on "new" religions and who has a history of defending controversial groups such as Jim Jones' People's Temple. When questioned in 1988 about the Jim Jones group, Melton said, "This wasn't a cult. This was a respectable, mainline Christian group."[14] Melton also appears on the Cult Awareness Network's online list of "Professional Referrals."[15] In a recent issue of *Nova Religio*, Benjamin Zablocki, a Rutgers professor and thirty-year cult scholar, exposed how cult funding often creates bias in studies of controversial groups.[16]

Cult defenders confuse the public by promoting a primitive, robotic conception of mind control. They also proffer an erroneous picture of the viewpoints of both cult critics and ex-members. A popular argument among cult defenders is that the testimony of former members, or "apostates," should not be considered reliable, because such people may have been prejudiced by their departure from the group. According to Melton, "hostile ex-members invariably shade the truth. They invariably blow out of proportion minor incidents and turn them into major incidents."[17] Ironically, cult defenders appear to ignore the possibility that the testimony of cult members and leaders might be partisan.

The demonization of cult critics

When *Combatting Cult Mind Control* was first published in 1988, I became one of the most visible targets of cult disinformation campaigns. There are cult leaders who lecture their members on the evils of speaking with me and even reading the book. Scientology has a "Dead Agent Pack" about me. This folder contains material designed to assassinate my character—to "neutralize" me in members' minds as a respected person. Countless times, I've been threatened with lawsuits and have even received death threats from cult members. Several groups, such as the Moonies, tell their members that I am Satan's agent. Specific phobias about me have been planted in members' minds. Cult members are indoctrinated to believe that Steven Hassan is a "deprogrammer" who endorses and associates with people who kidnap, beat, and torture members of new religions until they renounce their faith in God. Cult web sites portray me as an evil, anti-religious bigot who is out to destroy religious freedom.

When a cult member raises such an accusation about any cult critic, I recommend that the family ask for proof: "Show us the evidence. Have your leaders documented the charges with names, dates, and places? Were any charges filed?" The leaders of the group will not want their accusations examined or challenged. Family members and friends should ask to speak with the individuals who purportedly wrote negative affidavits. Questions can be asked, and facts can be communicated. The deprogramming phobia can be dismantled piece by piece, exposing the lies and deception. This is a vital and effective strategy to promote reality testing.

FATHER: I'm looking at the cult Web site, and there are pages that criticize Dr. Robert Lifton, Dr. Louis West and Dr. Margaret Singer. What is this all about? How can we judge if this information is harmful or helpful?

When evaluating any piece of information, ask yourself:

- What is the source of the criticism?
- How is the source funded?
- Who, exactly, is making the accusations?
- What are this person's verifiable credentials?
- What is his standing in the academic and scientific community?
- What is his training? His experience? His reputation?
- What has this person published?
- Have you read his work?
- Does what he or she says make sense to you?
- When you question him, does he answer honestly and responsibly?

I have known Dr. Lifton, the late Dr. West, and Dr. Singer for many years. While I don't agree with everything they have written or done, I have great respect for their positive contributions to humankind, which have been substantial.[18] They were all United States military intelligence officers who studied Chinese "brainwashing" in the 1950's, and all were brave enough to publicly attest that such a phenomenon exists. Read the information and disinformation for yourself about these individuals. Form your own opinion.

We Americans tend not to realize that our Constitutional rights mean nothing unless we are willing to stand up and affirmatively assert them. Cults force many of us to act because they have shown a willingness to deprive people of their rights. Speaking personally,

I refuse to surrender my rights. The stories of abuse, betrayal, harassment, intimidation, fear, broken families, neglected children, financial ruin, and personal and emotional devastation that I've heard from so many ex-members over the years impels and inspires me in that struggle. I believe one of the most effective strategies to counter the disinformation and slander is to help ex-members tell their story, and I encourage former members reading this book to do so for their own good as well as the good of others. I also advise those with loved ones in a cult to seek out ex-members with stories to tell.

Do I believe every ex-member's story without seeking verification? No, of course not. Is it possible that some ex-members exaggerate their stories? Of course. Believing that all ex-members are credible or that no ex-member is credible is too extreme. I seek to evaluate each person's story and obtain verification. Naturally, when there are many people telling of similar experiences with a particular group, the information usually proves to be trustworthy. Most ex-members speak out at great personal risk and with little or no personal gain, other than the therapeutic effects of standing up to expose an injustice, and perhaps to help others.

Former cult members and their friends and family are survivors, and their testimony is powerful evidence that a person can walk away from a destructive group and go on to a lead a contented, productive life. Hearing their supportive and inspiring words can help set a confused, discontented cult member on the road to becoming a healthier, more fulfilled ex-member. By putting a face to the other side of the story, former members show your loved one that leaving is an option. Once this becomes a viable choice, it is usually only a matter of time before the person decides to leave the group.

Chapter 8

Interacting with Dual Identities

Time after time, friends and family of cult members have told me, "It's like he's a different person now," or, "We don't know her anymore!" Such a stark description of a split personality may seem simplistic, but anyone with a loved one in a mind control cult will recognize the portrayal. It is an eerie experience when, mid-conversation, you sense a different identity has assumed control. Recognizing the change, and acting appropriately, is one of the keys to unlocking your loved one's authentic self and freeing him from cult bondage. In this chapter, we will prepare for interactions with your loved one by learning what to expect.

In the following conversation, Arthur, the friend of a cult member named John, describes several of his traits that are common to the cult identity of many members.[1]

SH: You've already looked at some of the material on my Web site. Have you seen John yet?

ARTHUR: We talked on the phone.

SH: How did it go?

ARTHUR: Strange! He told me he reads *The Wall Street Journal*. That's not John! And another strange thing was the way he avoided my questions. He was more interested in what I was doing than telling me what he was up to, even when I asked. I was doing things he thought were exciting. I asked him if we could get together. I figured he might say, "I'm not sure," but he said, "Let's do something next weekend."

SH: It will be difficult to know how John will behave when you see him. It's hard for you to imagine where he is—and how far he is from where he used to be. It will be striking when you get together. Now, in the conversation over the phone, you said he steers it towards you. That tactic sounds familiar. He's probably not going to want to reveal a lot of his beliefs, because he knows you won't accept them without questioning him. It's easier to talk about you. Wait until you see how he is around you. Members of the Lenz group (to which John belongs) are living a very difficult existence. They're under a lot of stress. John will be different than you remember, maybe even by a frightening amount. It might be easy to get to the "old John" in certain areas, harder in other areas.

ARTHUR: Sure. That will be true pretty much for anyone who approaches him. I know about the authentic John and the cult John. It's sort of creepy to think I might not be talking with my old friend. You know, he introduced himself to me as "Jonathan" on the phone the other night. It's probably nothing....

SH: It's probably something....

As we've seen, members of mind control cults suffer from a dissociative disorder which causes them to vacillate between the authentic identity and the cult identity. When dealing with a cult member, be sensitive to the differences between the two identity patterns. Pay attention to the following in your interactions:

- Content (what the person talks about).

- Communication patterns (the way the person speaks—mannerisms, gestures, vocabulary, expressions).

- Behavior patterns (the way the person acts).

The cult identity (Cultist John) and the authentic identity (Authentic John) will look and sound quite different: Cultist John will often seem to stare through people. His eyes may look glassy, cold, or glazed. His posture may be more rigid, his facial muscles tighter. If fact, he may make you think of a robot or zombie. Authentic John's posture will appear looser and warmer. Eye contact will be more natural. Cultist John will sound like a tape recording of a cult lecture. He may speak with inappropriate intensity and volume. He might whisper, mumble, or chant unintelligible syllables. Authentic John will speak with a greater range of emotion. He will be more expressive and share more willingly. He'll be more spontaneous and have a sense of humor.

Of course, in reality, the differences may not be so extreme, but the model is still useful.

SUB-PERSONALITIES

Now, I have mentioned that cults use significant parts of the pre-cult or authentic identity to create the cult identity. In particular, cults tend to focus on elements of the psyche formed early in childhood. It's not coincidental that many destructive cults tell their members to become "children of God." They encourage their members to psychologically regress to a time when they exhibited little or no critical thinking, and when whatever they were told went directly into the mind with no conscious evaluation or rebuttal.

During recruitment and indoctrination, cult members sometimes share activities—like sitting around the campfire, enacting skits, playing games or sports, and singing songs—that bring new recruits back to a childlike state. Leaders encourage members to talk about what they were thinking and feeling when they were little children. Indeed, several religious groups talk about being "born again."[2]

In "rebirthing," a controversial technique supposedly used to help people recover from early childhood trauma, people are age-regressed back to re-experience birth. One ex-member of an Indian

Guru cult told me of her experience squirming and writhing in pain on the floor as cult "therapists" showed her a picture of the so-called perfect "master." She and others were told that the "master" was the reason they were being born—so they could become his disciple and submit totally.

The creation of my Moonie self

My cult self was the devoted son of the "True Parents," as well as leader in the Unification movement, witnesser (recruiter), fundraiser, lecturer, celibate, holy, humble, self-sacrificing, small messiah to ten generations of my ancestors.

I have since come to realize that my cult identity was not entirely new, as elements of my pre-cult identity were the seeds of its formation. My work and experiences with former members confirms this basic point: indoctrination anchors itself to parts of our past, forgotten, outgrown, or discarded authentic self—not just the child but other aspects of the self. Analyzing my own psyche—and my own indoctrination into the Moonies—I have identified four distinct sub-personalities that were co-opted by the cult.

The young child part

To a child, parents are omnipotent authority figures. As we grow older, we inevitably become disillusioned by our parents' limitations, frailties, and especially what may be downright abuses, but the needs, perspectives and priorities of the young child remain embedded in our psyche.

Fairy tales play on the almost universal desire of children for a perfectly safe world, with perfect parents. Especially for those who grew up in orphanages, or whose parents were abusive or divorced, the child part hungers for the perfect father and mother. Cults insist on a very literal transfer of family loyalty. Jim Jones was one of many cult leaders to insist that his followers call him "Dad." When the illusion of parental perfection is combined with singing, games, and other age-regressing techniques, the universal young child can present itself quite forcefully as the foundation for the new cult identity.

The idealistic part

I was an idealistic child of the 1960s who believed in a world of truth, goodness, and justice. I was taught that honesty was rewarded, and misdeeds were punished. I was trusting and naïve, and I was in for a rude awakening. People lied, cheated and stole. I felt betrayed, again and again, by people who I considered my friends. My idealistic child part was hurt and horrified. As I grew older, I read utopian novels and longed for a day when the world would become a better place. I was told, "Don't be a dreamer! The world isn't like that. It's a cold, cruel place. Grow up!" I did grow up, and after many bitter lessons, this part of my authentic identity got pushed aside until I was approached by the Moon cult.

I was nineteen-years old, sitting in a group workshop, where young adults from different countries were talking about God's original plan to create a world of peace, harmony, and goodness. The idealistic part of me said, "How wonderful! I want that!" My cynical voice chided, "That's childish! That's silly!" Still, the cult activated a piece of me that grew to form an important part of my cult identity. The teachings were given in lectures, stories, and metaphors. My Moonie mind was filled with the fantasy that the group was creating the Kingdom of Heaven on Earth. In this world, there would be no crime, poverty, or suffering. All people would be part of our one world family under the True Parents. Peace would reign.

Though my idealism helped my recruiters to control me, ultimately, it was my idealism that motivated me to leave the group. I realized that Moon and the leaders of the Unification group lied, cheated, stole, and enslaved its members. This realization—that Moon was the complete opposite of everything I believed in—so repulsed me that I left the group.

The religious/spiritual part

During my childhood, my family belonged to the conservative Hillcrest Jewish Center in Queens, New York. My mother kept a kosher home, and I attended Hebrew School several afternoons a week, went to Sabbath services, and observed Jewish holidays. By the time I had my Bar Mitzvah at the age of thirteen, I found I didn't understand or agree with some of the concepts of Judaism. I was uncomfortable with what I felt was an overemphasis on rituals and the past. Still feeling deeply spiritual, I continued to pray to God, but I stopped going to Hillcrest, except to use their basketball court.

When I was nineteen-years old, I was not searching for another religion. I was Jewish. I had been to Israel, the Jewish Holy Land, where I participated in an archeological dig of the Biblical city of Beersheba in the Negev desert. I was trying to understand the nature of reality and my place in the universe. I loved to read philosophy and thought a lot about the meaning of life.

When I first encountered Moonie recruiters on the campus of Queens College, they identified themselves as a student group. They completely lied about being a religious group. Later, they sidestepped the entire issue of Jesus and Christianity and emphasized the Jewish belief in the coming of the Messiah. In that way, they were able to tap into the religious/spiritual part of my being. Since the Unification Church claims to be a religion, the indoctrinators knew my religious/spiritual part would be an essential contributing factor in the shaping of my cult identity. My belief in God was altered to accept the Moon doctrine as the "truth." Ultimately, it was my faith in a God of truth who wants His children to have free-will that played an important role in my decision to exit the cult.

The warrior/hero part

I was born in 1954 and grew up during the Cold War. I learned to hate and fear Communism. My childhood experiences taught me to be patriotic and proud to be an American. At ten years old, I wanted to be a hero and sacrifice my life in heated battle. One of my favorite television shows was a World War II action series, *Combat*, starring Vic Morrow. In fantasy war games with friends, I often pretended to be the heroic soldier. My friend Marc had a tree house in his backyard, and I remember taking turns attacking and defending the "fort" with dirt bombs (clumps of dirt) and water pistols. I even remember having war dreams at night, assaulting enemy machine gun emplacements, throwing grenades, and fighting for freedom. The enemy was always the Nazis or the Communists.

As I grew up, I began to recognize the horrors of the Vietnam War. By the time I graduated from high school, I had become an anti-war activist. I grew my hair long and participated in peace protests. What happened to the young patriot carrying a toy gun? I had grown up and renounced the warrior/soldier identity, but it was buried inside me. I was not drafted into the Army, but I was recruited to join the One World Crusade, a front group for the Moon cult, as a Heavenly Soldier fighting Satan's Communism. One of the group's favorite songs was "Heavenly Soldiers for God."

The universal theme of the hero who fights against Evil accounts for much of human history, art, and literature. The warrior/soldier mentality is another essential part of most cult identities. In a destructive cult, the soldier mentality is made to believe:

- I must follow orders from my superiors.
- We are good. Our enemy is bad.
- Sacrifice for the greater good makes you a hero.

In the Strategic Interaction Approach, we learn how to recognize when our loved one is speaking and acting from his cult identity. We try to build rapport and trust with his cult identity. One key to communicating with that identity is to acknowledge that these sub-personalities have good intentions. Our aim is to help the loved one liberate the parts of his pre-cult identity that were co-opted by the cult identity and integrate them back into his authentic self.

In my case, the young child part wanted perfect parents and perfect security. The idealistic part wanted a perfect world. The religious/spiritual part wanted a perfect relationship with God or the Creator. The warrior/soldier was willing to sacrifice life itself to achieve this perfection. After I left the group, the sub-personalities that formed the core of my Moonie identity needed to be identified, liberated, and ultimately integrated into my post-cult identity. I needed to love and accept my idealistic part, not merely cast it aside. Indeed, my adult idealism is preserved with the help of my child part. I needed to let my religious/spiritual part search for healthy alternatives, and I have recently joined a non-aligned Jewish synagogue.[3] My warrior/soldier part is engaged in a mission to combat cult mind control—hopefully, in a healthy, balanced manner.

In my work with clients, I try to promote holistic healing through in-depth counseling. During a Strategic Interaction with your loved one, your aim will be to honor the core of the cult self and help to integrate it into a new authentic, post-cult identity. When this deep therapeutic work of integration is not completed, former members remain in conflict, sometimes even at war within themselves. They can be afraid to open the Bible. They may be afraid to pray or even think about God. They hate the part of themselves that wants to be spiritual. They remain stuck with a black-and-white view of reality.

I want to educate former members that spirituality is not about black-and-white thinking or having blind faith in absolutes. The essence of faith is not having all the answers but trusting that there is goodness and truth, and that God exists. I consider it a tremendous setback if a person leaves a destructive cult and feels he must abandon or denigrate the religious part of his authentic identity to do so. There are countless people who have done just that by allowing their negative cult experience to hamper their free will.

When our loved ones leave a cult, we want to acknowledge their idealism. At the same time, we want to help them question the assumption that they had "God" or were working toward creating a perfect world while they were in the cult. We want to reassure the part of the self that is searching for an ideal world that, after they leave the group, they can continue working towards that goal.

DEVELOP RAPPORT AND TRUST WITH THE CULT IDENTITY

I have never met a family member who felt comfortable talking to a loved one who was in a cult. It is natural for a person to become uneasy and frustrated when normal means of communication are not successful. Keep in mind that you are trying to help someone whose behavior, information, thoughts, and emotions are being manipulated by the group. The more you encourage non-cultic behavior, information, thoughts and emotions, the more productive your goal-oriented communication will be. Approach your loved one on all these levels.

In my first book, I focused my advice on eliciting the pre-cult self. With the development of the SIA, I now encourage a dual focus which also includes the cult identity. If you understand the cult identity, you can use it to help liberate your loved one. Instead of waiting for brief encounters with the authentic identity, you can seek rapport and trust with the cult identity and enlist its positive qualities—like dedication and idealism—to help liberate the authentic identity. And rather than discarding the entire cult identity, we attempt to create a new, post-cult identity that incorporates the most valuable and healthy parts of the pre-cult, cult, and authentic identities.

Side-step thought stopping

Thought stopping is used by the cult identity to block out any idea, statement, or piece of information that challenges the group's doctrine or leadership. In the Hare Krishna, members are not permitted to question, doubt, or "speculate." They are taught to chant, "Hare Krishna, Hare Krishna," whenever such "speculations" arise. The original intent of Hindu meditation is to connect with God, but the International Society for Krishna Consciousness turned it into a thought-stopping process.

FORMER SCIENTOLOGY MEMBER: In "Bull Baiting," which happens during Scientology trainings (TRs), your coach's job is to get you to react. Whatever funny, embarrassing thing they say or do—no matter how outrageous—you must sit there like a robot or zombie. You can't smile or show any reaction. You're taught to disconnect from your feelings and thoughts. They'll even say in a taunting voice, "Oh you're in Scientology—you must be brainwashed! You're in a cult!" If you smile, you flunk. They'll go on and on baiting you, until you get to the point that you hear all kinds of criticism of the group and don't react. I actually used a similar technique on my father when he tried to talk to me three months after I joined. He said he was concerned about me, but he was directly attacking the group. He showed me articles and a book called *The Scandal of Scientology*, by Paulette Cooper.[4] It was the first critical book ever written about the group. He provided me with all the information I needed to leave the group, but I just shut it out.[5]

Trying to talk to a cult member who is using thought-stopping techniques can be a frustrating experience.

FATHER: How can we communicate? If I say anything, he'll start praying or chanting. He speaks very quietly and quickly. I'm not even sure what he's actually saying. He's repeating some phrase over and over. It's like he's a thousand miles away. I get so flustered, I can feel my blood pressure going up!

Perhaps the best way to counteract thought-stopping techniques (chanting, praying, speaking in tongues) is to avoid triggering them in the first place. Remember, thought stopping occurs in direct response to what are perceived to be negative comments. Be careful not to make remarks that are critical of the leader, the group, or the doctrine. Your loved one has been programmed to block out this form of communication.

When I was a member of the Moonies, I believed Scientology was a cult. I believed the Krishnas were a cult. I believed TM was a cult, but I was convinced I was not in a cult. When my family confronted me with a news story about Sun Myung Moon owning an M-16 gun factory, I shut down and started to chant, "Crush Satan!" If they had known better, they might have first fully engaged me in a conversation about Scientology or the Krishnas. I would have paid attention. Had they introduced me to a former Krishna who could explain how he used to chant to shut out negative thoughts, I might have listened. By circumventing my thought-stopping programming, they would have freed me to gain the framework for understanding mind control.

If you find you have inadvertently triggered a thought-stopping technique, you basically have two choices: be patient and wait for the process to end (it usually is over in minutes), or try to distract and interrupt it. Being patient and waiting is less risky than trying to change the subject, or interrupt. But as your relationship improves, you will be able to experiment with different methods. Learn what works.

Show interest in the cult identity

A good way to develop rapport and trust is to begin a dialogue with the cult identity. When he or she tells you, "Oh, it's incredible! I'm doing these amazing things," you can say, "Give me an example of something that was really important to you this week. Describe it in detail. I'd like to know," or, "Give me an example of how you feel." Asking for examples, and counter-examples, is crucial when you are gathering information. Your loved one might say, "When I was meditating, I had a really profound experience." In that case, you could say, "Tell me how it felt. Have you ever felt that way before? When?" This kind of question might help the cult member reconnect with his non-cult past. If your loved one replies, "When I was fifteen and fishing on the lake," you have just elicited the authentic identity. That is an important step. Then you can introduce a counter-example: "Did you have any experience that left you feeling lonely or disoriented? What did that feel like?"

While you gather information, you are helping the cult member to reality-test. The conversation below is an example of effective goal-oriented communication with a cult member.

CULT MEMBER: I had a profound spiritual experience today.

SISTER: What kind of experience did you have?

CULT MEMBER: Oh, it's too deep, too complex for me to explain.

SISTER: Give me the feeling associated with it. If you drew me a picture, what would be in the picture? If it were a melody, what would it sound like?

CULT MEMBER: Oh, you wouldn't understand. It's too deep.

SISTER: Try me!

CULT MEMBER: Well, it was like I was surrounded by a warm cloud of God's love. I felt like I was not only hearing Bach, I was the actual music.

SISTER: Wow! I was in Church last Sunday and I felt almost exactly what you felt. Isn't it an amazingly wonderful feeling to have such a sense of grace?

Getting the cult member to verbalize an experience provides an opportunity to build bridges. If you have had a similar experience, talking about it can build rapport and trust. If spiritual experiences are important to the cult member, your sharing could help pave the way for him to leave the group. Experiment with other ways for the cult member to provide you with information about his experience. If your loved one is artistic, ask him to write you a poem or a song. Do any of the family members or friends practice meditation? If so, that person could say, "When I was meditating the other day, I had this warm feeling. I felt totally immersed in love," or, "I was doing Yoga this morning and I had the exact same feeling. It was wonderful, wasn't it?" By developing rapport and trust with the cult identity, you are communicating to the cult member, "You're not alone. You don't have to be in a cult to have that experience."

MOTHER: How do we know if we have rapport and trust?

SH: Ask your loved one: On a scale of one (low) to ten (high) "How much do you trust me?" Remember, this is a process. Ask, "What can I do to make you feel more comfortable with me?"

If the response is to read a cult book, or attend a cult meeting, then do what was requested. Families sometimes miss opportunities and get into trouble when their expectation is merely to convince the person to leave the cult immediately. An impatient approach will only lose rapport with the cult identity and reinforce cult indoctrination.

RECONNECT WITH THE AUTHENTIC IDENTITY

When the cult identity takes over, a person's past is redefined and often distorted. After Moon recruiters convinced me to divulge a few painful experiences in my childhood (one big one with my father), the group magnified the negatives and minimized the positives of my past. My cult identity was taught to suppress good experiences and exaggerate painful ones. I came to believe, "My childhood was lonely and miserable. I experimented with drugs. I had pre-marital sex. It was horrible. Thank goodness the Father (Moon) showed me the way to happiness!"

When I got out of the group, I needed a reality check with my family and friends. I needed to sit down with old photograph albums and home movies. I needed to be reminded that I used to go fishing with my father on Sunday mornings, and that when I had bad times, both he and my mother were always there to comfort me. I had to take the experiences that were exaggerated and put them back in their proper perspective. I had to reconstruct the pre-cult Steve Hassan.

My old teachers, neighbors, friends, and family helped me remember the fun things that I did: I had bicycled across America when I was sixteen; I had canoed and fished my way across Canada to Alaska with my friend Lenny; I worked on an archaeological dig in Israel with my friend Marc; I enjoyed camping, hiking, and horseback riding. I loved basketball, reading, and writing poetry. When I was in the cult mindset, all of those experiences were trivialized, distorted, or manipulated.

Eliciting the authentic identity

As much as cult indoctrination attempts to suppress and destroy the authentic identity, it never completely succeeds. There are too many experiences, too many positive memories that don't disappear. The cult tries to bury these reference points and submerge the person's past. Yet, over time, the authentic, pre-cult self seeks ways to regain its freedom.

The authentic identity continues to play an active role in a cult member's psyche by:

• Creating illnesses, such as skin problems, asthma, or severe allergic reactions that give the cult member an excuse to sleep and take some time off from his grueling work schedule. If the illness is life-threatening, the cult member may feel justified in seeking outside medical attention.

• Exerting pressure on the cult identity to go home for a visit. It is creative in inventing excuses to go home, such as to collect clothes or funds, or to find new recruits.

• Dropping hints when speaking to family members or friends, that they want to be rescued. I have had several families contact me after their cult son or daughter told them not to get a professional counselor to get them out. Before the cult member made that remark, the families had not realized that they could contact someone like me for help.

• Generating thematic dreams. Former members describe recurring nightmares of being hurt or trapped while a member of the cult. I know people who have had cult dreams of being lost in a menacing dark forest, being choked or suffocated, or being imprisoned in a concentration camp.

• Having spiritual experiences (such as receiving a revelation) that the member is meant to leave the group. The cult identity does not want to leave the group, but the experience is so powerful that the person follows his unconscious and runs away, hopefully getting support and counseling.

When I was in the cult, I thought the old Steve, the "evil" Steve, was dead. After a near-fatal accident that landed me in the hospital, I was out of the cult environment for over two weeks. To keep my cult self centered while in the hospital, I listened to Moon's speeches, in Korean (with a simultaneous English translation), through headphones. When I left the hospital, my parents arranged for former members to conduct a deprogramming. I discovered that "I" was still there. The human mind and spirit are resilient. It is amazing to me what people can endure and be able to survive and thrive.

The Strategic Interaction Approach accelerates this process because it teaches family members and friends to:

• Reconnect the person to his or her past memories and experiences.

• Facilitate positive exposure to non-members.

• Provide enhanced access to outside information.

• Bring to consciousness the accumulation of negative experiences the person has had while in the group.

Helping your loved one reflect on his experiences

Because mind control cults never deliver what they promise, it is likely that your loved one will have many disappointing experiences with the group. Deep down inside, the authentic identity sees contradictions, asks questions, and records the disillusionments. An essential part of the SIA involves bringing a person's own experiences into the light, so that he can process them.

During the later stages of the SIA process, cult members are able to verbalize specific negative incidents that occurred while they were members. They will sometimes recall traumatic experiences; for example, being raped by the cult leader, or being forced to lie, cheat or steal. Even though they knew at the time that they were doing something wrong or were being abused, they were not able to process the experience or act on it while the cult identity was in control. It was only when the authentic self was given permission and encouraged to speak out that these experiences came into consciousness.

Sharing feelings and perceptions, not judgments

The difference between perception and judgment is sometimes subtle. In the following example, a Team member, whose name has been changed here to Danny, makes the common mistake of drawing a conclusion instead of making an observation.

DANNY: I feel if I were to ask [my loved one] a specific question, like, "What research have you done about mind control?" I would feel him get closed and withdraw.

SH: Do you ever point out to him that when you ask a specific question, you feel him closing down? It's not like him to act like that, so what's going on?

DANNY: I think I pointed out to him that he is defensive.

SH: Saying he is "defensive" is a judgment. It's an evaluation, whereas if you're just reporting a feeling you're having and ask him, "What's that about?" — it's giving him feedback and asking him to reflect and perhaps have an insight.

Rather than making statements, ask open-ended questions to elicit the most information:

• "Tell me what you think (feel) about your relationship with Dad."

• "Tell me what you think (feel) about your relationship with Mom."

• "Tell me what you think (feel) about your relationship with your siblings."

During most Strategic Interactions that I organize, family members quickly realize that they do not always know what the person previously thought about specific people and things. In addition to teaching the family communication techniques, I try to make them aware of how much they don't know and motivate them to learn more. I encourage them to go through an information-gathering process from the pre-cult point of view to the present cult member point of view.

YOUNGER BROTHER: I don't know how to answer some of the questions on the Background Information Form.

If you do not know the answers, ask others, but especially ask your loved one. This is another opportunity to build rapport and trust while you gather information. Some of the questions you might ask include:

- I really don't know you the way I want to. Tell me how things were before you got in.

- How would you describe your relationship with Dad three years ago, before you joined?

- What would you like to change about your relationship with Mom or Dad?

- What about when you were growing up? What about now?

- How would you have wanted Dad to be different?

The cult member might respond:

- I wish Dad were more verbally approving.

- I wish Dad were more supportive.

- I wish Dad showed more interest in me as a person.

- I'd like him to hug me, praise me, and listen better.

On the second day of my deprogramming from the Moonies, my father broke down and started crying. He asked me how I would feel if my son, my only son, dropped out of school, moved out, and joined a controversial group. At that moment, my father's emotions reached through the cult's indoctrination to my heart. I felt, "He really loves me!"

Remember, you will get a very different answer to these questions if the cult identity is the one responding. Be prepared to hear some painful, sometimes arrogant answers, but make sure to listen carefully. Not everything the cult identity verbalizes will be false. If the cult identity gives a negative generalization, like "Dad never listened to me," acknowledge it, and if you know of a time when his father did listen, remind him of it.

Cultivating rapport and trust

Rapport and trust building should never be underemphasized or underestimated. This is so in any counseling situation or interpersonal relationship. If you do not have rapport, the person will not tell you the deeper things that are going on with him. He will not feel safe. He will not trust you. When you give him good ideas, he will not listen to you. If a member has had eight years of confrontational and condescending remarks from certain friends or family members, it may take a year or maybe longer of positive, constructive interactions to reverse that.

If you have had an honest relationship with your loved one, there will be a lot to work with. If the relationship doesn't have a high level of rapport and trust, you will have to go back to stage one and develop it. The healthier the pre-cult family relationships, and the stronger the member's sense of identity prior to being in the cult, the easier it will be to reconnect and get the person to open up. Until you have a sense of closeness, you shouldn't even mention his leaving the group. Instead, get involved doing things that will build the relationship.

Connecting with your loved one's authentic self

As part of the rapport-building process, I invite parents to open up and connect with their loved ones. Imagine how powerful it is when an "unemotional" father starts sharing his emotions with his son.

In many cases, I'll ask the father in private about his childhood and his relationship with his own father: "How would you have wanted your Dad to be different?" Almost universally, the father will have the same wish list as his son. When I ask, "Have you ever sat down with your son and shared what it was like when you were little?" most fathers say, "No." Then I suggest, "Next time you are alone together, go for a walk and start talking about your childhood." Sharing that conversation allows the son to identify with his father because he had the same experience. There is automatic empathy. It opens new areas to discuss: what it's like being a father; what it's like being a son; and how to improve their relationship.

It is essential for family members and friends to step out of their own reality—to think, feel and imagine what the other person's reality is. That is how you really get to know other people; how you show that you really care about them as individuals. You do not have to accept the group's teachings or the leader's authority. You have to recognize the cult member's reality is real for him and ask your loved one to share it with you.

We are all different. Let us honor and appreciate the differences. Let's not assume we know what others are thinking and feeling. Remember, Strategic Interaction is about asking questions, learning, and experiencing. It is a process. It involves creating a flexible, trustworthy relationship. I can respect other people's sincerity and intention for spirituality and fulfillment. There are many different orientations and spiritual paths. I believe we are all just doing the best we can based on our knowledge, information, and experiences. The thrust of my approach in the Strategic Interaction is to meet the participants where they live—in their models of reality.

Create a model of your loved one's present self

I encourage family and friends to engage in a socialization process that activates their loved one's authentic identity. Each person is unique and has his own story to tell. In any case, family and friends should say to the loved one, "Tell us about yourself. Tell us about your experiences. We want to understand. We want to know you better." This helps the person to be in touch with his feelings, to know his own thoughts.

MOTHER: "I want to be able to step into your shoes and know more about what your inner experience is like. Teach me! I'm curious! What are you thinking?"

CULT MEMBER: "You don't care about me. What I do is not important to you. You don't love me."

MOTHER: "I want to be involved with your life. I do care about you!"

CULT MEMBER: "How come you didn't write to me in two years? How come you didn't visit?"

MOTHER: "Forgive me. I had personal problems. I couldn't handle it. I was too upset. I felt it was my fault. I blamed myself. Now I've gone into therapy. I want to build a relationship with you. Help me. You're my son and I love you."

This approach works much better than saying, "You idiot! Can't you see the WatchTower (or the Divine Principle, or Dianetics) is all wrong?" or "You put the group ahead of your family and friends. Get out!" or "You're no longer a member of this family!" In cases where families have uttered these sentiments out of pain and frustration, the cult member will need an apology and time to heal, to trust that "Dad really does love me. He wants to hear what I think now. He wants to understand what the group is all about."

Build bridges to life outside the cult

There are many ways to remind your loved one that he had a good life outside of the group.

- Look at photographs and home movies or videos.
- Cook his favorite dinner or send home-baked cookies or other goodies.
- Take him to a favorite restaurant that evokes old positive memories.
- Invite him to do things he once enjoyed. Go bowling. Go to sporting events. Go shopping. Go fishing.

Look for opportunities to show your loved one a picture of his authentic self. Remind him of special pre-cult experiences.

Remember, there is a part of him that does not want to be in the cult, that wants real love, that wants honesty, that wants to grow and learn. When rapport and trust are developed, you can elicit the person's authentic self. Then, your loved one will tell you what needs to happen for him to leave the group.

An important part of rapport building between yourself and a cult member is establishing a firm mutual commitment to being in a relationship. In the following discussion, two Team members, one an ex-cult member (whose name has been changed here to Billy), learn how to ask a cult member (who I will call Jeff) for such a promise.

BILLY [EX-MEMBER]: Lenz would say to us, "You are all unhappy. The reason is you're remembering the old times. You still have attachments to your past, your parents, your friends, your possessions, the place you used to live. Cut them! Get them out of your life! Throw away your pictures. Throw away anything that reminds you of your past life." He does everything he can to cut you off from who you are.

SH: That's why it's so important to connect with Jeff's authentic identity.

DANNY: It's pretty scary. I love my brother. I don't want to lose him.

SH: Since he's just beginning to get really sucked in, I think the tack you should take is to tell him, "Promise me we'll be close forever and that nothing will ever come between us." If he says, "Of course," then you can say, "I have a fear I want to get off my chest. What happens if you move, and six months from now, Lenz tells you never to talk with me again? I'm worried you might dump me." Let him respond, "No, no, that would never happen." Then, you say, "But what if it did? I want your commitment that you and I are going to be able to communicate no matter what, even if I'm doing something you don't like, or you are doing something I don't like. We're brothers."

Pursue as deep a commitment as possible. If he asks, "Anything else bothering you?" you can say, "Yeah, a million things, but as long as we keep talking about it and we keep an open mind—looking from different perspectives, looking for information—I know things will work out." Remember, in spite of his cult indoctrination, Jeff still has many connections, and that's why we are doing this Strategic Interaction. We want to prevent him from moving and cutting off from everyone he loves and cares about, and becoming more controlled.

Connecting with the pre-cult and cult identities is an essential ongoing process in the SIA. In the following chapters, you will learn how to use your understanding of both identities to show your loved one that mind control exists, that other groups use mind control techniques to control their members, and, finally, that their group is a destructive cult. But before discussing any specifics about cults or mind control, we will prepare ourselves for such conversations by learning and practicing new modes of communication that will help you get your message across without alienating your loved one.

Chapter 9

Communication Strategies

One of the hallmarks of the Strategic Interaction Approach is its focus on effective, goal-oriented communication skills. Without clear-cut objectives and techniques for achieving them, people can easily feel frustrated and burned-out when interacting with a loved one in a cult. Communicating with a cult member can be a difficult and emotionally draining experience. This chapter introduces skills that you will use to facilitate interactions with your loved one—whether it is by letter, on the telephone, or face-to-face.

Step-by-step, you will learn, rehearse, and implement these skills. After each phone call, letter, or visit (what I call a mini-inter-action), you will assess where your efforts are being rewarded and where they need adjusting. One of the goals of your interactions is to gain information about your loved one, what his life in the group is like, how he has been affected by his cult involvement, and to educate him about other destructive mind control cults. Ultimately, your aim—indeed this is a critical objective of the Strategic Interaction Approach—is to motivate the cult member to begin to question his own cult involvement: to research and consider alter-native points of view and to think critically and independently.

Rather than attempt to try for a knock-out blow, the objective will usually be achieved as the cumulative effect of many interac-tions in which you have built rapport and trust. Along with information-gathering, rapport and trust-building are the foundation stones for using the more advanced techniques for promoting freedom of mind presented in chapters 10 and 11.

After every interaction, you should try to assess where you are in the process and develop an idea of the next several steps that need to be taken to assist the cult member. When planning future interactions, each Team member should ask himself: "Will this step bring me closer to the goal, or take me further away?" Only say and do those things that enhance your relationship and assist the cult member to act independently.

One of the most common mistakes made by the friends and family of cult members is to approach the person prematurely with facts about the group. I recently received a telephone call from one such woman whose husband had joined the Jehovah's Witnesses. After reading my first book, she had started gathering information to discredit the group, articles pointing out contradictions in its doctrine, and was trying to force her husband to look at it. She kept at it for over two years, but didn't stop to think that each time she criticized the group, she was losing rapport and trust with him. She thought that by repeatedly bringing up contradictions and problems with the group, she would "wake him up." At the point that she contacted me, their marriage was falling apart. I told her that she needed to back off, learn how to communicate effectively, and rebuild her relationship through marriage counseling—before even thinking about raising any more criticisms about the group.

Remember, in most cases, Team members will have to engage in a series of mini-interactions over days, weeks and, possibly, months before the cult member expresses the first inklings of doubt about his cult involvement. We will learn a multi-step approach to give the Team the necessary resources to see members through this period. Each prepared interaction should advance our goals of building rapport and trust, gathering and providing information, and sowing seeds of doubt. By rehearsing actual conversations that

you plan to have with your loved one, you will learn how to anticipate his responses and react appropriately.

REHEARSAL STRATEGIES

The best way to prepare for a telephone call or face-to-face
meeting with a cult member is to rehearse what you will say and
how you will say it. Once you have acted out your approach, and
anticipated your loved one's possible responses, you will have a
foundation of experience that makes goal-oriented communication
much more effective.

Families sometimes underestimate how helpful such preparation can be. For example, I recently met with a couple whose
daughter had broken off contact a year earlier. While we were discussing their options, I asked, "What would happen if you saw her
on the street or in a shopping mall?" The father looked bewildered,
and told me, "I don't know what I would say!" "We just don't think
fast on our feet," added the mother. I replied, "The only reason I
think fast on my feet is that I practice. I make it a habit to imagine
different scenarios—from the best possible to the worst possible,
and rehearse my best response to each scenario in my mind. That
way, I already have a range of choices that I've thought out before
I speak directly to the person." Over time, practice can give you
the confidence and mental readiness for virtually any situation.

Preparation

Before you speak with your loved one, visualize seeing yourself
having a conversation with the cult member. Imagine three variations of what could happen: the best possible scenario, the worst
possible scenario, and what will probably happen.

For example, picture yourself asking the cult member to spend
some time alone with you when you next visit.

Best possible scenario:

- The cult member says, "I have the day off. We don't have to be here. Let's go into town or somewhere fun."

You already have a few places to visit picked out and several things you want to talk about, for example, the phobia cure (chapter 10).

Worst possible scenario:

- The cult member is suspicious. He says, "I don't trust you; you've never come to visit me before. Maybe you want to deprogram me."

You have a lot of rapport and trust building to do. You might ask, "What can we say to reassure you that we would never violate your rights and force you to do something against your will?"

What will probably happen:

- The cult member says he's asked "a friend" to join you for the visit and adds, "it's better if we stay here." You say, "Okay, if that's what you want, this time." Then you ask the other member, "What's your name? Where are you from? How long have you been involved?"

By having a pleasant, non-confrontational meeting, the cult member and leaders will think you are a nice person and hopefully, no longer a threat. They will think that you love your child. You will probably be invited to come back again to visit. Next time, you might be able to have some time alone. They might even allow both of you to leave cult property by yourselves.

By thinking through and preparing yourself for all three of these scenarios, you will be eliminating many of the unknowns that create fear and anxiety. Rehearse different variations. If you find yourself saying something that is bound to have a negative response, try something else. The better you understand the cult member, the more accurately you will be able to predict his response. For many people, learning to be deliberate in your communication with a family member is awkward and strange. Indeed, this kind of rehearsal strategy is often taught in the business world, especially in sales, in order to teach salespeople how to make money. The more you rehearse, the easier your task will be to constructively influence the person in the cult.

Intention-delivery-response

An important part of goal-oriented communication is the ability to assess your intended message, your delivery, and your loved one's response. When you practice asking a question or conveying a piece of information, keep in mind these three stages of communication:

- Intention: what you mean to express, like "I love you so much."
- Delivery: the words you use and how you say them—your facial expression, tone of voice, and speed.
- Response: the reaction you get— what that person "heard."

For example, a cult member's father may want to tell his son, "I care about you." This is what he feels. But perhaps he is shocked by his son's appearance, so he asks, "Why are you dressed that way?" The delivery is sarcastic and critical, so the cult member's response will probably be defensive. He may express his feelings with body language—by diverting his eyes, furrowing his brow, or crossing his arms—or with words: "This is who I am. If you can't accept me, that's your problem." Focus on reaction. If you don't get the reaction you are looking for, building rapport and trust, giving information, planting seeds, then rethink your choice of words and delivery. Think back to what you meant to express, and find another way to say it.

If what you are doing builds rapport and trust, then you are on the right track. If what you are doing has a destructive response, like alienating your loved one, then stop doing it. Minimize the damage. You want to develop communication patterns that are flexible, creative and constructive. They will maximize rapport and trust-building responses. Rigid, habitual, destructive patterns will produce alienation and frustration.

However, Team members should not become frustrated or impatient when they do not see immediate results. When they are doing the right things, they may not get the best response possible—but they won't get negative responses, either. Think of your relationship with your loved one as a cup with holes in it. During the SIA, you fill the cup with love, rapport, and trust, but the cup continues to leak until you figure out where the holes are. Once you identify what needs to be changed below the surface—what phobia you have to undo, what information you need to get and give—you will begin to see positive results.

Role-playing

The next level of preparation, beyond visualization, is to role-play. At first, most people need to be coaxed into doing a role-play, but find that the more they practice, the easier it becomes. Most clients like it when I engage in it with them a few times to warm up. I usually start by playing the role of one of them (a family member or friend), while they play the cult member. We focus on a situation where they typically find themselves getting stuck and do not know what to say, for example, why they think their loved one is being misled by the cult leader. Putting themselves in their loved one's shoes, and hearing my response, can sometimes give them new ideas about how best to express themselves. After a while, everyone on the Team takes a turn.

During role-playing exercises, you also play yourself and share things that you want to say to the cult member (played by another

Team member). This gives you the opportunity to rehearse responses to different points that the cult member might make. Acting out the interaction in advance can help put you at ease during an actual meeting, and can help you achieve a higher level of rapport and trust.

Former members will be especially adept at teaching you what to expect and how to act. The more experience you have talking to former members who can role-play the typical cult member, the more accurately you will predict how the loved one will respond.

A sample role-playing exercise

Below is a transcript of an extended role-playing exercise that I performed with a former member of the Jehovah's Witnesses (I have renamed him Steve W. and changed other identifying features.). Your first attempts will most likely be shorter and less polished, because we have more experience to draw on. In fact, I reprint the exercise in its entirety to show you the various aspects involved in communicating with a cult member.

It is a scene that is familiar to most of us: a man comes to my door, ready to hand me the *WatchTower* publication. Very few people understand that the Jehovah's Witnesses fulfill the criteria of a mind control cult. Until former members educated me, I didn't believe it was.

SW: (knocks on door): I'm Steve. I am here to ask you if you are interested in a Bible study. Time is running out. I can offer you irrefutable evidence that in months to come Armageddon will be here. You need to get into God's Kingdom!

SH: What was your name again?

SW: Steve W. And your name?

SH: Steve. I think we can remember each other's names. I'm interested in what you have to say, Steve. Would you tell me a little about yourself? How long have you been involved with the

WatchTower Society?

SW: Most of my life. My mother became a Jehovah's Witness (JW) when I was five and brought us kids up in it. It's been a way of life for me.

SH: Do you remember when your Mom joined?

SW: Yes, I even remember one Christmas—you might know that JWs don't celebrate Christmas.

SH: Oh, really? But you remember celebrating a Christmas when you were five?

SW: Yes, and even an Easter egg hunt at my grandmother's house.

SH: Was it fun?

SW: Yes, but I'm not here to talk about that. I'm here to talk about God's Kingdom.

SH: Do you live in the neighborhood?

SW: I'm one of your neighbors.

SH: How old are you?

SW: Forty-four.

SH: And have you lived in this neighborhood for long?

SW: Oh, about twenty years.

SH: So, you're going door to door because you want me to know that the end is near?

SW: We offer free home Bible studies. You can find evidence from the Bible that the end is near. You'll find out what you can do to get your life in order so you can get into that new world.

SH: Uh-huh. What would be different once I became involved with your organization?

SW: You would find out for the first time how you fit in with God's purpose. You'll see Jehovah has a purpose for you.

SH: I believe already that God has a purpose for me.

SW: Do you? What is that purpose?

SH: I've done a lot of research, counseling, speaking and lecturing.

SW: What would be the nature of that research and counseling?

SH: Steve, I'm really interested in who you are as a person. Could you tell me a little more about what's happening in your life? What's important to you? What questions do you have? That will help me understand what your group is all about. Could you tell me your thoughts?

SW: As a Jehovah's Witness?

SH: No, as a person.

SW: When you're a JW your whole life is wrapped up in Jehovah's organization. Everything about you as a person is your purpose to spread the Kingdom of good news. If you pile up enough good works, you'll survive the battle of Armageddon. I'm looking forward to that.

SH: Steve, I need to ask a question and I hope it doesn't upset you. I'd really hate that. Is it OK to ask?

SW: Go ahead.

SH: When I hear you to talk the way you're talking, I feel like there's something else going on with you. There is a part of you that doesn't believe completely what you are saying.

SW: I think you'll find JWs are not perfect. We're not perfect.

SH: That's good. I'm not perfect. I don't know any human who is.

SW: We alone have the truth, but as individuals we're not perfect. We have our problems. I have family problems.

SH: I hear you! None of us is. We agree with that. JWs claim to have the truth—there are a lot of organizations that claim to have the truth. Have you noticed that?

SW: To my knowledge, Christian Science, Mormons, Roman Catholics, and Seventh-Day Adventists claim to have the higher truth.

SH: What about Scientology? They're the ones who advertise the book *Dianetics*.

SW: Oh, yes.

SH: They believe they alone have the Truth. They can help save the earth. What about the Moonies?

SW: They all believe they have the truth?

SH: They are convinced Sun Myung Moon, their leader, is Christ returned. The members completely dedicate their lives to help people come to God through what they believe is their interpretation of Bible. I have some friends involved with that. What about the Multiplying Ministries?

SW: I never heard of them.

SH: That's a very fast growing group. They tell their members it's proof they are God's chosen because so many people are joining.

SW: It's presumptuous of them to say that.

SH: Yeah, I think so. Members believe that Kip McKean is God's anointed on the planet earth, and that only they are practicing true Christianity. They also believe the end is near. I know people involved with that group. It's amazing. If you step back and think about it, there are thousands of groups. Each one claims it alone has the truth. If you step out of that particular group you're basically going to hell. Can you imagine someone being afraid to leave the Moonies because they believed they would be going to hell? Isn't that ridiculous?

SW: They have been lied to in the first place. But we have the Bible to back up everything we say. I know it sounds preposterous for me to stand at your door and say, "We have the Truth!" but we do. We can prove it by the Bible. I don't think these other groups can.

SH: Steve, I completely believe that you feel that way. You've been involved since you were five years old. I'm sure I would feel the same way. I think it's curious to realize there are other groups out there, and their members are being brought in and told that they alone have God's truth and any other group is an inferior group. They alone have the truth! They are even given phobias—can you believe that? If they leave their particular group, bad things will happen to them. They are told they will go to Hell. They will get cancer or get hit by a car or lose their salvation. They believe another person is so much closer to God than they are, that whatever the leader says goes; even if it is against their own inner yearnings for truth. Even if it goes against their desire to question, think and exercise their free will. You would agree God wants us to have free will. Isn't that incredible?

SW: I don't feel like talking about that. I'd like to talk about the *WatchTower* we have right here.

SH: I think that would be valuable. I'd like to think a little more about our conversation. I know you're going to want to do that too. I do want to mention a few other things that seem important for me to say right now. My friend in the Moonies was told that if he ever questioned Moon or the Bible as it was taught by the Unification Church, evil spirits or Satan were trying to tempt him or test him. He was taught to shut off any doubts. Just follow. Just surrender to God. Everything would work out. When anyone would try to talk with him, "Hey, did you read this?" or, "Did you talk to this person?" or, "Study this," he would automatically say, "Satan is trying to take me out of this group. Satan is trying to tempt me away from God. I can't listen to it." The more he tried to suppress his doubts, the bigger they grew. He really wanted to know what the truth was. Isn't that amazing?

SW: I've got to go.

SH: It's been a pleasure meeting you (shaking hands). I'm sure you'll consider what I've said and feel free to come back and we can talk some more.

Remember, when speaking with a cult member, your thoughts and judgments about the cult member can be communicated in seconds with a few words, a look, a tone of voice, or a gesture. During the exercise above, I tried to communicate a non-confrontational, curious, yet concerned attitude. Practice creates experience and I have over twenty years under my belt. I don't consciously think about all that I will explain, I just do it naturally. For teaching purposes, I will explain some of the main points.

Smile on my face

He knocked on the door, and I opened it and smiled. If I had scowled, he would have gotten a negative message. Remember the old phrase, "Looks can kill." I wanted him to instantly know that I was a friendly person.

Calm, friendly voice

How you speak is as important as what you say. I spoke calmly and didn't whisper or shout. I let him introduce himself, asked him what his name was, and then shook his hand. I didn't speed up or slow down. Mirror, match, and pace the conversation.

Body language

I initiated body contact; I shook his hand. The importance of body language was demonstrated in a social psychology research project where a person in front of a pay phone asked people passing by, "May I have a quarter for a phone call?" A certain percentage of people would hand over the coin. When the caller touched the person's arm or shook their hand, the percentage of people who agreed rose dramatically.[1]

A touch of the hand makes the person real to you, not an abstraction. I always try to shake a person's hand. If he is uncomfortable and his hand doesn't come up to meet mine, I'll put it down quickly. But it's important to try to connect on a physical level.

Sometimes family members don't make the effort to extend their hand or give the hug or kiss, especially if the cult member looks rigid or distant. Go ahead and shake your loved one's hand, or hug him. A short, warm hug is worth initiating. When giving a hug, the friend or relative shouldn't let go too early. Wait until you sense that the cult member wants to let go. If you have a history of not hugging or kissing, warn him and ask for permission: "I really have a strong desire to give you a hug! May I?" See if he will reciprocate. You're better off trying than not trying.

Consider spatial distance—too close feels intrusive, too far away seems too impersonal. To gauge his comfort zone, I try standing a little closer and see if he backs off. When Steve shifted his weight, I tried to shift my weight as a way of creating rapport. I also look for an opportunity to pat the person on the back, perhaps as we walk out of the room together.

Pay attention to your hands. When I was talking to Steve about the other cults, I gesticulated with my hands to imply: "Over there," and "groups other than yours." At the same time, I wanted him to follow my gestures with his eyes in such a way that he could imagine stepping into the shoes of a Moonie. I wanted him to feel that, as a Moonie, he couldn't have doubts about Moon or God. I wasn't talking abstractly about it, because I wanted to shift his perspective.

Eye contact

For some people, eye contact is reassuring because it makes them feel that you are paying attention to them. For others, direct eye contact makes them nervous. These people tend to concentrate on auditory rather than visual cues. It is not natural for me to make extensive eye contact when I talk to people, but I have trained myself to do that. Watch for nonverbal responses from the person to discover what he needs for rapport and trust building.

Elicit the pre-cult self

I try to access who the person was before his involvement, in Steve's case, a young child of five. I would much rather talk with the authentic identity than the cult self. If I can access the pre-cult self in the first moments, as I did with the reference to Christmas and Easter, I have already established a connection I can return to.

Work with the cult self

If the cult identity is the only part that I can interact with, then my approach is to try to expand the cult identity's world. You might try asking him why a member of the Governing Body (the elite leadership of the *WatchTower*) has left the group, is still a believer in God, and has written books about his sixty years of experience within the organization.

Establish your "territory" and avoid getting drawn into his territory.

I choose not to talk about the *WatchTower*. An old strategy used in debating is that whoever defines the territory of the discussion has the edge. Rather than discussing the doctrines of his group, I shifted the focus to the beliefs of other groups.

Find areas of agreement

I didn't tell Steve how I disagreed with him. Instead, I defined the territory in terms of: "I am a human being and you are a human being. I am interested in who you are." I tried to make it clear that it mattered to me what he thought: "Can you imagine? Have you ever thought?" I wanted to know his name, and it turned out to be the same as mine. With religious cults, it helps to talk about your spirituality and faith, if you are a believer. If you can find common ground, it will be easier to talk about other things. Having things in common builds rapport and trust.

When I first opened the door, I didn't have the agenda to get him out of the cult in ten minutes. I was thinking, "I'm going to spend ten minutes or so with him. How much can I do to establish rapport and trust?" I tried to cultivate a relationship. If I could then get the person to agree, "Yes, this 'other' group is a cult and it uses mind control techniques," then I would have accomplished an important goal. Spell out criteria that you can agree on. This takes you a step closer to the goal of helping the person broaden their perspective.

INTERACTING WITH YOUR LOVED ONE

Letters, telephone calls and visits are your primary modes of contact with your loved one.[2] Your communication might very well be the most important link the cult member has to the "outside" world. Every time you interact with your loved one—in letters, by telephone, or in person—you are creating an opportunity to influence the cult identity and the authentic self.

A. Writing letters

Letter writing is a powerful medium of communication, and I recommend making each letter count. It is the one mode of communication in which you have total control. You should think, plan, and utilize letter writing as the foundation of your communication efforts. As always in the Strategic Interaction Approach, your first goal is to develop higher levels of rapport and trust so that he will look forward to hearing from you and want to correspond. The next goal is information gathering. Once you have achieved a high level with these two goals, you can move on to advanced techniques. The following suggestions may help you in composing your letter:

- Start warmly and end warmly.
- Keep it short (avoid long-winded treatises).
- Focus on one or two key points.

- Restate points raised in past telephone calls and letters.
- Ask follow-up questions to past interactions.
- Coordinate letter-writing efforts with others.

The great thing about letter writing is that you don't have to mail a letter, or even show it to anyone else. You can simply read it and throw it away, or put it in a hiding place. I find that for some people, letter writing is an incredibly helpful way to "purge" their anger, frustration and hurt. Team members can write a "purge" letter to the cult member as often as they need to, saying exactly what they want to say, holding nothing back. This is an effective way to maintain your sanity. You might be surprised at some of the thoughts that come out of your unconscious.

Strategy for effective letter writing

What I have found to be the most effective strategy involves a multi-step writing and editing process. First, write the first draft of the letter. Put the letter aside for a few hours or a few days. Open it again and pretend that you are the cult member. Imagine what he or she might think and feel as you read each line. By putting yourself in the shoes of the cult member, you can best appraise the effectiveness of what you have written. As the cult member, do you feel closer to the author of the letter? Does the letter motivate you to share yourself with him? Does it encourage you to reflect about your experiences? Edit the letter as many times as necessary, until you believe it has achieved maximum effectiveness. You can also ask siblings and former members what they think of the letter and get suggestions. I spend a good deal of my time helping family members and friends edit important letters.

Sample letter to a fictitious cult member, Alex, from his father

June 1, 1994

Dear Alex,

I've been thinking about you almost all the time since we spoke last Saturday. It was a good talk, one of our best, I think, although I got off the phone thinking how much better I wished I knew you. You are a fine young man and I'm proud of you, although I struggle to understand some of your choices.

What did you think of last week's conversation?

I hope we can spend some quality time together—soon. Perhaps, you could get some time off and we could go on a fishing trip together, just the two of us. Wouldn't that be great? I remember the times we went up to the mountain cabin when you were younger. Which memories stand out for you? I'll never forget the time when I got so excited by that big fish on my line that I stood up in the canoe and tipped us over—and how we laughed!

I wish I had spent more time with you as you were growing up. I guess I was too busy trying to be a "good provider." Often when I got home from work, I was so tired that I just sat down and watched TV. I wish I could go back and do things differently. I wish I had spent even more quality time with you. Was I a bad father?

But one of the things you'll learn as you grow and mature is how to make wise decisions—ones that you will feel good about ten, even twenty years from now. What do you see when you imagine yourself in ten years? Twenty years?

I would very much like you to send me that book you mentioned that you think I should read. As I said to you on the phone, if it will help me to understand you and your group better, I will do almost anything. I promise I'll take notes and ask you all the questions that come to my mind, as long as you promise to take the time to answer them for me. I don't want you to have someone else explain the group's philosophy to me. I want you to do it. You're my son and I trust you.

I'm sending along a copy of a recent photo of your mom, Billy, Sandy, and me at the last family reunion. Everyone asked about you and hopes to see you soon. I'll speak with you again on Saturday, right?

Love,
Dad

Photocopy every letter that goes out

If a letter gets lost or the person never receives it, you can say, "Don't worry. I make a photocopy of each letter that I send you. I'll mail a copy of it tomorrow. It should arrive in 2-3 days. Look for it." I recommend writing letters, even if you don't get a response. When you finally do manage to re-establish contact, your loved one might tell you that he never got any of your letters. When you see him in person, you can give him the pile of letters and say, "Here are all the letters I wrote you." Seeing the sheer effort that was put into writing is usually a very positive and emotionally powerful experience for the person, not to mention sitting and reading all of them.

Privacy and censorship issues

Some groups go so far as to screen members' letters and telephone calls. Some secretly destroy letters and will not allow private telephone calls. Politely ask your loved one if anyone else reads your letters. Ask former leaders of the group if they are aware of any policy to read members' mail. If you don't know for sure, you should assume the letters are read by others.

If you're concerned that your loved may not be getting your letters at all, tell him when you speak that you will write once a week or once every two weeks, and that if he doesn't get a letter, he should look for it. If your loved one works outside the cult, you might consider sending the letter to his place of employment. You can even offer to open a post office box for him, if he wants it. If your loved one has a family and lives in a house, try sending picture post cards. That way, everyone might take a "peek."

For most cult members, knowing that their mail is intercepted or even thrown away by leaders is a major source of discontent. It is a very graphic demonstration of information control and has led to many people becoming disillusioned and walking out of their groups. Make sure to do everything in your power to help the cult member become aware of this control. You can ask questions like, "Isn't it strange that letters I write to you seem to disappear? When I write to your brothers and sisters, they always get my letters!" Avoid the temptation to say something critical like, "They are deliberately withholding my letters to you."

Frequency of contact is important

It is better to write a short note once a week than to write nothing for months and then send a long letter. Cultivate an ongoing relationship. If the cult member asks you, "Please write to me," then tell him that you will do your best to write regularly, at least once every week or two. If the cult member ignores your letters, try to make a verbal agreement that he will call or write: "I would like for us to have regular communication. Our relationship has not been on the same level as it was before."

If the cult member is a rebellious nineteen-year-old, he may not want the parent to write or call once a week. Find out what will work. It might be once every two or three weeks.

Coordinate letter writing

It will be suspicious if no one in the family has been writing for months and all of a sudden everyone on the Team starts writing. It usually takes some kind of explanation to avoid suspicion. The most common one is that everyone in the family recently got together (at a family event—birthday, anniversary, or even a family counseling session), and talked about how much they all love and miss the individual.

When you initiate a new pattern of communication, contact your loved one, preferably in person or on the telephone and say, "I really miss you. I want to stay in touch. Let's start corresponding. I'm going to write a letter every week or two." Just receiving a letter from the outside world is positive because it reminds cult members that they are special, that their friends and family care about them, and that there is an outside world with people who are important to them.

If there is a large family and circle of friends, it is best to prioritize who should start communicating first. People who were closest to the individual before the cult involvement should be the first to call or write. Once the most important relationships are re-established, other members of the Team can join in and initiate contact.

Follow-up

People in cults are usually kept tired and busy. They often don't even remember what they wrote or spoke about last week. Do not assume that the cult member remembers what he wrote in his last letter or conversation. Remind him and restate: "When we were talking on the phone, you were saying..." or "I've been thinking about the issue you wrote about in your letter...."

Choose what will be most beneficial to discuss. You can avoid some comments or statements he made, and choose the ones which will help you advance the relationship. Do not remind the cult member of things that will move you away from your Strategic Interaction goals.

Be creative

Enclose a poem, watercolor, joke or cartoon (make sure it will be funny to him or her). You can ask if your loved one wants any music tapes or CD's, preferably music he used to enjoy. Some cult groups allow videotapes of popular movies. Some movies can be very positively influential. When you write, try to periodically include photos of yourself and the person. Whenever you visit, take photographs of you and your loved one, as well as other Team members and cult members. Your aim is to create as many positive bonds as you can. Sometimes photographs can be used for reality-testing, especially if the cult member looks uncharacteristically thin or overweight, or even depressed. As often as possible, the Team should help the cult member to feel loved and missed.

Send gifts

When the cult member receives a package of Grandma's home baked cookies and shares them with everyone, other members will enjoy them, too. They may even feel jealous, and it might make them miss their families. It will give your loved one a good feeling about the "outside" world.

It is generally not a good idea to send money. This is because cash usually has to be turned over to the group. The last thing you want to do is enrich the coffers of the cult. However, you might consider sending an occasional small gift of cash ($20-$100) in a letter. You might say something like, "Buy something for yourself," especially if that is something you would normally do for a birth-day or holiday. By sending some cash, you might actually help to create constructive dissonance, especially if the long-term cult member is married and has children. On the one hand, the cult self knows he should surrender the money to the group. On the other hand, the real self might want to buy something that he needs.

In some cases, offering a laptop computer is a great thing—if the cult member promises he will be the primary user of it. This way, your loved one can use the Internet and you can exchange email. You can suggest that he "check it out with his superiors," and make sure he will be able to keep it. If for some reason, the leaders make an excuse to commandeer the computer, it can be a great source of frustration for your loved one. It might even lead to his leaving the cult. Some family members have sent a non-cashable return airline ticket with a note that says: "Please use this anytime. Whenever you have an impulse to come home, just get on the plane!" Arrange this with a travel agent, who can advise you the best way to get such a ticket.

B. Telephone calls

Practicing specific communication skills will help you make more effective telephone calls to your loved one. Make a tape recording of each session so that you can listen to, and evaluate, the conversation. Focus on how to improve your skills. Role play on the phone, paying attention to what people at the other end say, and how they say it. Try to match their style:

Auditory Level: Whisper if they whisper; speak loudly if they do.
Speed: Talk as quickly or as slowly as they do. Allow exaggerated pauses after asking a good question, even if it's a long-distance call.
Diction: Use words that are neutral for rapport building. Do NOT use words such as "brainwashing" or "cult," which can be alienating.
Mood: If they're in an upbeat mood, join them. If they're down, don't tell them to cheer up. Ask them why they're feeling the way they do.

Content: Seek areas of agreement to establish rapport. If it's a religious cult, talk about spirituality.

As always, in the Strategic Interaction Approach, it is a good idea to begin each telephone conversation warmly to build rapport and trust. Show interest in how the cult member is feeling. Ask what new things he is learning. Give plenty of reinforcement: "I really enjoy talking with you. It helps me to feel closer to you."

Periodically assess your level of rapport and trust. Ask him, on a scale of one to ten: "Where am I now—a three? What can I do to make it a four, five, or six?" In general, rapport and trust is heightened when you find areas of mutual interest and identification. The closer you can mirror, match, or pace the person you are talking to, the more rapport and trust you will build.

Pay attention to the cult member as well as to yourself. Ask yourself: "What's going to help me be most effective while I'm on the phone?" For example, some people are more resourceful standing up than sitting down. Other people might feel comfortable sipping a cup of tea. Remember to pay attention to the volume of the conversation. You don't want to find yourself raising your voice and shouting into the receiver. Some cult members may speak very quickly. Try to match their speed.

Visualize

Visualize your loved one when talking on the telephone. Imagine the expression on his face. It may be more helpful to close your eyes. Listen to your loved one's tone of voice. This process will give you more information than merely listening to the person's voice.

Silence is valuable communication

If you ask a question and there is silence on the line, wait at least five full minutes before gently repeating the question. You want the cult member to think and reflect. Sometimes, people do not wait for long silences because they worry about the expense of the long-distance telephone call. It's worth waiting for the response. Do not let the cult member change the subject. Gently restate the question you asked, or remind them what they were last saying.

Prepare for future calls

Have a list of things to talk about in front of you:
- Something you enjoy doing
- Something you want to do in the future
- A book or magazine article you are reading
- A movie you saw
- New friends you made
- Positive spiritual experiences
- Information about other groups or cults
- Questions you would like to ask to follow up on previous conversations

It is better to make one good point over and over in different ways. In a telephone conversation, a barrage of questions will lose rapport and trust. It is easier for the cult member to think about one question. When faced with too many, he will just shut down. Remember, declarative statements or judgements won't build rapport and trust, either. Again, when you ask a good question, make sure you allow up to five full minutes of silence.

Take notes

Each time you make or receive a telephone call, take notes:

carefully record the date, time, and what is discussed. This will allow you to track your progress and maintain continuity in your communication. For those people with computers, write up your notes and e-mail pertinent points to others on the Team.

When you call your loved one and another cult member answers, ask for information about that person: "What is your name? What do you do? Are you a leader?" If this person fails to give a message that you called, you can identify that person to your loved one, a potential source of dissonance.

Access the pre-cult self

Team members should learn to recognize whether their loved one is in cult mode or not. If he is warm and friendly, bring up positive pre-cult memories, tell jokes, tell him about other family and friends. If he's hostile, arrogant, or defensive, this is not a good time to ask the person to come home and visit; it is time to build rapport, change the subject or end the conversation. When you feel you are losing your resourcefulness and the cult identity is in full gear, be patient. Wait for another time.

When is the best time to call?

Try to find out when there will be no others around so you can talk undisturbed. Find out from your loved one what his schedule is like: How much time does he have to talk? If he has ten minutes, use it. Let him tell you he has to go. Don't tell him his ten minutes are up. If he is enjoying the conversation, keep talking.

In communal cults, there are usually only one or two telephones. These are usually monitored. If so, your loved one is probably standing there with other members nearby, or the phone might simply be wire-tapped. If other cult members are listening, you will probably be speaking to the cult self. This may seem like common sense, but most people don't stop and think, especially when they can't see or hear the other cult members. In other situations, private time is usually late at night or early in the morning. Begin the conversation with: "Is this a good time for us to talk? Are you free?" If not, ask when you can call again. They may only be able to talk privately when off the compound. Offer a pre-paid telephone card for them to telephone you when they have a moment.

Minimize distractions

Try to make your telephone calls during periods where you can give the conversation your undivided attention. People visiting, animals barking, children crying, a television blaring, or a doorbell ringing are not conducive to goal-oriented communication.

You should also consider your privacy when talking on the phone to your loved one. Calling from work may seem convenient, but your employer or co-workers may be listening. When such people have not been coached as part of the Team, their negative comments and attitudes might be counterproductive or downright discouraging.

Pass the telephone to others

When you talk to the cult member during a family gathering, try passing the phone around to key people. Try to maintain a sense of normalcy. Describe what you see, hear, and smell: how people are dressed, what you've been discussing, the smell of a favorite food. Tell your loved one you wish he were with you to enjoy the occasion. Make him want to be there.

Emergency telephone calls

Tell the cult member that if he ever needs to speak with you, to call collect anytime. Parents can also give the cult member their calling card number, but ask him to use it to call family and friends only. Since you will get the bill, you will have a record of all the phone calls and numbers. You won't have that advantage with a pre-paid calling card. Some parents have even installed an 800 number so the cult member can call any time. If you don't have an answering machine or voice mail, install it immediately. You do not want to miss any messages.

When your loved one calls in the middle of the night, it is usually an important telephone call. Chances are you'll be awakened from sleep and very disoriented. Take a moment to turn on the light, sit up and wake up. Your first task is to assess if the cult member is upset and is reaching out to you for help. Ask, "Where are you? What is happening?"

The cult member might be deliberately trying to catch you off guard, to tell you he can't come home for a visit, or to pressure you for money. If this is the case, tell him politely that he woke you up from a deep sleep, and that you would like to speak with him about his request tomorrow, when you are awake. If he is in his cult identity, try to get off the telephone as quickly as possible, and go back to sleep.

On the other hand, late night emergency calls can happen when the person wants to run away from the cult. If the cult member is crying, seems upset or confused, comfort him and tell him that you are glad he called you and that you are there for him. Tell him to start from the beginning and tell you everything that is going on. Be prepared for long silences. If there is no response after waiting several minutes, gently ask him if he is still there, and repeat your last question or what he last was saying. Be confident, reassuring and directive. After you find out what has happened, try to tell the person to go somewhere unknown to the cult and wait for you to come get him. If he lives in another city, state or country, try to place him in contact with a local resource person. But don't get off the phone too quickly to make arrangements. Keep him talking as long as possible.

Hopefully, you will have a emergency plan all ready to go before such a telephone call is received.

Learn from each interaction

Typically, family members will get off the telephone and say, "I wish I had said this," or "I should have said that." Instead of dwelling on something you cannot change, accept what happened as part of the learning experience. Visualize yourself having the conversation; only this time, saying what you wanted to say. This way, you rehearse effective communication and feel good about it. Remember, in the SIA, you must keep a positive focus.

- What is our goal?
- Where are we now?
- What will advance us to our goal?
- What did I do right?
- How would I do it differently in the future?

When there are interactions that do not go as well as the family had hoped, remember that every Strategic Interaction is an opportunity to learn and grow. One way to learn from your experience is to tape record conversations with the cult member in order to assess the conversation later. In many states, recording is legal if one party in the conversation consents to it. If you feel uncomfortable with the idea, check your local laws.

C. Face-to-face Interactions

Seeing your loved one for the first time since his recruitment can be an emotionally charged event. During face-to-face meetings, Team members must remember that they are allies of their loved one, not foes. Make win/win suggestions, not yes/no, win/lose demands. Ask non-threatening questions, but don't make assumptions or critical statements. Pose hypothetical ("What if...?") questions, and remember to speak about other groups. Give specific examples. It is likely that you will be communicating with the cult identity most of the time, so be prepared.

During face-to-face conversations, remember to allow for periods of silence—up to five full minutes to allow your loved one adequate time to process the thought. During that period of silence, try not to fidget or wriggle your leg or arm, look out the window, tap your fingers, or jingle coins. Calmly wait for his or her response and remain relatively motionless, but not staring. Hopefully, at the end of a visit, your loved one will be left with feelings of love and warmth. He will wish you weren't going, or better yet, that he could leave with you. Each visit should improve upon the others. Even if your loved one lives far away, try to visit at least once every six months.

When to ask your loved one to visit home

A positive home visit is essential, but your invitation must be timed strategically. Any cult member's commitment to the group will vary over time. There will be peaks and valleys. If the member has just returned from a three-week cult workshop, you should expect him to be zealous. Conversations will be saturated with loaded language. This is not a good time to ask for a visit home.

On the other hand, your loved one might be at a point where he is disillusioned with the group, the leader, or the doctrine. If his closest friend in the cult has just been transferred to another state, he might be especially receptive to an invitation to visit home. For a variety of reasons, your loved one could also be at a stage where he feels more in touch with the non-cult world and his authentic identity. A young man I recently counseled left the Moon cult after secretly reading *Combatting Cult Mind Control*. One of the things that set his exit into motion was his first visit home after three years of being in the cult. During his visit, he was able to see old photographs of himself and his family, meet with old friends, and sleep in his own bed. The visit reactivated a big part of his old self.

If you have rapport and trust, your loved one will share disappointing and disillusioning experiences with you, through letters and on the telephone. These are the best times to invite your loved one home for a visit. It is essential to keep inviting, even when the person does not come. It is possible he is being discouraged, or even denied permission, by the cult. The more opportunities you can create, the sooner your loved one will realize there is a cult plan to keep him away from his family and friends. Other approaches you can take:

• Become friendly with your loved one's immediate superiors and ask them for help in making sure that your loved one can come home. Remember, cult leaders want to recruit others. They want good public relations.

• If the cult member never seems to be allowed home to visit, suggest that he bring another cult member with him. This will give the group and the cult member a sense of security.

• Invite your loved one to specific events on specific dates.

Broken promises

Consider the following reaction to a cult member's promise:
BROTHER: So, you're coming home? I'll believe it when I see it. You never keep your promises. We asked you if you were coming home for Thanksgiving, and you said, "Sure!" The family got all

excited. Then you never showed up. You had something more important to do—like saving the world by selling candy bars on the street corner.

Let's review the intention— delivery— response exercise:

INTENTION: "I want my brother to keep his promise. I want to see my brother."

DELIVERY: "I'll believe it when I see it." He sounds angry and sarcastic.

RESPONSE: The cult member doesn't want to come to visit or even speak with his brother.

To Do

- Have a list of things to talk about.
- Call when the cult member is most likely to be alone.
- Start warmly and end warmly.
- Assess whether you are talking with the authentic identity or the cult identity.
- Speak about other groups.
- Minimize distractions.
- Make one or two good points well and repeatedly rather than using a shotgun approach.
- Restate and follow up on topics and questions.
- Allow for silence.
- Pass the telephone around during family gatherings.
- Accept collect calls at all hours.

In fact, the cult member may have wanted to come home but was detained at the last minute by the cult. This happens time after time. Cult members are often led to believe they will be going home in a month or two, but when the time comes for the visit, a leader will say, "We need you right now." Sometimes, the cult member will become angry at the leader for breaking his word.

This is a positive step forward.

When a cult member breaks a promise, it is important to express disappointment. Don't get angry at the cult member—it's not his fault. Creating some feeling of responsibility is good, but go easy on making him feel too guilty. You want him to want to see you.

Don't think your loved one isn't disappointed, even if he sounds happy. He has been conditioned to hide negative thoughts. But beneath the surface, there is always dissonance between the cult identity and the authentic identity. If a cult member is denied permission over and over again, the dissonance may grow into disillusionment, which will be a good thing.

Don't take the experience personally by thinking, "He doesn't love us," or "She only cares about herself and her group." Remember, the authentic self probably does want to come home. The authentic self is registering every disappointment and broken cult promise.

If your loved one has broken a promise several times, you might ask him to think ahead: "Will you give me your personal word that, even if you are asked to do something at the last minute because it is an emergency, you'll still come?" This is future-pacing: you're asking the person to go into the future and anticipate a behavior. The disappointment and disillusionment they will feel if they are once again denied permission will be even greater.

Reinforce the authentic identity, not the cult identity

During home visits, family members sometimes go out of their way to remind their loved one of his cult responsibilities—such as eating only vegetarian food, calling the group regularly, waking up early for cult practices, and even being on time for the train ride back to the cult. This is counterproductive! You never want to remind your loved one that he isn't being true to the cult, or that he is breaking cult rules. Doing so will just reactivate the cult identity. If the cult member's behavior shifts away from the cult norm, go along with the change. Reinforce the positive!

Think of the future

Team members sometimes get stuck and can't see that their future dealings with the cult member will be different. During a conversation, a family member might say, "She doesn't ever let me talk about that." More constructive would be to say, "I haven't yet figured out a way to talk with her about that subject." Both in your attitude and in specific interactions, you want to find ways to learn constructive communication patterns.

MOTHER: He said he couldn't possibly come home for a visit.
SH: Try asking him what would need to change so he would want to come home. Get him to tell you what's blocking him or what is missing that would motivate him to visit.

Assessment and feedback

One of the most critical aspects of the SIA is evaluating the impact of your actions on your loved one. "What works?" and "What helps?" will be crucial questions. Always watch your loved one's reactions. If your approach isn't working, try something else. Don't rely solely on your opinion of the situation. Talk it over with other Team members. Did they have the same impressions? By paying attention, we will be in a better position to know if our efforts are effective or misguided. Assessing your loved one's responses may be confusing. At any given moment, the cult member could be expressing the authentic self, the pre-cult self, or a mix of both.

When asking the cult member a difficult question, it helps to take it one step at a time.

Step One: Visualize talking with your loved one.

Step Two: Hear yourself asking a question: "How would you feel about a meeting with a former member of your group?"

Step Three: Listen to the imagined response: "Oh, I wouldn't want to talk to any apostates."

When I make that visualization, I already know it will bring up the cult identity and shut off the dialogue. When your visualization tells you that something will shut a door, change gears. Find a less threatening way to discuss issues and accomplish your goals. For example, try another question: "How would you feel about meeting a former member of a different group?" Perhaps you can see the cult member saying, "I don't know if it would be useful, but sure—if you think it would." If so, then you might try asking the question. If your loved one responds as you imagined, you'll know your model of the cult identity is accurate. If the actual response is nothing like what you imagined, your model needs refining.

Family and friends should develop an accurate model to predict how their loved one will respond with each interaction. Keep tracking your loved one's responses over time. Remember, when you learn how to ask questions, your loved one will give answers that reveal how he makes sense of "reality." Your loved one's authentic identity will be speaking, helping you to enter his world. From there, the next step will be to help him to identify implanted phobias and dismantle them. Doing so, you will help him open the door to freedom of mind.

Chapter 10

Unlocking Phobias

I first learned about phobias in 1980. I immediately realized that cults systematically instill phobias in their members' minds. To help a cult member regain freedom of mind, I had to help him overcome his phobias. This realization led me develop a new therapeutic technique, the three-step phobia intervention. It will be crucial for you to learn this new method, since it lies at the heart of the Strategic Interaction Approach.

Phobia indoctrination is the single most powerful technique used by cults to make members dependent and obedient. I have encountered innumerable individuals who had long ago stopped believing in the leader and the doctrine of the group, but were unable to walk away from the group. They were psychologically frozen with indoctrinated fears, which often functioned unconsciously.

Psychological prison

Several years ago a former member of a small music cult in a northeastern city contacted me. He had read *Combatting Cult Mind Control* and wanted to help his friend. The friend, whose name I have changed here to Michael, had been imprisoned by the cult leader—locked in the study of his own home—for twelve years. He

233

had been ordered by the leader to give up his successful career as a psychologist and to spend his time composing and copying music for him. The leader also broke off his engagement and persuaded his fiancée, whom Michael had recruited, to become his jailer. She brought him food and let him out to use the bathroom. Through phobia indoctrination he had come to believe he would go insane, hurt himself or turn criminal if he ever left his house.

I asked the former member if he knew how to get in touch with Michael's family, and he told me that another family member had been in the cult but had left ten years earlier. I encouraged him to get in touch with that person to see if he would be willing to read my first book and to help. Fortunately, he was.

Meanwhile, his twin brother sent Michael a computer along with a music copying program. Surprisingly, the cult leader allowed Michael to leave his house unescorted to attend computer courses to use the program. After being outside and interacting quite appropriately with strangers, he realized that he wasn't going insane. Nor was he going to commit any violence. In fact, he loved being outside, even though he was still phobic about breaking away from the cult leader. A while later, he was given permission to attend his parent's fiftieth wedding anniversary. Using the techniques outlined later in this book for communicating with cult members who are still under mind control, the family member talked to him. He got Michael to contact the former member, who told him about the cult leader's abuse of many other members, including himself. Michael decided to leave permanently.

Soon after, he did some counseling work with me. This therapy helped him to get free of his fears about the future and to reconstruct a normal and positive life. In the spring of 1998, while I was teaching a workshop for the Society of Clinical Hypnosis in Sweden, I was surprised to see Michael in the audience. He had moved to Denmark, resumed his profession as a psychologist, married, had a daughter and was doing very well. On his next trip to the United States, he again consulted me. As a result of our counseling sessions, and a two-week stay at Wellspring Retreat in Ohio, he was able to turn his cult experience into a source of strength. He is now engaged in professional cult recovery work.

A cult phobia is a human-made mental illness that is an integral part of the overall mind control regime. Older rescue methods like deprogramming and exit counseling are inadequate because they attempt to persuade cult members to change their beliefs without first dealing with the phobias that paralyze them. In the Strategic Interaction Approach, we acknowledge the importance of phobias by learning to recognize and cure them before we engage our loved one on a rational, cognitive level.

WHAT IS A PHOBIA?

There are many different kinds of phobias, but their structure is always the same. A phobia is a persistent, irrational fear of an object or situation. All phobias are triggered by a cue that initiates a closed cycle of fearful images, thoughts, and feelings. The cue can be any internal or external stimulus, such as a thought, image, word, smell, taste, feeling, or behavior.

This stimulus causes the phobic individual to generate negative images, often unconsciously, and engage in fearful self-talk, such as expressions of impending doom uttered in a frightened tone of voice. During a phobic reaction, the body's automatic physiological survival ("fight-or-flight") response is activated. This panic response causes a number of physiological symptoms, including a racing heart, a shortness of breath, dry mouth, cold, clammy hands and sometimes nausea. The most common coping mechanism for a phobic individual is avoidance of the provoking stimulus.

Phobias destabilize and undermine a person's view of reality, emotional and intellectual control, self-confidence, and judgment. Typical non-cult phobias include fear of public speaking, heights, dark places, drowning, snakes, and so on. It is estimated that over 30 million Americans suffer from some type of phobia.[1]

Cult phobias

As I reviewed my experience as a cult member, I recalled specific incidents where fears were either installed or activated by my recruiters. During my initial three-day workshop, cult leaders implanted the fear that I couldn't trust my own thinking capacities due to unseen negative spiritual forces (Satan) that were supposedly affecting my mind and spirit. I had never believed in Satan or any such evil metaphysical entity, but by the end of three days, part of me (the nascent cult self) had come to fear these unseen forces.

Later, I was told that "ten generations of my ancestors were stuck at a low level in the spirit world, and were depending on me for their salvation." I was told that if I didn't follow Moon, all of these ancestors "would accuse me throughout eternity of failing my responsibility." The powerful, though, in some aspects, irrational, image of hundreds of angry relatives bound me to the group and helped push me through the low periods during my membership.

Members are taught that they are completely responsible for what happens to them, that there is no such thing as an accident, that everything has a spiritual cause, and that the group or leaders are almost never responsible for bad outcomes. If something bad happens, it is because the cult member did something wrong. In the Moonies, this is called "Indemnity" (sins of the past).

Moon also made efforts to instill more direct, personal, and graphic phobias. For example, in 1974, all New York members (myself included) were taken to see *The Exorcist*, a movie about a young girl who is possessed by an evil spirit. Moon then held a meeting at his Belvedere estate in Tarrytown, NY, and told members that this movie was "made by God and was a prophecy of what would happen to anyone who left the Unification movement."

During any cult recruitment and indoctrination, phobias of the outside world, and even of the pre-cult self, are methodically implanted, fertilized, and utilized. The critical faculties of discrimination that would allow a non-phobic person to examine objectively the claims of the leader and the doctrine are often short-circuited by such phobias. Independent thinking or action is precluded. Fear prevails over logic.

Common cult phobias

Cult leaders elicit intense feelings and are able to manipulate them in followers, so that they can easily activate panic and fear. I have compiled a list of some of the most common phobias indoctrinated into members experiencing mind control. Because these fears are part of an entire belief system, and actually become part of the cult identity, their impact is more extensive than any single common phobia (like fear of a snake). It's also important to understand that the cult identity has a host of phobias to keep it imprisoned.

One of the most universal cult phobias is fear of the anti-cult network. Members of large, established cults are told that they will be kidnapped, tortured, even raped by deprogrammers and exit-counselors. Cult leaders claim that these deprogrammers brainwash parents to hire them. These stories not only make members fearful and distrustful of their families, they bind members in fear of what they believe is a massive, well-funded network of hate criminals. If you are aware of the actual facts, this belief would be laughable, but millions of people actually accept this nonsense.

If you are up against a well-known cult, you may learn from former members the specific phobias that are used to program cult members. When dealing with a smaller, more obscure group, you may have to rely on reading cult literature, attending cult functions, and discussions with current members. I have attempted to create basic categories for cult phobias, but some phobias can belong to several categories.

Cult members may be programmed that, if they disobey or leave the group, they will suffer in some of the following ways.

Physical health

- Die painfully, be murdered, or commit suicide
- Become ill and die (of cancer, AIDS, a heart attack)
- Cause their loved ones to become ill and die
- Be hit by car, bus, or train, or die in an airplane crash
- Be beaten and/or raped
- Be robbed
- Be disfigured
- Become (or remain) overweight
- Become anorexic and not eat
- Become homosexuals
- Become drug addicts
- Become prostitutes
- Develop sexual perversions, or contract incurable sexually transmitted diseases
- Become deaf or blind
- Die from drugs or poison
- Have problems sleeping
- Be subjected to invisible toxic rays
- Cause their children to be stillborn or deformed at birth
- Cause their children to become sick or die young
- Cause their children to be killed
- Cause their children to commit suicide

Psychological health

- Go insane
- Be committed to a mental institution
- Be subjected to drugs, electroshock, and given a lobotomy

- Be a failure
- Be a sexual deviant
- Become less intelligent
- Lose their memory, talents and abilities
- Lose control completely
- Never be happy
- Be controlled by past traumas
- Never develop their minds properly
- Suffer for the rest of their life
- Lose their dreams

Spiritual life

- Become unspiritual or unbalanced
- Lose their relationship with God
- Be attacked by supernatural entities
- Be possessed by evil spirits/demons
- Lose their chance of redemption/salvation
- Miss, reject, or persecute "the Messiah, Apostle, Avatar, Enlightened Master"
- Never make it up "the Bridge to Total Freedom"
- Be spiritually attacked, raped, or killed while they sleep
- Never achieve enlightenment
- Be beset by lower spiritual forces
- Not be saved
- Be reincarnated 10,000 times as a roach, or other odious creature
- Be trapped in "illusion" forever
- Be haunted by problems from their past lives (they murdered people in a past life, and without the group's help they will kill again)

- Have problems with future lives
- Be judged unworthy when Armageddon takes place
- Burn in "the eternal lake of fire" when Jesus returns
- Find their souls rotting in hell forever

Social life

- Lose the safety and security of the group
- Be unloved
- Never be able to trust anyone again
- Be rejected by others
- Never find a good wife/husband
- Only attract people who hurt, victimize, rape, beat, torture, or rob them
- Be controlled by others
- Be rejected by family and friends
- Be abandoned
- Never speak to their children or grandchildren again
- Be harassed
- Disappear
- Lose their job
- Never get a good job or promotion
- Never be financially successful
- Commit crimes
- Be accused unjustly
- Be put in jail
- Be abducted and held prisoner
- Be persecuted by evil agents
- Be persecuted by psychiatrists or any mental health specialist

More paranoia instilled in cult members

- Fear that they are being spied on and followed
- Fear of race wars
- Fear of rioting or other criminal activity
- Fear of nuclear holocaust or cosmic cataclysm
- Fear of alien beings who kidnap people and perform bizarre experiments
- Fear that the earth will be destroyed
- Fear of terrorist attack, biological warfare
- Fear of an evil conspiracy by a covert group (Satan, A One World Government, the Antichrist, the Illuminati, the CIA, etc.) to take over the world and enslave everyone

Not all groups use the same phobias, and some just focus on a few. Some of these fears may be grounded in fact; some groups have spied on ex-members who are actively fighting them. There is still a social stigma attached to being an ex-cult member. Cults do try to keep family members still in the cult away from ex-members. Some groups have even gone so far as to kill perceived enemies. Fortunately, these are the exceptions.

Programmed phobias can be so strong that cult members cannot imagine themselves happy, safe, and fulfilled outside of the group. They can generate only negative images of life outside of the cult. When they think of leaving the group, they imagine themselves being destroyed, along with all other nonbelievers, by the fiery judgement of Armageddon. When they picture another member leaving the group, they see him being hit by a car, falling deathly ill, being locked up in a mental hospital, or committing suicide. Their internal voice expresses only fear, dread, and worry regarding the outside world. In addition to these images and voices, cult members often experience a host of physiological symptoms that propel them to block out any thoughts of leaving.

METHODS FOR PHOBIA INSTALLATION

Mind controllers install phobias through a variety of methods and techniques. A common first step is to induce the cult member to enter an altered state of consciousness or a trance. As we've discussed, in such a state, the analytic mind is side-stepped and information comes in with little or no critical evaluation. Many cult leaders have members meditate, pray, sing, or chant—sometimes for hours—before a lecture or sermon is preached, often inducing states of consciousness similar to those created under hypnosis or the influence of certain drugs.

In the Moonies, we would often be robbed of precious sleep so that we could drive to the Moon estate early in the morning. We would sing "holy" songs for an hour and then pray for an hour (first individually, then in unison) before listening to Moon speak. That way, our minds were much more "spiritually open" (cult lingo for "receptive"). In reality, we were in a trance, and certainly not thinking analytically or critically about what we were hearing.

Direct suggestion is one of the most common installation techniques. For instance, a leader will say: "You will die of a heart attack if you ever lose faith and leave." Typically, his tone of voice is one of absolute authority and confidence, his eyes are usually fixed, and his index finger is often pointed directly at members of the audience. Since cult leaders typically claim to possess divine powers, their words carry tremendous weight.

Indirect suggestion is less specific, but can be even more effective. For example, cult members may be told that "Whenever a member loses faith and leaves, something bad happens." By not stating specifics, the indirect approach allows for individual members to fill in the blanks with their own greatest fears: the ex-member could get trapped in a room full of rats and be eaten alive; be possessed by evil spirits and machine-gun his entire family; set fire to himself and jump off a building into a troop of girl scouts. No one knows for sure. Indirect suggestion invites the projection of the person's deepest and darkest fantasies. In many ways, these are the most powerful—suggestions that emanate from within your own psyche.

The use of stories and testimonials. Cult leaders often use stories about defectors to reinforce phobias: "Do you remember Alice M.? She left the group last month, and we just got word that she hung herself. See what happens when you leave the protection of the Almighty?" These stories are often total fabrications. Sometimes, they are partly true—the person did leave the group.

Former members who have returned to the group are often asked to speak with the membership about the sin, greed, or suffering that they encountered in the outside world. They describe how they were mugged or raped, plagued by terrifying nightmares, or suffered unrelenting migraine headaches until they "came back to God's family." The more horribly graphic the story is, the more effective it is.

Books, movies and news stories. The late Frederick Lenz ("Rama") often told his followers to read Stephen King novels and later used the frightening stories to make them afraid of losing Lenz's protection from lower spiritual forces.[2] He would also recommend Carlos Castaneda's books, which speak of evil entities and demons, to inculcate in members the need for his spiritual "protection."[3]

I have already mentioned how the movie *The Exorcist* was used to instill phobias in the minds of Moonies back in 1974. The horror movie genre offers many tools for cult leaders to use to manipulate people through the emotion of fear.

Though not used, to my knowledge, by destructive mind control cults, I believe Steven Spielberg's *Jaws* is one of the most effective phobia indoctrination movies ever made. It made more people afraid of swimming in the ocean than any other movie or book.

Media news items are excellent at eliciting fear and inculcating phobias, as well. Cult leaders like to tell members about floods, earthquakes, fires, famines, plagues, and wars, and use them as proof that the "Last Days" have arrived. They love to proclaim the destruction of the non-believers of the world. Besides Biblical prophecies, there are increasing numbers of extraterrestrial-oriented cult groups. Many of these say that the world will soon perish, and that only believers will be taken away to safety or be put in place to run the "new world order."

Utilizing existing phobias and fears. Potential converts are encouraged to reveal detailed information about their past, particularly any traumatic events or psychological disorders. Cult leaders can then exploit these existing fears to activate old phobias or create new ones. Traumatized parts of the pre-cult identity are often elicited and used to help create a dependent, phobic cult member. It is as simple as finding out finding out about a person's fear of being buried alive and telling them, "Hell (which you face if you leave the group) is like being put into a deep hole in the ground and having dirt slowly shoveled onto you throughout eternity." If someone was suicidal before his involvement, leaders might say, "Go ahead and leave. You'll only wind up wanting to kill yourself." If the person had been a drug addict, he might be told that if he left the group he would go back to drugs.

The cult member's fear is then generalized to include anything which is designated as a threat to the cult identity:

- Any thoughts, feelings, or information critical of the cult leader, doctrine, or organization.
- Former members or critics of the group.
- Doubts or thoughts about leaving the group.

Once these phobias are in place, the cult member becomes a dependent personality, filled with a sense of helplessness and hopelessness about escaping the group. Cult leaders want their members to be filled with such fear and self-doubt. They want to cultivate low self-esteem and manipulate members to work harder for praise and promotion.

In smaller, personality-type cults, control can be much more intense, because there is more direct contact between master and slave. These abusive relationships are often less ideological, with little or no formal doctrine or rituals. Nevertheless, the mind control processes are quite effective, especially when exploiting existing fear and guilt.

Small personality cult

Some time ago, I was asked to help with one such case that involved a three-person cult composed of a father, his son, and my client's daughter, whom I shall call Joanne. (Please note that all personal names and identifying characteristics have been changed in this story.) Only eighteen-years old and Roman Catholic, Joanne was afraid to tell her parents that she was pregnant. She told herself that it was "no big deal," and impulsively had a secret abortion. In a position of great emotional and psychological vulnerability, Joanne was befriended by Gus, a stranger, on the bus home after the abortion.

Joanne went to the house where Gus lived with his son, Alan, and quickly joined their "family." At this time, her parents knew nothing about the pregnancy or the abortion. They only knew that their daughter, a recent high school graduate, had suddenly decided to leave home and live with these strange men. They hired a private investigator, who was able to locate Gus's house.

Frustrated and anxious to see their daughter, they waited outside the house and surprised her. When they saw her, they were shocked and horrified. Gaunt, dirty, and wearing baggy, paint-splattered overalls — a far cry from the designer jeans she previously wore — Joanne's blank expression made her look like a zombie. In a monotone she told her parents that they were trying to control her and were jealous that she had found people who truly loved her.

Joanne's parents contacted me, and we arranged a preparatory meeting and brainstormed. When I initially spoke with them, they seemed to be quite kind and loving. I did not have the impression that they were domineering or controlling personalities. Her parents knew that something terrible had happened to Joanne and were committed to helping her break free. But they didn't know what to do and that's when I became involved. Unlike cases that involve a large, well-known cult, I had little information about Gus and Alan. The family was desperate to try something immediately. I agreed, but felt strategically limited because I had so little information about the situation.

Parents often call me when their loved one makes this kind of radical change and cuts off contact. Sometimes it turns out there are serious underlying family problems. Other times, it's a simple case of a young person trying to spread his wings, to do some experimentation. Between the ages of seventeen and twenty-one, it is developmentally healthy behavior for a young adult to rebel and try to find himself.

Unfortunately, this was not the case with Joanne.

Gus, a tall, strong man with a confident, deep voice and penetrating eyes, had suffered episodes of excessive drinking and had a history of being verbally and physically abusive. He implemented a crude yet effective mind control regime over his son and Joanne, who was isolated from her family and friends and was never left alone. Gus and Alan forced her to work long, unpaid hours in their small house painting business. She was taught to be unconditionally obedient, and was yelled at and occasionally struck by Gus — particularly if she disobeyed a direct order. I later learned that Alan was also subjected to verbal and physical abuse by his father. It didn't take long for Gus to force himself sexually on Joanne, who passively submitted. I later discovered that Alan had secretly been having sex with Joanne behind his father's back.

I decided to make an exploratory call to Gus and Alan. I told them that I was a counselor who had been contacted by Joanne's parents and was looking into the situation. I took the tack that the parents were probably trying to control their daughter, who was probably just acting out and enjoying her new found freedom.

Gus was suspicious of me at first, but within a few minutes, he was doing his best to con me into thinking that Joanne had been mistreated by her parents, and that he was doing her a favor by letting her stay at his apartment. It didn't take much for him to agree to let me come over to talk further with him, his son, and Joanne. Before I hung up the telephone, Gus unexpectedly told me that I could bring Joanne's parents along too. He wanted to prove to me that he was acting in Joanne's interests. We were nervous, but delighted.

When the meeting started, Gus seemed to regret his suggestion that the parents come along. He obviously had been drinking too much. He had counted on Joanne's complete submission to him, but her secret relationship with Alan had caused dissension in the ranks. Alan had already told her how much he hated his father.

I did my best to act as a facilitator and let everyone take turns talking. Within an hour, it was clear that Joanne was happy that her parents were there to tell her how much they loved her. She clearly wanted to escape from Gus, but still cowered in fear of him. We were shocked when Gus threw up his hands and blurted out, "Go ahead! Go back to your family and get back on the abortionist's table." He had apparently used Joanne's guilt and fear caused by the abortion to control Joanne. The controlling belief was, "Leaving us means getting back on the abortionist table."

The parents were totally aghast, but to their credit, they didn't say or do anything to alienate their daughter. The pieces of what had happened had quickly fallen into place. Joanne's parents told her that they loved her and begged her to come home with them. Their love and acceptance opened the door. Joanne had been afraid that they would reject and condemn her for actions. Fortunately, they didn't.

THE THREE-STEP PHOBIA INTERVENTION

The three-step phobia intervention is a safe, effective method that people can use to unlock cult phobias. Unfounded fears are stripped of their power and seen for what they are, proof of the group's banal destructiveness. I have been teaching my clients and other mental health professionals this three-step method for years with success. You can't expect to be as effective as a therapist when implementing this approach with a cult member, but a well-prepared, well-rehearsed family member can do the job.

Anyone can use this approach, although it is often the case that one of the Team members will stand out as the best choice for implementing the process. A once-phobic family member who is now cured makes an especially powerful force. A family member who is a psychologist, social worker, or member of the clergy would also be in a good position to talk about phobias with professional authority. In my experience, almost all cases of phobia are cured through visualization, suggestion, and experience. Most of the time, this method takes surprisingly little time.

The three-step phobia intervention, which I will describe at length, can be summarized as follows:

Step One

The cult member is told what a phobia is and how it differs from a legitimate fear. You describe the structure of a phobia and its impact. Using examples of different phobias, you explain how a cure is possible.

Step Two

Next, you explain how other destructive groups or people deliberately install a phobia in order to control people through fear. Again, you will provide several examples of cult phobias, and ask the cult member what he thinks of these other groups. You will give examples of how former members left these other groups, came to understand phobia indoctrination, and applied the cure to themselves.

Step Three

Finally, you discuss the specifics of your loved one's group. When the time is right, you will ask the cult member, "Is it possible to leave the group and be happy and fulfilled?" If not, why not? How is this group different from other groups? Once the cult member sees that his group, like the other groups you discussed, practices phobia indoctrination, much of the mind control hold will loosen. Ask your loved one if he has ever talked with a former member of the group who is happy and fulfilled? Would he be open to doing so, even if only to show the family that he isn't controlled by fear?

It is probably best not to attempt to do all three steps at the same time; nor is it wise to spread them out over many weeks. Timing the steps so that there is continuity makes the intervention much more effective. Ideally, you want cult members to make their own connections at their own pace.

STEP ONE: PHOBIAS AND THEIR CURE

Discrimination: respecting legitimate fear and identifying a phobia

Fear is not an inherently bad thing. To the contrary, it's one of the most important of human emotions: it promotes survival by alerting us to potential danger and mobilizing the body to either fight or run away. The crucial difference between a fear and a phobia is that a fear is based on a realistic danger or threat, whereas a phobia is based on an irrational or unrealistic thought. People with strong elevator phobias cannot get into any elevator, even one in a modern building that is equipped with a telephone, emergency brakes, and a current inspection sticker. They can't distinguish a safe situation from a potentially dangerous one.

I recently had a discussion with a thirty-two-year-old, athletic man named Eric who had a fear of drowning due to two traumatic childhood incidents in water. He told me he was participating in a triathlon in the coming weeks and asked me if I had any ideas of how to eliminate his fear.

Assessing danger: the need for competency

Competence means having the necessary knowledge and behavioral skills to perform appropriately. I noted the two traumatic events, but rather than probe, my first step was to assess Eric's competence in swimming. "Have you had swimming lessons? Have you practiced long enough to feel confident?" I asked. "No, not really," he replied, and added that he didn't even know how to float. I told him the key to floating was learning how to hold a lot of air in his lungs, and to take calm, shallow breaths. I described other competence-building steps, like learning to tread water comfortably for a long time, and knowing how to massage away a leg cramp.

Eric realized that he had good reason to fear the water, given his lack of swimming skills. Naturally, as Eric learns how to float or tread water for thirty minutes, he will develop more competence and confidence. At that point, it will be easier to clear up any residual traumas from the past.

What if your worst fears came true?

Drowning is a scenario that needs to be taken very seriously indeed. But many phobias have much less serious consequences. Pretend that all of your worst fears are realized, and ask yourself: "Then what?" This question often takes people by surprise because they are unaware of the negative images in their minds. I have found that getting people to describe these images and articulate their fears helps to drain phobias of their power.

People with phobias of public speaking (one of the most common phobias) have told me they see members of the audience getting bored, falling asleep, walking out, or telling one another how stupid or ill-prepared the speaker is. Some people even imagine that members of the audience will throw rotten tomatoes at them. Once they verbalize their fears, they usually chuckle at their absurdity.

Other people worry that, once they're in front of the audience, they will freeze up and forget what to say. As with any legitimate fear, practice can provide them with the skills, competence, and confidence necessary to make it through a speech. "Do you know the material? Do you have note cards, or an outline of your major points in front of you? You can always pause and take a long sip of water while you reorient yourself," I tell them. "I don't know a single professional speaker, including myself, who hasn't experienced the panic response. We just have learned how to manage it so we can do what we want to do."

The bottom line is that, even if these people give the worst talk of their life, the worst scenario they can imagine is one in which they survive. There will be another day and another opportunity. Perhaps their ego and reputation will be temporarily bruised, but they will go on. Hopefully, they will become stronger from the experience, rather than quit and avoid the situation for the rest of their life.

The physiology of panic[4]

Panic attacks affect us both mentally and physically, although the symptoms vary from person to person. As the panic response takes over, people may feel confused, disoriented, or cut off from their surroundings. They sometimes begin to hyperventilate, a state in which a person takes many short, shallow breaths in a row. This can make them feel dizzy, nauseated, or faint. Frequently, their heart will beat faster, their muscles will feel tense, and they will start sweating. Their eyes may twitch. Often, their mouth will become dry and their voice will tremble. These physical sensations make people feel even more anxious, thereby feeding the panic cycle and intensifying the attack. Once a panic response is triggered, it takes the body approximately three minutes for the physiological reaction to pass.

Controlling panic in your own life

Virtually everyone has experienced panic sometime in their lives, perhaps during a piano recital in grade school, a difficult math test, or a first date. You may recognize many of these symptoms of anxiety in yourself. Finding a way to relate personally to a panic attack will help you understand how they work, how to cure them, and, eventually, how to explain them to your loved one.

First, identify that you are having a panic response. Next, determine whether there is a danger that you need to avoid. Assessing danger will allow you to take appropriate action. For example, if you're on an African savannah and a rhinoceros is charging at you, you will know to run for cover — but if you're sitting in your easy chair at home, watching a movie in which a rhinoceros appears to be charging you, then a simple reality check (like squeezing the chair) will suffice. Once a person is able to identify that he is experiencing an inappropriate panic response, the next step is to intervene in the panic cycle.

Breath control

One of the most common responses to panic is to either hold one's breath or hyperventilate. Therapeutic breathing techniques can help to counter this reaction and relax the body. Begin by taking a slow, deep breath to the count of four. If you're not sure how fast to count, say, "One one-hundred, two one-hundred, three one-hundred," and so on. Then, when you are ready, release the breath in an even slower, more controlled exhalation to the count of eight. Repeat these deliberate, calming inhalations and exhalations for several cycles. Nothing changes your consciousness faster than changing your breathing pattern.

Focusing your attention on a slow, deliberate exhalation will profoundly influence your body's function, bringing a sense of calmness. Once you have mastered the technique, you will be in a position to explain it to the cult member and demonstrate the actual breathing technique.

Controlling internal imagery

Mental images, memories or figments of imagination, come in one of two forms. Mental pictures are either associated or dissociated. In an associated image, you are in your own body within the image, as in real life. You see the scene from within, experiencing all of the feelings and sensations. For example, an associated memory of a roller coaster ride would bring you back to what you saw and felt while speeding around the tracks. On the other hand, a dissociated memory of the same event is one in which you are an observer, watching from a distance, as you would an actor on television. Associated images carry all of the original emotion with them. Dissociated images create a sense of detachment.

Understanding this distinction in memory coding enables us to control our own minds. Ideally, we want to experience positive memories as associated images, and negative ones as dissociated images. Rather than avoiding unpleasant memories, or panicking when they arrive, we can face them with a realistic optimism by viewing them from a distance. Also helpful is reminding ourselves that these negative memories happened to a younger, less-experienced person, not to our present selves.

A Team member should explain these distinctions to the cult member. Ideally, he will be able to draw from his own experience to describe how internal imaging has made a difference.

Positive visualization

During a panic response, people engage, often unconsciously, in a process of negative associated visualization. In Eric's case, whenever he was near water, he unconsciously experienced the traumatic memories of his childhood when he almost drowned. I asked him to deliberately remember each incident, but this time imagining that he was standing by, safely, as an observer, watching the younger Eric flail around in the water until he was rescued. By teaching Eric to make his unconscious images conscious, I was teaching him self-awareness. By teaching him to make a new set of dissociated images, I was freeing him to be in control of his own mind.

In the three-step phobia intervention, my aim is to promote freedom of choice. A person can always have the choice to relive a traumatic episode, but now, there is a new choice— that of positive visualization. I teach people to make a dissociated movie from images of the past trauma, while keeping in mind that the younger self had fewer resources than the present self. For example, Eric should be able to watch the near-drowning scene again and again from different visual angles, while maintaining a strong sense of resourcefulness and detachment. There are many other ways to alter the visualization to gain distance; for example, by making the image larger or smaller, color or black-and-white, in-focus or blurred, speeded up or slowed down, even played backwards.[5]

Once my clients feel comfortable with this dissociation method, I ask them to construct a new movie of the past events to which they bring all their current resources. I ask them to see themselves engaging in the behavior safely, happily, and in control. At first, this visualization will be seen as a well-focused, dissociated movie with full color and sound. I then ask the phobic individual to step into an associated version of the movie.

Using this visualization helps people to replace a traumatic memory with a new, positive alternative. A person who was once phobic about elevators comes to see himself riding safely and comfortably, over and over again. A person who is afraid of drowning sees himself swimming with confidence.

As long as the person is competent, has evaluated the situation thoroughly, and knows that he is safe, this kind of reprogramming of the mind is necessary, natural, and healthy. It is an ethical use of self-directed mind control designed to promote free will and enhance quality of life.

Positive self-talk

All day long, every day of our lives, we are busy talking to ourselves. The voice within explains and interprets reality, most of the time in an automatic and unconscious fashion. During a phobic attack, people will typically hear an inner voice that is panicked and fearful. I tell them to first identify that voice, making it conscious, and then to evaluate the situation to determine if there is any cause for danger. If there is none, I urge them to self-soothe: talk to themselves in a calm, controlled, manner.

Learning to pay attention to the way we communicate with ourselves is a powerful step to greater self-awareness. The realization that you can deliberately change how and what you say to yourself is tremendously liberating. For example, labeling a feeling of panic "excited anticipation" can be used to generate a positive experience. Call it "terror or fear," and it can become a phobic reaction. Cultivating a confident, soothing inner voice can help redirect your attention, for example, to counting as you perform calming breaths, or to focusing your visual attention on scenes of being safe and in control. Sometimes, an inner voice can speak to you from the perspective of an objective observer: "Everything is going to be fine. The elevator is safe. You're in control. There's an emergency stop switch. There are emergency brakes. There's a telephone so that you can communicate."

Other times, you may speak directly to yourself: "I am a competent swimmer. I'm strong and in good health. There are other swimmers nearby who will assist me if I need help."

Systematic desensitization

You can also eliminate triggers and other vestiges of phobias by desensitizing yourself to the source of fear. Desensitization is a form of behavioral reconditioning in which a phobic individual confronts his fear through firsthand experience. It is essential to begin this process slowly by planning small, manageable steps. People who are afraid of drowning can take trips to a pool (with a support person) and stand near the water until they feel safe and comfortable. Next, they can put on a bathing suit and stand in the water up to their ankles. Then, they can go into the water another few inches. The key is to make slow, steady progress, so that new, positive associations are made. A person can then go into deeper water and wear a life jacket. Over and over again, the person experiences support and resources as he develops his own confidence.

When taken slowly and systematically, behavioral reconditioning is an effective way to neutralize phobias. The once-phobic person can seek out past negative triggers and create a new, empowered association based on the resources of the present. It is essential to rehearse scenarios that might cause a stress reaction and make sure the individual has multiple strategies for coping, such as calming breaths and positive self-talk. By orienting the person to new ways of coping with future situations, you can ensure that the phobia cure will be permanent.

Discussing phobias with your loved one

As the cult member listens to all of this information, he might become suspicious, and ask, "Why are you telling me all of this?" If this happens, ask the cult member if he has any phobias, or knows anyone who has a phobia. If the answer is yes, then a simple reply that "This information could be helpful" will suffice. If the answer is no, a family member who was cured of a phobia or knows someone who was cured can discuss the benefits of understanding phobic reactions.

SISTER: Do you remember how I was afraid to go into elevators? Well, I'm cured!

CULT MEMBER: How did you do that?

SISTER: It turns out that a phobia is an irrational fear. I didn't realize it but I was seeing negative images in my mind. I saw myself plummeting out of control, to my death. I'd scream to myself, "Oh no, the elevator cable is going to break!" My heart would race. I'd breathe fast, which made me really panic and avoid even the thought of an elevator. I went to a therapist who taught me to discriminate between rickety, old elevators and safe, modern elevators. I learned to visualize myself going up safely and comfortably to my floor. I learned how to pay attention to my breathing, to breathe very slowly and deeply.

If you're not sure whether the cult member has digested this information, ask questions and spend more time talking about other phobias and cures. If he becomes defensive while you are explaining phobias, it is likely that the relationship lacks sufficient rapport and trust. Back off! Don't try to force this on your loved one. It is better to wait and find the right time, place, and person to deliver the phobia intervention. The foundation of the intervention must be solid, because the next two steps are built on Step One.

STEP TWO: EXPLAINING HOW OTHER GROUPS USE PHOBIAS

Now that you have laid the groundwork by explaining the difference between legitimate fear and phobia, the structure of a phobic response (negative images, negative self-talk, and physiological reactions), and strategies to cure phobias, you can proceed to Step Two.

During the next conversation, perhaps a few hours (or a few days) later, the sister would describe how she met a former member of another cult group. That person described how phobias were put in his mind. He was programmed to believe that, if he ever left the group, terrible things would happen to him. It kept him trapped in the group for a long time, until he met other people who had left the group. Contrary to what he had feared, these ex-members were happy and fulfilled. This knowledge made him question whether his fears of leaving the group were real fears or phobias.

It is essential to continue communicating with the cult member in a way that doesn't trigger thought-stopping. Remember, cult mind control subjects are not allowed to think negative thoughts about their leader, doctrine or group. By being indirect at first, you can give your loved one information about phobias without triggering one. Choose your words carefully. Use terms like "cults," "brainwashing," and "mind control" only if you can do so without jeopardizing rapport. Other loaded terms include: "closed organizations," "destructive groups," "authoritarian societies," "indoctrination," and "closed mindsets." If you press on without waiting, the phobia may persist, and you may lose rapport with the cult member.

Using examples of other groups

To prepare for this step, you should educate yourself, through research on the Internet or at a library, about three different mind control cults. Find out how they use phobias to control their members and imagine how you might explain their methods to your loved one. It helps to talk about a group that the person considered a cult before their own involvement. The focus of concern should be how the organization undermines the personal autonomy of its followers. Some of the higher-profile cults include: Jim Jones and the People's Temple at Jonestown, Guyana (the 913-person mass murder/suicide on November 18th, 1978); kidnapped heiress Patty Hearst and the Symbionese Liberation Army;[6] David Koresh and the Branch Davidians (the standoff between that group and the FBI in Waco, Texas); Luc Jouret and the Order of the Solar Temple (mass suicides in Canada, France and Switzerland); Shoko Asahara and Aum Shinrikyo (who reportedly staged the nerve gas attack in Japan); Marshall Herff ("Do") Applewhite and the Heaven's Gate suicides. I frequently hear from my clients that the Unification Church (the Moonies), Scientology, and the Jehovah's Witnesses are often thought of by the individual as destructive cults. If so, these will serve as good examples.

Be sure to include a cult that has similarities to your loved one's group. If the person is in a Bible-oriented cult, use at least one example of another Bible cult in this step. If the group is a therapy cult, learn about other therapy cults. The same applies to political cults, large group training programs, business cults, and so on. Rapport and trust with the cult member are crucial to accomplish this step effectively.

Breaking the ice

During a conversation with your loved one, raise the subject of how you've been thinking about a particular group after reading an article or book, seeing them featured on television, or having been approached by them recently. This should be part of a two-way dialogue and not a lecture. Start with a group that is not like the cult member's group or a group that he would agree is a destructive cult. Pacing is vital. Go step-by-step and don't rush. Remember, most cult members believe that there are destructive cults. They just don't think their group is one of them. This is your chance to discuss that issue with the cult member.

Explain how amazing it is to you that a particular group (Group X) actually installs phobias in its members' minds in order to keep them dependent and obedient. Review the material in Step One, but this time apply it to Group X. If you think the cult member will be responsive—rather than suspicious and defensive, tell him that you spoke with an ex-member of this other group. It's always best to use real ex-members as examples because then you can ask the cult member at a later time if he is open to speaking with this individual.

Talk about how members of these other groups are trained to have only negative images and negative self-talk about the outside world or their past. Discuss how they are given phobias that they will die, go insane, or be possessed by demons if they consider leaving that group. Try to cover a number of phobias that apply to your loved one's group, but do so in another context to camouflage the approach. We want to deliver the information in a way that will be heard and digested, so it can slip past the cult identity's filters.

Talk about how members in those other groups are taught to think there is no legitimate reason to ever leave, and how defectors are always considered to be weak, deranged, selfish, and no longer spiritual. You can combat these phobias by having your loved one talk with former members. It will become apparent that these ex-members are good, responsible people who have seen through the lies and manipulation, and have moved on with their lives. You might even try to arrange for your loved one to see how such phobias are indoctrinated in members of another group, perhaps by attending one of their meetings. When the cult member understands that there are other choices and that a person can leave and live a fulfilled life, the process of positive visualization comes much more easily.

You will know that you have communicated effectively when the cult member agrees that other groups control their members with phobias and that bad things do not actually happen to members when they leave those groups. You have made exceptional progress if the cult member agrees that these other groups vilify former members and critics in order to deprive them of information necessary for reality-testing.

Don't be disheartened if you are not able to cover these points sufficiently in one conversation. Be careful not to force information on a cult member who is being evasive or resistant. This does not mean that you've failed. It just means there needs to be further rapport and trust building.

STEP THREE: DISCUSSING THE SPECIFICS OF YOUR LOVED ONE'S GROUP

At this point, your loved one should understand what a phobia is, how to cure one, and how other groups use phobias to control their members. It is essential that the first two steps of the phobia intervention be performed properly so that you can begin discussing your loved one's group without triggering a phobia and losing rapport and trust.

The goal of this final step is to have the person make the connection between his group and the other groups you've discussed. You want your loved one to see that his group, like these other cults, manipulates its members, causing them to fear that if they ever leave the group, terrible things will happen to them. Your purpose is not to prove that you are right or to attack the cult member, but rather to get the person to apply the phobia cure to himself. You want to help your loved one to visualize himself out of the group, happy and fulfilled.

Ask the cult member to make a comparison

If sufficient rapport and trust has been established, you should be able to build on the discussion of other groups that you began in Step Two. You can start by asking the cult member if he has ever thought that his group does anything similar to these other groups. If he asks, "What do you mean?" you can say, "I was just wondering, when you think about leaving your church or organization, what comes up in your mind?" Of course, allow a long, silent pause so that he can think about the question.

Typically, the cult member will play it safe by asking, "What do you mean by that?" This gives you the opportunity to go one step further and ask, "I was wondering if it's possible to leave your group and be happy and fulfilled." You might also ask, "Do you believe it's possible that someone could leave your group and still be with God and be happy and fulfilled?" Again, you want to wait patiently for an answer.

Encourage the authentic self to speak

One of the most powerful questions you can ask a person is: "If the group never existed, and you were happy and fulfilled in your life, what do you think you would be doing?" My experience in asking cult members this question is that, at first, they will look at you blankly and ask, "What do you mean? I'm happy in the group right now!" If you get this response, you can repeat the question,

this time emphasizing the hypothetical *if:* "But I'm just curious —
if this group never existed, for example, *if* the Moon organization
or *if* the Bhagwan Shree Rajneesh (Osho) group never existed, and
you were happy and fulfilled, what would you be doing right now?"
If the person replies, "Oh, I would be a drug addict," or "I would
commit suicide," you will know you may have discovered the actual phobia in the person's mind. If the person refuses or is unable to
give a positive choice, then back up a step. Ask a more general question: "Do you believe anybody outside the group is happy and fulfilled in their life? If so, can you give me an example of the kinds
of things people could be doing that would make them happy and
fulfilled."

You want to get your loved one to say things that are meaningful to him, such as, "I'd be married and having a child," or "I'd be
a teacher, a dancer, a poet, a musician," or "I'd be sailing a yacht
around the world," or "I'd be fighting poverty." In this step, our
aim is to engage people's authentic selves and get them to visualize
this happy, fulfilling behavior. Ideally, once they visualize it as a dissociated image, like a picture on a screen, you can have them step
into an associated picture and describe what it feels like, for example, to actually stand at the front of a classroom teaching children
and feeling gratified by the experience. If the person has problems
visualizing, you can encourage him to get in touch with the positive
feelings first and then develop a picture. Remember, this is a
process, so it is not something that you have to complete in one
particular conversation.

Discussing former members

Another goal of Step Three is to motivate the person to meet
with former members of the group. Toward this end, you can ask
your loved one, "Do you know anyone who left the group and is
happy and fulfilled?" This is a very important question. Typically,

cult members will say things like, "Well, I know someone who left and she committed suicide," or, "I know someone who left but he no longer believes in God." They might even say, "No, I don't know anyone who has left and is happy and fulfilled." In that case, your next question could be, "Do you believe it's *possible* to leave your group and be happy and fulfilled?"

An alternative strategy is to follow up on Step Two—when you talk about other cults like David Koresh's group, Jonestown, or Heaven's Gate—by saying, "Well, help me out here, but it seems like you're giving me the same kind of answer as the people we talked about earlier." You might ask, "Where did that belief come from? Are you open to the idea that maybe there is such a person in the world?" You want to get the person to actually speculate about and visualize a person who has left the group and is doing well. Then, you can ask your loved one, "If such a person existed, would you be willing to at least meet with him or her and evaluate for yourself?"

The point here is that you are working on multiple levels. You're dealing not only with the cult identity but also with the person's authentic identity. Hopefully, by covering all the issues — what phobias are, how to cure yourself of a phobia, and how phobias are indoctrinated into people's minds — the person will connect the dots and begin to see the big picture. My experience when doing this intervention is that it is most effective when I don't expect the cult member to admit, "Ah-hah! I have a phobia so, therefore, I'm under mind control." Instead, I try to engage people in an open conversation that allows them to draw their own conclusions. When you are really curious, and you're trying to understand how the person's group is different from these other groups, that is when you make the most progress. Ultimately, you want to help the cult member develop a ready facility in his mind to see himself out of the group, happy and fulfilled.

Chapter 11

Promoting Freedom of Mind

In the Strategic Interaction Approach, we want to help the cult member to grow both on an emotional level and on a cognitive level—to feel more free and to think more freely. A successful three-step phobia intervention will cultivate emotional growth by helping your loved one overcome fears implanted by the cult. In this chapter, we will discuss how to encourage further cognitive growth and, ultimately, freedom of mind, by helping your loved one think more critically and independently.

From this point, the Strategic Interaction Approach will consist of a series of mini-interactions—phone calls, letters, visits—each of which is designed to help open your loved one's mind to points of view beyond the cult perspective. Building on the skills you learned in previous chapters for interacting with dual personalities and for communicating effectively, your aim in each strategic interaction will be to progressively move your loved one through a series of steps.

- By asking hypothetical "what if" questions, you will help him to see alternative points of view and to think more critically.

- By talking about the negative experiences of people in other cults, you will plant seeds of doubt that could blossom into concerns about his own cult involvement.

• By encouraging him to reflect on the history of his cult involvement you will help him to reality-test, and ultimately to see how his cult has not lived up to its promises.

Ultimately, your aim is to motivate him to begin asking his own questions and to research his own cult involvement by speaking with former members and by reading. This step is critical because, when your loved one looks beyond the group perspective, he will be using his own mind rather than the cult-controlled mind. Through creative story-telling and metaphors and by encouraging him to consider exciting possibilities in the future, you help him to imagine life outside the cult, a stepping-stone to actually leaving it.

CULTIVATING A QUESTIONING PERSPECTIVE

With a curious yet concerned attitude, ask your loved one to help you understand how and why he joined and what his life in the cult is like. If you show that you are genuinely interested in his point of view, you will model the kind of open-minded perspective that we hope to nurture in him.

Confrontation is the least effective way to get cult members to talk about their involvement. In the heat of the moment, family members sometimes forget that their loved one is under mind control. They might make declarations and try rational argumentation, forgetting that the cult identity has been trained to block out discordant information. Rather than making statements about his cult or about cults in general, begin by asking your loved one questions.

Ask the cult member about his new circle of "friends." Often, families don't pay enough attention to other significant cult members and their backgrounds. This is usually a mistake. It is also tactically important to find out the names of immediate superiors as well as the overall group hierarchy. These questions should be asked with a "matter of fact attitude" and from a purely rapport-building, information-gathering perspective.

Important Ideas about Reality[1]

- Every individual has his own sense of reality and is connected to a shared reality with others.
- Our perception of reality is influenced by our inborn characteristics and abilities, psychological development, emotional states, and belief systems.
- Our view of reality is influenced (positively and negatively) by memories, beliefs, needs, and social influence.
- We all filter and edit the information detected by our senses: we emphasize some things and eliminate others. Otherwise, we would be overwhelmed by a flood of information. In fact, much of the brain's function is to inhibit incoming information.
- We can never be 100% certain that our picture of reality is objectively correct.
- We never fully know another person's reality.
- We are not capable of fully communicating all the things that make up our sense of reality.
- We can't assume that what we believe is more than a "constructed" view of reality.
- Our internal self-talk interprets, and sometimes distorts, our sense of reality.
- We can control some of our inner and outer reality. Total control is impossible, although through discipline (meditation or hypnosis), the mind can develop greater degrees of control.
- We can't control all of our reality all of the time.
- No matter how much we improve and work to enhance our sense of what is real, it is always incomplete, imperfect, out of focus, and distorted.
- The more distorted our sense of reality, the more certain we will be that what we believe is accurate.
- The more insistent a person is about the accuracy of his or her observations, the more likely it is that his or her sense of reality is distorted.

Appropriate questions to ask your loved one

Remember to take your time and be patient when waiting for a response. Allow long silences and gently re-ask the question if the answer is off track. Ask for specific examples: really try to get the person to access their memory.

- What are the positive things about the group and about being a member? What are the negative things?

- Who are your closest friends in the group? Tell me about them.

- What jobs do you do? How much say do you have about your job and how it is performed?

- What have you been learning?

- Have you had any interesting experiences? Tell me about them.

- Do you travel? Where do you go?

- What is your schedule?

- When do you wake up?

- When do you typically go to sleep at night?

- Where do you sleep? In a bed or on the floor? Do you have privacy?

- When is the best time to telephone you?

- Do you have questions or serious doubts about the group? Can you share them with the group? If so, how are your questions answered? If you have doubts, would you feel comfortable sharing them with me?

- What were your lifetime goals before joining the group?

- Have they changed? If so, how have they changed? Do you think they might change again?

- What independent research have you done concerning the group? Are you open to learning more?

- How much do you actually know about the leader's background?

- What sources of information, in addition to the group, do you have?

If you get vague, evasive answers like "I don't know," work on building rapport and trust. If your loved one seems truly unable to provide requested information about the cult, he may still be on the fringes; or he simply may be afraid to ask. Posing questions with open-mindedness and genuine curiosity, rather than a show-me attitude, will encourage him to seek answers. In his research, he may discover that he has been told a lie. If he knows he has been lied to, you might ask "How can you trust other things that you've been told?" By encouraging distrust of the cult hierarchy, you are helping the individual to think critically and independently. Encourage his integrity and self-trust whenever and wherever you can.

Ask for examples and specific details

An important part of learning about your loved one's perspective, and ultimately helping him to expand it, is asking for details and specific examples. If he says:

- "I'm having spiritual experiences all the time," say, "Give me an example of a spiritual experience you had today."

- "I don't like everything about the group," ask, "Like what specifically?"

Use counter examples

If your loved one says:

- "My leader is a Prophet whose prophecies always come true," ask, "You mean if we check all his prophecies, we'll find none that was wrong?"

• "I know our group is God's because we are 'fruitful,' we are growing so fast," ask," Does that mean that if you find a group that is growing faster, then God wants you to join that one instead?"

Find out what attracted your loved one to the cult

It's best to ask your loved one to describe step-by-step how he first heard about the organization and how he came to join. Reviewing in detail just how and why he joined the group is often illuminating and therapeutic. For example, he may have been attracted to the recruiter or some other group member, who has long since disappeared from the group. People often join for quite personal reasons. Realizing this can help them see their involvement from a new perspective.

When first recruited, most cult members don't think they are making a lifetime commitment. They say to themselves, "I'm going to check this out for a little while. I'll see if it fits." Family members and friends should not miss the opportunity to remind their loved one that, initially, they were just looking instead of making a lifetime commitment.

Try asking:

• What was it that made you first pay attention to the group and take it seriously? What were your thoughts and feelings at the time? Your expectations?

• Was there a person who was particularly influential in your conversion experience? Was it a social service project or some other experience that drew you in?

• Why did you think that becoming a member was an important thing for you to do, more important than your prior commitments?

• How long did it take for you to make a commitment? If it happened quickly, why? What factors do you think influenced your joining?

A person in a science fiction cult will give different answers than a person in a Bible cult. For example, a surviving member of Heaven's Gate claimed that he didn't think of the group as a cult, but as a class for higher learning. Many cult members are seeking spiritual growth, but this is not always the case.

In a business cult, the motivating factor is usually success, typically expressed in terms of money. If the cult member is involved with multilevel marketing, ask him if he looked into other ventures, such as an internet or mail-order business. You want to respect his intention and expand upon it by offering alternatives. Ask him if he has set a maximum for the length of time for he would be involved with the group's products and methods before deciding it was time for a change. Would it be three months, six months, or a year? If he is in debt, at what point would he leave the group? Again, your aim is to help him think beyond his cult experience.

A person in a therapy cult wants to be healed. He might be indoctrinated to believe he has to keep re-experiencing his traumas until they are "discharged", like electricity from a battery. Tell him, "That's only one of several methods that can be used to deal with traumas. Are you open to learning a faster, easier technique, one that promotes choice as well as healing?" For example, some of the techniques mentioned in the phobia chapter can ease past trauma faster and with much less pain. We want to challenge the rigid, black-and-white model that says the cult's way is the only way to get better.

Ultimately, we will want to use what the cult member says about the reasons he joined the group to help him reality-test: What was he promised would happen when he joined the group? How does it compare with what he is doing in the group today? With the information you have gained about his life in the group, you can ask specific questions:

• Did you know that you would be working in a fish factory sixteen-hours a day?

• Did you expect to be sleeping only five hours a night and eating fast food?

• Did you ever dream that you would be discouraged from seeing your family and friends?

You do not want to assault your loved one with such questions, since that may make him defensive. Rather, use them over a series of mini-interactions, as your loved one reveals the details of his life. Pursued skillfully, this line of questioning can give him many reasons to question his involvement with the group.

PLANT SEEDS OF DOUBT WITH HYPOTHETICAL QUESTIONS

Ultimately, you want to motivate your loved one to leave the cult—for cult members, an unimaginable prospect! To begin, we ask him to imagine hypothetical circumstances under which he *might* leave. We ask "what-if" questions that present negative possibilities about the group that the cult member might not have considered. At first, your loved one may protest, "But I don't want to leave." Tell him that you're not trying to take him away from the group, you just want to understand his commitment better. Say, "Wait a minute, let me explain myself." Then introduce an example: "What if you knew someone in The Way International? People in The Way believe they're doing God's Will. They seem to know the Bible really well — they can quote Bible verses extensively and very quickly. Now, what if they discovered the leader's credentials weren't what he claims? He says he has a Doctorate in Theology, but what if, in fact, he got a mail-order doctorate. I guess you would have to conclude the leader was misrepresenting his credentials. If you were in The Way, would that be enough to get you to leave? What if the leader then said, 'God wants us to lie.' Do you believe that God needs to lie, trick and manipulate?"

This issue of whether God lies or encourages lying arises in many Bible cults. Some even use Bible stories justify lying. Here you might ask, "Could a leader who claims God condones lying really be doing God's will? Is that a possible criterion for leaving a group, having a leader who lies?" Your loved one may not believe it a sufficient reason to leave. If so, encourage him to think about it. "How can a God of Truth encourage lies? How can you ever trust such a God?" Ask the cult member to identify specific qualities of God, again by asking questions: "Is your God a God of truth?" Here you might agree that if God existed, it would be a God of Truth.

Another question you might ask is: "*What if* someone asked you to talk to a former member from a group some consider to be a cult?" Again, you're asking indirectly—"*what if* someone"—which allows you to gain information without losing rapport with the cult member. If the cult member's response is "No, no way!" it's clearly not the right time to bring in an ex-member to speak with him. Instead, you might relate a story about a specific person you have met or heard about who has left a particular cult.

FORMER MEMBER: When I was in the Moonies, I was in charge of a mall store where we sold colored lava lamps. We'd show the customer an expensive lamp, and then sell them a box containing a cheap imitation. I secretly bought a copy of *Combatting*. It got me to thinking. I decided it was against my integrity to sell these phony lamps, no matter what the cause.

Inviting him to step into the shoes of an ex-Moonie, your underlying aim is to get him to imagine circumstances under which he might leave a group. Rather than making statements and judgments, you suggest and elicit. You might talk about how difficult it was for this person to leave because he came to equate the group with God's will. Leaving the group meant leaving God. After he got out, he realized the belief was not correct, indeed, the opposite. It was promoted by the group to retain its members, recruit others, raise money, and enhance public relations. It took some time for him to realize, "I can leave the group and still have a relationship with God." If your loved one can identify with an ex-member's story, he will begin to see that there is a way out.

At some point your loved one may become downright defensive and say, "I don't want to leave the group!" Remind him: "I'm asking hypothetically. If this happened to you, would you leave the group? Is there ever a legitimate reason to leave a group—any group. A fraternity, for example?" Open your discussion to all kinds of groups—political groups, psychotherapy groups, the military, gangs, and business groups.

  • "What if you're in a gang that is going to rob a bank? Is that a legitimate reason to leave? What if you're afraid the gang will pressure you or come after you? Would that be a legitimate reason?"

  • "Say you belonged to a therapy group that asked you to reveal intimate secrets confided to you by another member, would that be a legitimate reason to leave?"

Don't hesitate to use the word "legitimate," although you might ask the cult member, "Who defines 'legitimate' for you?" In a mind control group, there is never a legitimate reason to leave. Typically, you are betraying God or you're possessed by Satan, or some other absurd claim. Avoid talking directly about your loved one's group, but do build your case in the abstract by asking hypothetical questions. This will help create a new frame of reference for your loved one to think about his own cult.

Dealing with unfamiliar religious beliefs

Asking creative questions is a key to the success of the SIA, but to do so, and to evaluate answers, may be difficult if you have little understanding of the group's beliefs. If the cult member is in an eastern religion cult, it is imperative that you have at least a basic understanding of the history, beliefs, and practices of the original religion, whether it be Hindu, Buddhist, Taoist, or some other. Many eastern cults are split-offs, and sometimes hodgepodges, of mainstream religions. Your knowledge of these well-established religious doctrines may prove to be invaluable in helping your loved one see how he is being misled.

When it comes to Bible-oriented cults, if the loved one's family and friends are not religious, I advise them to learn the basics of Christianity through books, and by speaking with knowledgeable people. I am not a Christian and don't consider myself to be a Bible expert, although I have considerable experience helping people trapped in Bible-oriented cults. As I mentioned earlier, I have developed a close friendship with a mainstream minister, Bob Pardon, and his colleague Judy Barba, of the New England Institute of Religious Research. They are able to share the depth of their knowledge and personal faith with me, the Team, and ultimately, the cult member. Some cult members find it easier to talk with a believer like Bob or Judy before meeting with me. Others who have been programmed to fear "Christians" might find it easier to relate to me first.

If the family is religious, but of a different faith from the cult member, you would be wise to consider carefully the minister you enlist. For example, if the individual went from a Roman Catholic upbringing to an extremist fundamentalist Bible cult, then it might be inappropriate to ask a Roman Catholic priest to be involved too early— unless the cult member asked to speak with one.

Dealing with a proselytizing cult convert can be quite an ordeal, especially if it is your loved one. Proselytizing is a powerful method for reinforcing new beliefs and behavior in the person doing the proselytizing. For this reason, new members are told to recruit aggressively, and they may even try to recruit Team mem-

bers. Family and friends often do not know how to respond constructively when the cult member says, "You are going to hell!"
They may be tempted to retort that he is the one possessed by
Satan. Take the high road. Try saying, "I thought the Bible teaches
love, not fear; forgiveness, not guilt-tripping; prayerful acceptance,
not condemning judgment." Establish a clear understanding of
your own religious beliefs and learn how to communicate them
effectively. Prepare yourself. If you are a devout Christian, don't
argue the Bible. It will only result in a win-lose situation, and the
relationship will suffer. Emphasize the mutual, positive points of
both your respective belief systems.

If you don't believe in God, don't lie. You can say, "If I did
believe in a God, it would be a God of Truth and free-will. He or
She would want us to live our lives with love and compassion." If
until now you haven't discussed such a possibility, your loved one
may believe that positive changes are taking place because of God:
"He is helping to heal the family." Nurture this belief, but encourage also the idea that God transcends any one group's beliefs. By
simply acknowledging the possibility of a higher power, you will
have more leverage during future discussions of spiritual issues.

If you don't know what you believe, then I strongly
suggest finding out. Start with the Golden Rule or the Ten
Commandments. Establish for yourself what you believe and why.
If you are a complete skeptic regarding spiritual issues, be prepared
to discuss why that is. Demonstrate open-mindedness and a willingness to consider alternative points of view. Talk respectfully with
the cult member and, hopefully, he will show respect for you.

Getting your loved one to consider past events and possible future ones

A cult member's attention is usually kept focused on the immediate task at hand or on future projects. Memories of the pre-cult

past—especially positive childhood memories—are suppressed, and even distorted. An aim in your mini-interactions will be to loosen the cult's grip by getting your loved one to move freely in time, backward and forward, and to remove the cult's distorting lens by helping him see his own past and future more clearly.

Telling family stories, singing childhood songs, cooking familiar foods, showing old photographs that trigger positive childhood memories, (as we have seen in Chapter 8) can bring out your loved one's authentic identity. In addition, try getting him to reflect on the time when his cult self was just forming.

- "Go back to the time when you first heard about the group—did you think you would commit your life to it? What were your first impressions when seeing or meeting the leader? When you first joined, what did you think would happen in one year? Two years? Three years? If you knew then what you know now, would you have even gone to the first meeting?"

A crucial aim is to have him imagine circumstances under which he might leave the cult. Ask him to consider looking into the future:

- "What if, in two years, five women told you that the leader raped them, and you knew in your heart that what they were saying was true? Would you decide to leave the group?"

- "What if the leader said, 'Tomorrow, we're going to drink fruit punch laced with cyanide.' Would you consider that a legitimate reason to leave?" The cult member will usually say, "That would never happen!" Ask, "But what if it did?" If you can get the person to say that he would walk out, you have started him thinking about an alternative future.

The next step might be to get him thinking about life after the cult. Here you might say:

• "It's three years from now and you're no longer working with the group. You feel happy and fulfilled. What do you think you'd be doing?"

Be prepared to wait many minutes for an answer. A common mistake families make is to not give their loved one enough time to stop and think. Be patient. Ask the question two or three times, if necessary. By waiting for the response, you show your loved one that you're asking the question seriously, that you care about his answer, and that he is capable of finding an answer.

Sowing more seeds of doubt

Bible-oriented cults often quote passages out of context, cite Greek texts inappropriately, or make inaccurate translations. In such cases, you might ask the following questions:

• "What if you found your Bible group leaders were making inaccurate translations of key passages? What if you realized the meaning of the Bible is different from the group's interpretation—would that cause you to leave?" If your loved one admits to some doubt, you might say, "I'd be happy to introduce you to people who can help answer your questions about the Bible. Of course, you have to want to know those answers. Do you want to know?"

Team members may also appeal to the cult member's sense of responsibility and personal ethics. Here you might say:

• "What if it turned out you belonged to a group with a leader who is hurting people? How would you feel? Would you feel responsible for the people you influenced to become involved with the group?" Don't make accusations, threats, or judgments, but do try to help your loved one see that there is a lot at stake. He could be wasting valuable time and money, compromising his integrity, recruiting innocent people, and raising money for a destructive organization.

Remember, it is much better to ask a hypothetical than a direct question such as, "Are you going to leave the group or not?" If the person says "No," you may reinforce his devotion. Be creative. For example, you might say: "If the leader got up one day and said, 'I'm so sorry. For the last fifteen years I've been telling you I'm God's enlightened being. I'm not! I realize I've been on a power trip. I'm disbanding the group.' What would you do? Would you believe him, or would you think he was testing you to see if you were faithful?" A question like this could prod a cult member to begin to question his own leader.

CUSTOMIZING YOUR APPROACH

Thinkers, Feelers, Doers, Believers

A critical key to the success of your interactions will be to direct your questions and comments in such a way that your loved one's authentic identity is most likely to hear them. This requires knowing whether your loved one is a Thinker, Feeler, Doer, or Believer.[2] Thinkers are analytic; Feelers values emotion over rational analysis; Doers are activists and workers; Believers most value intuition and spiritual experience. Thinkers, Feelers, Doers, and Believers will all respond differently to questions asked by Team members, so determine which term best describes your loved one. Some people will fall into more than one of these categories, but each Team member will usually have a sense of the best approach. Decide which model is most appropriate for your own relationship with the cult member, then concentrate on framing the most effective questions.

Thinkers

When asked why they joined, Thinkers will be most apt to say, "Because I've found the truth," or "All of my questions about life have been answered," or "I was impressed with the group's science conferences (with Nobel Laureates) and their claim to be bringing together science and religion." To shift a Thinker's perspective, you might ask questions such as:

- What if you found out the Divine Principle isn't true?

- What if you found out a Bible quote was taken out of context by the group and is wrong?

- What convinced you that this teaching, and not any other, was the highest truth?

- Have you gone back to the original source material to validate or confirm the claims, quotes, contexts, and conclusions of the teaching?

- How would you know if there were a Higher Truth? What would it look, sound, and feel like?

- What would you do if you found an even higher Truth?

- What if you discovered that the teaching of your group has changed over time?

- What if you discovered parts of the teaching are wrong?

- What are the arguments that critics of your group use? If you don't know the specifics, how can you refute them?

Feelers

During my recruitment into the Moonies, I was "love-bombed." My recruiters told me over and over, "Ours is the one true family. We practice unconditional love, higher love than any other group in history. We love you! Come join, and we'll love you forever." The Feeler in me responded to their entreaties. Of course, the group's love was conditional. If you questioned and decided to leave, you would not be worthy of love—to the contrary, you would be worthy of scorn and even hatred. If you stayed and did not obey the rules of the group, love and approval would be withdrawn. In fact, all cults practice this kind of conditional love. Consistently expressing unconditional love, encouraging your loved one to act with integrity, being creative, learning, growing, and participating with family and friends to improve the world will remind the authentic member of the cult's broken promise. Love is stronger than anything, even stronger than sophisticated mind control techniques. Some useful questions for feelers:

- How did you know that this was the group for you?

- If your group teaches unconditional love, what happens to those who decide to leave? Would the group still love that person, spend time with that person?

- What if the people you think are your best friends in the group refuse to be your friends any more because you asked a question that the leader criticizes or refuses to answer?

- What would you do if you saw someone suffering? Would you help them if they were not a member of your group? What if they were a critic of your group?

- What would you do if you felt anger toward another member of the group? Are you allowed to feel such emotions, or are you expected to suppress them? If you must suppress them, does your leader always suppress his anger?

- Do you ever see leaders being hypocritical? Does it ever upset you?

- Do you ever miss your friends, your family? How does it make you feel when you want to see them and you have to ask permission to do so?

- Do you ever feel like you need a vacation?

- Do you ever feel like just walking out of the group?

- Do you ever feel that whatever you do, you just aren't good enough?"

- What would need to happen for you to feel that it is time for you to leave?

Doers

Doers are activists who like to perform deeds and achieve goals, such as getting a project accomplished. If your loved one tells you that he is in the group because of its important humanitarian work, such as working for world peace, ask him to detail the specifics of how the group is actually making that happen. Groups often have beautiful brochures but there is usually little or no real activity. If they are giving out free government surplus food, but are keeping most of it themselves, this is not an example of humanitarianism. Doers especially hate to work hard and see that they have accomplished nothing, or worse, actually undermined their original purpose. Here are some questions:

- How did you know that this was the group for you — the one that would accomplish your goals?

- Did you check out the actual accomplishments of the group before you joined?

- Did you look into any other organizations before deciding to commit to this one? Which ones?

- What were the specific goals of the group that first attracted you? What events or activities were you told would accomplish those aims? Were they achieved? Have you set a firm date in your mind for a specific goal or event to occur—or else you will walk out of the group?

- Would you do anything you were ordered to do by the group? What if it was something you didn't want to do— would you do it anyway? Why? or why not?

- What if you're asked to commit a crime?

- If you found a group that was doing more to accomplish your goals, would you consider joining them? What about Red Cross? Amnesty International? The Salvation Army?
- What kind of group experience would it take for you to know it was time for you to try something different?

Believers

Believers have a decidedly spiritual orientation. They are attuned to and seek out religious and spiritual experiences. In fact, believers often get involved with a cult because they've had an experience they think is a message from the Divine. By the same token, they usually leave because of a spiritual missive. If your loved one tells you, "I joined because God told me to," then you should get a detailed description of how and when he received God's message.

- When you first heard about the group, what was it that encouraged you to believe?
- Tell me all about your spiritual path. What were the most important spiritual experiences you've had in your life?
- How much exposure have you had to different spiritual teachers and traditions? Were you ever in a group where the leader turned out to be less than responsible? Have you ever spent time in cult groups? What do you think of the people you have met in these groups?
- What questions did you ask when you first considered getting involved?
- What would you do if you were praying tonight and you had a spiritual experience that clearly indicated you had to leave the group? For example, what if God came to you in your prayers or meditations and said, 'I want you to leave.' Would you stay in the group, or would you follow God?

The cult member might reply, "Oh, God would never do that." Try to steer him back to the hypothetical: "But what if He did?

Where is your commitment? Is it to your friends, to your status in
the group, or is it to God?"

Motivational styles

The way your loved one interacts with the world, the goals he
sets and the decisions he makes, depends on his motivational style.
If a person tends to seek out good or pleasant things in life, his
motivational style is assertive, or "moving toward a positive." If he
tends to avoid bad or painful things, his motivational style is defensive, or "moving away from a negative." Although people typically
rely on both styles in different situations, they will generally favor
one style. Try to determine what motivational style your loved one
used before becoming involved with the cult.

When you plan your approach, consider all of the variables. For
example, a Thinker might say, "The teaching of my group is the
highest truth." If his motivational style is defensive, you can offer
specific criteria: "A higher truth should not contain contradictions,
and a higher truth should not change over time — as yours does!"
You want to motivate him "away" from the negative of a false
teaching. If his orientation is assertive, then offering him an even
higher truth would work best.

If a Doer whose motivational style is assertive says, "Show me
a better group, one that does more," find out what matters to him.
You might ask, "What are your criteria for doing more? Do you
want to feed the hungry, clothe the poor, and visit the sick, as the
Bible says? Have you ever investigated, in a concrete, practical way,
what the Salvation Army is doing?" If the Doer's orientation is to
"move away from a negative," then you might find evidence of how
his group is violating his ideals, and possibly hurting people, and
bring it to his attention.

REALITY-TESTING: REDIRECTING THE NEW PERSPECTIVE

The way you look at things impacts the way you experience them. For example, if you're wearing rose-tinted glasses, everything will appear rosy because the glasses create a filtering lens for incoming information. In fact, the human mind needs filters in order to function. Change the filter, and the information coming in will be interpreted in a different way.

When people are subjected to mind control techniques, along with social influence processes, their mental filter becomes distorted. Events that have been calculated in advance are seen to be spontaneous. Mere coincidences are construed as revealing a "cosmic message." Mundane experiences are attributed to a spiritual force. Members, reinforced by leaders and each other, come to see the world according to the cult perspective. In the Strategic Interaction Approach, we help the cult member step out of that perspective and test his reality. We do that by getting him to see through our eyes and, even more importantly, through the eyes of his authentic self. Of course, we must do this in a non-confrontational, non-judgmental way so that we don't alienate the cult identity.

Clarifying intention, method, application, and consequence

Most cult members have noble intentions. Believers may want to achieve enlightenment, and Doers may want to make the world a better place. While these are honorable goals, cult members, despite their efforts, usually do not achieve what they intend to accomplish. By asking your loved one to discuss his intentions, you help him develop a filter for evaluating his reality, in particular, his actions and their outcomes.

MOTHER: My son tells me he has been meditating three hours, twice a day. Afterward, he feels spacey and has a headache.

The problem here is not with the son's intention, which is to achieve spiritual growth, but with his approach. Begin by acknowledging the good intent. In addition to building rapport, this validation will also move the cult member back in time: "What were your original intentions when you first got involved with the group?"

The next step will be to draw his attention to method. If group doctrine says there is only one way to meditate — that is, chanting for three hours, twice a day — suggest alternatives like a breathing meditation, visualization meditation, or walking meditation. The application is the second place to intercede: "What about meditating for fewer minutes each time? See how you feel." It might be too much to suggest stopping the meditation altogether. This approach will allow your loved one to make small, gradual changes in his behavior without feeling that he's guilty of disobeying cult rules.

The bottom line is the consequence. Are the method and application producing positive results in your loved one's life? Encourage the cult member to ask questions: "What happens when you tell the leader that you are having headaches or muscle spasms?" A cult's answer might be, "Do what you are told!" or "Follow instructions!" or "You are 'unstressing'" or "You are liberating problems that have been held in your body. Keep meditating!" As long as the member is obedient, the symptoms get worse. Reality-test the cult's explanation for the consequences, and offer alternative explanations:

- "Maybe you're meditating too many hours."

- "This type of meditation may not be healthy for your physiology. Maybe you need a different method."

- "How long will you continue to use this method, with these results, before you realize a change is in order?"

Therapeutic stories and metaphors

Stories and metaphors are among the most compelling vehicles for communicating information and changing attitudes and behavior. They are especially powerful in their ability to sidestep the cult's thought-stopping methods. One of the most effective therapeutic metaphors is that of the hero story: At the beginning, a person (the hero) is "stuck" but may not be aware of it. After a series of events, he becomes aware of the problem and seeks out new resources (people, information). These resources in turn provide new perspectives that lead to new behaviors. At the end, the hero is not only free from his problem, but leading a happier, healthier life.

This story-structure could be used again and again by different Team members who tell different stories. For example, someone who has just stopped smoking cigarettes might begin telling his story by saying how he knew it was unhealthy, but felt stuck and hopeless. He could go on to describe how he found resources—a nicotine patch, a hypnotherapist, or a course to give up smoking— and saw new perspectives, and how he was able to find healthy substitutes for smoking, like therapeutic breathing techniques. Finally, he can tell the loved one how much better he feels and how happy he is to be back in control of his life.

Another approach is to use actual metaphors to draw parallels between cults and other destructive situations. An especially powerful metaphor for the cult experience is that of an abusive relationship, and the abuse may be psychological, physical, or both. Here you might look for an example of an unhealthy relationship in your past, and talk about it in a way that helps the cult member draw connections to his own situation. If you can't think of a personal example, describe someone you know or heard about who suffered from battered wife syndrome. Talk about how people warned her of her future husband's temper; how she was unable to see his flaws; how he controlled her with fear, guilt, and pain; how he isolated her from family and friends and made her dependent; and how she ultimately got help and escaped from the relationship.

Questions to Help Reality-Test

- On a scale of one to ten, how would you rate your leader's moral qualities? How does he compare to religious figures such as Jesus and the Buddha?
- On a scale of one to ten, how would you rate your commitment to the group when you first joined? How about now? How about five years from now?
- What is your view about people who are not members of your group?
- What is your view of the world outside of your group?
- How do you feel about your parents?
- How do you feel about your siblings?
- How do you feel about your other relatives?
- How do you feel about your old friends?
- What do you think about people who help get others out of cult situations? Why?
- Have you ever talked with someone who was helped to exit a cult involvement? Are you open to it? If not, why not?
- What is your attitude toward leaving the group?
- What did you say your attitude was toward former members? Why do you seem so willing to globally dismiss so many people without making an effort to get to know them first?

Other therapeutic metaphors may seem irrelevant, but if told properly, can be very effective. For instance, you might talk about becoming lost in a forest while on a hiking trip with friends. Describe how you came to realize that you were lost, and how you climbed a tree to get a better perspective on where you were. You might also describe how you built a fire and put wet leaves on it to make a smoke signal that was spotted. The message of your story might be, "Sometimes you need help to get out of trouble. It's okay to ask." Another powerful medium for therapeutic metaphors is movies. Two of my favorites are *The Truman Show* with Jim Carrey and an old movie with Walter Matthau and Robin Williams called *The Survivors*. In *The Truman Show*, Jim Carrey's character chooses personal freedom at the end, rather than living an illusion. In *The Survivors*, Robin Williams' character gets recruited into a survivalist cult and realizes in the end that the leader is a phony who is just trying to make money by promoting fear.

Switching roles

This technique is an incredibly powerful way to open new perspectives, improve communication, and create a more intimate relationship. Unlike role-playing, where you are stepping into the cult member's shoes for the purpose of planning and rehearsing mini-interactions, here you are asking him to step into your shoes so that he will see from your perspective. One way to do this is to respond to a question your loved one asks with another question:

Cult Member: How do you feel about my joining the group?

Stepfather: If you were me, how do you think I would feel?

This role-switching technique causes the cult member to adopt his stepfather's perspective. Of course, you must be prepared to reciprocate. In fact, you might explicitly ask your loved one to switch roles with you. Can you defend his position on a particular subject, for example, his love of his leader, as if it were your own? Team members who feel they cannot take on the perspective of the cult member should spend more time with him in order to understand him better. Ask more questions, and learn about his world.

You might try practicing this powerful technique with another Team member. In the following exercise, I took the mother's position and the mother took her daughter's as a way of preparing for an actual role-switch with her daughter.

SH: (as mother): "You know, Kristi, I really wonder how you can be so willing to allow your guru to decide whether you can come visit us when you've always taken such pleasure in making up your own mind, and even going against authority."

MOTHER (as daughter): She'd say, "My guru has shown me that my rebelliousness was just a way of trying to control things that are out of my control. Mom, when will you let go and just accept things?"

SH: (as mother making role switch): "I'll do my best to accept things, but you also need to step into my shoes. How would you feel if your beautiful spirited daughter whom you loved, and whose company you enjoyed so much, had to ask someone else whether she could even see you?"

In asking such a question, your aim is to not only elicit the authentic identity, but also to get the loved one to go inside to get in touch with her own feelings as a way of getting in touch with yours. You will probably get a different response, depending on whether she is in cult or authentic mode.

CULT IDENTITY: "I'd just accept it."

AUTHENTIC IDENTITY: "Hmm... that's a tough one."

MOTHER: "So then what would I say?"

SH: Try this (as mother): "I want you to know how much I respect you and I hope you respect me too. If the leader of your group is who he says he is, and if the group's teachings are valid, then I, too, will see the light. Share with me and teach me; I want to understand you and your group! If the leader proves to be untrustworthy, then let's try to take what we've learned and move forward."

As she responds, show that you are listening. Say, "So what I hear you saying is...." and then repeat back what she just said, in your own words. Be genuinely, sincerely interested. Let her talk about herself. Let her tell you what she likes about being in the group. Remember, both identities (cult and authentic) want your love and approval.

The elitist cult mind set and reality-testing

Cult members have been indoctrinated to believe the outside world is hostile, hateful, and dangerous. They are often treated as if they were misfits and idiots by other people. When I was in the Moonies, I was punched and spit on by people on the street. I had beer thrown at me. These attacks reinforced the cult worldview. My commitment to the group was intensified by what I experienced as "persecution."

One hot day, as I was selling flowers on a New York City street corner, a man showed me compassion and offered to buy me a cold drink, my cult mentality was challenged. I will always remember the kindness that "outsider" showed me. Go out of your way to do things that communicate to your loved one that people in the outside world are kind and loving. Treat people respectfully and compassionately and be especially nice to members of the group. They are someone's children, siblings, or parents.

In some cults, members are told that the family is against them or trying to control them. You can effectively challenge that belief by showing that you want your loved one to think independently and make his own decisions. Find ways to convey the message that you admire the person's intentions and desires. Some of your concerns are directed at the way the leader is acting or how the group is asking members to fulfill their desires. By supporting the positive intentions, you will ally yourself with your loved one's real self. The authentic self gets the message, "Dad wants me to be in control. He isn't trying to control me, and he doesn't want anyone else to control me, either."

If the cult member believes he will be kidnapped and tortured by deprogrammers, then he needs to be reassured that it will never happen. Here you might ask your loved one, "What do we need to do to show you that we'll protect you? That we'll stand up for your right to be an individual? That we'll protect your right to do what you think is best for yourself?" Don't plant negative suggestions by saying, "We promise we won't let anyone kidnap or torture you." Plant positive seeds instead: "We're on your side, and we would protect you from anyone trying to force you to do something against your will."

If the cult member believes people leave the group because they are weak, possessed, sinful, or brainwashed, the most powerful antidote is meeting happy, well-adjusted former members. As a former member, I would tell the person, "I left the group because of my integrity — I couldn't go on deceiving and being deceived. I'm happier now, and I feel closer to God than when I was in the organization. I also understand the Bible better than when I was in the group." It is incredibly powerful to meet a former member who is happy and fulfilled. It undermines the phobia indoctrination.

Examining the cult's claims

Cults tend to make extraordinary claims for their leaders, doctrines, and organization: "Only we know the truth! We have the greatest Messiah who ever lived." But the burden of proof lies with them, not with critics. In other words, they must prove they are superior. We do not have the burden to disprove their claims.

FATHER: He believes the leader is the greatest figure in human history and has the answers for all questions, all problems and situations.

The most effective response is to point out that there are hundreds, perhaps thousands of people claiming to be Messiahs, Perfect Masters, and Avatars. We need to step back and examine these claims. If they turn out to be true, the group will be there tomorrow, next week, next month, next year. Why rush?

Morality systems based on absolute principles inevitably reach a point where some of the principles contradict each other. Cult doctrine is based on absolute principles. It will be instructive to discover the inherent contradictions. A productive strategy to gain rapport and trust with the cult identity is to use cult ideologies and behaviors to reality-test to see if the group is actually practicing its own ideals.

For example, Scientology has some teachings that can orient a member in a healthy direction. In one of Hubbard's heavily promoted lectures, the cult's creator describes Scientology as *The Road to Truth*, and says, essentially, that true steps must always be taken when seeking the truth. Jon Atack, author of *A Piece of Blue Sky*, told me that when helping members to re-evaluate their involvement, he would take an audio tape of this lecture with him.[3] Once the member had agreed that this teaching was essential, Atack would point out contradictions and deceptions made elsewhere by the cult's leader. In this way, the positive teaching of the cult can be used to help the member move back towards independent thinking.

Remember, cults often say one thing and then practice something else. They don't deliver what they promise. Examine the claims and promises that a group makes. If they promise that, using their methods, members can raise their IQs, ask for the scientific proof. If they promise people can move objects with their thoughts, have them demonstrate it. Look at reality and ask them to make an assessment.

Paradox

Paradox is a technique in which you encourage the cult member to do something that he is already doing. It must be used sparingly and cautiously, otherwise you risk losing rapport and trust, and may even seem to approve of his cult membership. I recently used paradox when I said to a client, "I think you should move to the headquarters to be closer to the guru so you can see what goes on at the heart of the group." This suggestion might sound shocking to the cult member and the family. However, I've found some people need to get even more involved. Then, when they experience the abuses of the cult, it is easier for them to decide to leave. Besides, when a cult expert actually recommends getting closer to the cult, the cult identity is forced to stop and think.

Sometimes a loved one needs to experience firsthand the discrepancy between his own idealistic beliefs and the reality of the cult and its leader. Using paradox can empower him to reality-test and, hopefully, to re-evaluate his cult involvement. Not all cases call for the use of paradox and, in fact, some may be damaged by the technique. For this reason, be very careful when you use it.

The Strategic Interaction Approach is designed to promote gradual, self-directed, positive change over time through a series of mini-interactions. Family and friends work together to help their loved one in the least intrusive way. Sometimes the cult member will make the decision to walk away after only a few mini-interactions, but this is not always the case. However, if a formal intervention is necessary, your hard work will not have been in vain. From the beginning, SIA Team members are planting seeds. During an intervention, you build on all of your previous efforts to see that these seeds come to fruition.

Chapter 12

Planning and Holding an Intervention

The main focus of the Strategic Intervention Approach is to empower the family and other Team members to do mini-interactions that will ultimately motivate the cult member to seek out information: to talk with former members, do research on the Internet, or to come to Boston to meet with me or others. Under ideal circumstances, your loved one will be ready to re-evaluate and, hopefully, leave the group after a series of successful mini-interactions, and there will be no need for a formal intervention.

Sometimes, the decision to leave happens quite suddenly and dramatically. Some time ago, I helped a family whose daughter was involved with the Moonies. I encouraged the sister of the cult member to attend a cult lecture. I educated her about the group, told her about the alleged sexual improprieties and cocaine addiction of Moon's son and suggested questions she might ask her sister.[1] After hearing what her sister had to say, the young woman quickly became disillusioned with the group and walked out. Later, she was willing to meet with me, explore more information about the group, watch videotapes, and get counseling.

Other cult members will need more time and experience to reality-test before making the decision to leave the group. One time I was asked to speak with a woman who was preparing to move to the Southwest to join the leadership of an unusual UFO channeling cult — a group whose leaders claimed to be from the eighth dimension. A friend of hers approached me and asked me my opinion of a videotape made by the group to recruit people. I found it to be very manipulative and hypnotic. He asked me if I would meet with her, and simply introduced me as his friend. I spent about an hour and a half telling her about my own experiences with the Moonies, and doing some of the suggested SIA techniques described in the previous chapter. While I was initially disappointed to learn that she did move in with the group, within two months she walked out and went on with her life.

Some members may be kicked out of a cult because of their questioning attitude, or because they are seen as a liability. I worked on a Transcendental Meditation (TM) case in which a young man living in the group's ashram was losing weight and acting oddly. After I met with and coached his family, they pressured one of the group's sub-leaders to take him to a physician for evaluation. We also asked his friends to visit the ashram, invite him on trips, and talk about old times, which provided opportunities to do mini-interactions and the phobia cure with him. It turned out that the physician was very concerned about the young man's health. Because the group was afraid of attracting bad publicity—and possibly a lawsuit—they told the young man to move out of the ashram and back home until he was well again. When I was brought in to do family counseling, I was able to address the cult issues with him directly and asked him to meet a former leader. John M. Knapp had been a "Governor of the Age of Enlightenment," a high level of attainment in TM, and shared some of his first-hand experiences as well as insider information, which enabled the young man to re-evaluate his involvement with the group.[2]

Even after cult members leave the group, there is still a lot of work that needs be done. They may make a clean break from the group but still be influenced by the residual mind control that was exerted on them. If they have access to a computer, they may get on the Internet and communicate with other cult members and ex-members. Often, these people need counseling to help them counteract the effects of mind control and deal with other psychological and social issues. They have several options. They could come to Boston and meet with me for a few sessions, or for an extended stay. If they live nearby, they could come in for ongoing therapy. If not, they could meet with a local, professional counselor who is familiar with cult related issues. Other options include ongoing telephone counseling or e-mail consulting.

Difficult cases

After a series of mini-interactions, your loved one may still be on the fence, not completely convinced that he should leave, but open to more discussion. For example, I once helped a Jehovah's Witness who, through many interactions, came to realize that there were problems with the WatchTower Society, but was unable to leave the group. Since he did not yet have the personal resources to make the move, I recommended that we do an intervention. First, we located a former member and friend of his who had left a year earlier. Then the cult member's brother contacted him and invited him and the ex-member to lunch. There, the former member discussed some of the mind control criteria from my freedomof-mind.com web site and introduced the idea of meeting with me. The cult member agreed to talk with me over the phone. During our conversation, I encouraged him to come to Boston and meet with me, which he did. Over a period of a few days, we were able to answer all of his questions, watch videotapes, and go over the mind control paradigm. He decided to leave the group.

It is also possible that, after months of work, your loved one will be completely resistant to further discussion of his cult involvement. Perhaps you've asked him to read critical literature about his group, speak with a former member, or meet with someone like me, and he has refused. If, after many interactions, your loved one is still firmly entrenched in the group, you may consider planning a formal, three-day intervention.

WHAT IS AN INTERVENTION?

An intervention is, in a sense, a ritual experience. It has a beginning, middle, and end. Team members—family, friends, former members, possibly clergy—are introduced to the individual not all at once, but according to a plan, which often changes to fit the immediate need. Like a religious ritual, an intervention is a moment of "sacred" time. During an intervention, everyone takes time off from work, puts their lives on hold, and lets the cult member know that he is important and that there's a problem that needs to be addressed. Adding to the feeling of ceremony, and this is sometimes what makes an intervention so powerful, is the fact that people may be traveling long distances to participate. Perhaps a cousin is flying north from South America, or a grandmother is flying cross-country. Former members are coming from distant locations to speak with the individual.

People with a loved one in a cult are often tempted to rush into an intervention even before they have given mini-interactions a chance. If the case was difficult to begin with, it will be even more so if there has been little previous communication with the cult member. The mini-interactions that have been done lay the groundwork that allows a family member to say, "I've really tried to understand you and now I need your help. I really need to hear you talk with other people (former members, cult critics) so that I can better understand both sides of the issue. If this group you've been involved with for ten years is really legitimate, then it will stand up to scrutiny. If it isn't, then let's cut to the chase! Let's find out from the people who have a critical opinion, hear what they have to say, and evaluate it."

An SIA intervention can be like an alcoholism intervention in that concerned family members confront their loved one by saying, "Hey, this is a problem. You may not think it's a problem but let me give you some concrete examples. It's a problem because you're missing out on your education; because if anything happens, you don't have health insurance; because if you have kids, they're not going to have a chance to get a proper education or medical treatment." Having laid out all the facts, we are then in a position to offer solutions to the problem.

However, the goal during an intervention, as with mini-interactions, is not to force your loved one to leave the group but to provide information and perspectives that were not previously available to the cult member; to promote informed choice; and to enable him to re-evaluate his commitment and make his own decision. You should not attempt an intervention without guidance from a professional who will have the necessary skills, information, and objectivity to guide the process safely and effectively.

A. Planning the Intervention

Your preparations for an intervention will go much more smoothly if you take a balanced, step-by-step approach. It is important to pace yourself while planning an intervention, otherwise you may become overwhelmed by the task and, consequently, delay or give up on the intervention. Using the information gathered by Team members during mini-interactions, take small, manageable steps. At each step, make sure to consider the possible positive and negative consequences of your decisions (regarding team members and location) and planned actions (who will say what and when) by visualizing what might happen. Imagine the best, worst, and most likely scenario. The main steps in planning an intervention are as follows:

Picking the intervention team

The first step is picking the intervention Team from members of the SIA Team. The intervention Team will be composed of those people who are most significant to the cult member and who will be most effective in communicating with him. When planning an intervention, I customize rather than taking a cookie-cutter approach, because what works terrifically for one case could be a disaster for another. I take what I know of the loved one and I try to put myself into his shoes and imagine, "What kind of intervention would motivate me, engage me, and make me want to participate?" In some cases, it is good to have a lot of loving family members there. In other cases, it is best to keep it small and intimate. Sometimes it may be most effective to have the intervention initiated by a sibling and not have the parents present at all. Perhaps a favorite aunt or best friend should take the lead.

Usually, one team member will lead the intervention. I take the lead and arrange the specifics for those interventions I am involved with. Generally, I find the best leaders are former cult members who have had formal counseling training. In the future, I will be devoting more time to training counselors to do effective interventions.

When picking ex-members to be part of your team (as leaders or as participants), try to choose people whose interests will help them relate to your loved one's pre-cult self. If the cult member used to play basketball, a basketball player or fan would have automatic rapport with the pre-cult self. If the cult member loved blues music, an ex-member who plays blues guitar would be a good match. Ask yourself, "Is this a person who could get rapport and respect from the cult member?"

Of course, a former member who knew your loved one while in the cult is an invaluable resource. There are many ways to locate former members, such as browsing newsgroups on the Internet or doing Web searches for stories written by former members. If you kept a record of the cult members you've met or spoken with since your loved one joined, you should be able to find out if they are still in the group. If there is a Web site put up by former members, e-mail them and find out if they can locate those members, or ask them if they know of others who might be willing to help you.

Arranging a time and place

Next, identify potential times and places for doing the intervention. In addition, think of possible situations that might get your loved one physically away from the group for an extended period—for example, grandmother's eightieth birthday party, or the annual family reunion in the country—and consider doing an intervention before or after. Doing an intervention during the first visit home after a cult involvement is usually discouraged because the member will be on maximum guard. Make that visit a wonderful experience so his fears will be abated and he will want to come home again. If the cult member is about to be married, that is not the time to try an intervention, unless it is an arranged marriage and you know your loved one doesn't really want to be with the person. Deciding when is the most effective time to do an intervention is a key to success. Ideally, it should be timed after a set of successful mini-interactions has been done and the three-step phobia intervention has been implemented, though in truly difficult cases this may not have been possible. If you have spent time discussing how other groups use mind control, you will be one step ahead.

Deciding where to conduct the intervention is another important decision. There should be positive, or at least neutral, associations with the location. If it won't be done at the parents' home, then it might be held at a sibling's or other relative's place. Also, check to see if the cult member and key Team members have major allergies. The Team's efforts will be hampered if someone who is allergic to cats (as I am) has to work for days in a house with four cats. Likewise, cigarette smoke might cause problems for the cult member and the team. Try to pick a place that is not known, or easily accessible, to the cult. As an obvious example, it should not be across the street from the cult center. The physical layout should be conducive to comfort and privacy. Lighting should be adequate, and there should be a minimum of noise and distractions, such as ringing telephones, barking dogs, or crying babies.

B. Approaching your loved one

The advantage of the SIA is that, after you have done many interactions, it will become easier for you to decide how to approach your loved one to obtain consent for a counseling intervention. The most honest and direct approach is to have family members discuss their desire with the cult member. The person with the most trust, respect, and emotional clout should be the person to ask the cult member. When approached in such an open, non-threatening way, and by a non-authoritarian figure, the cult member will feel control over the situation. This approach can also be a big plus because it sidesteps the fear of deprogramming. By being so open, rapport and trust are emphasized. The downside is that the cult may do everything in its power to make sure this meeting never happens. Leaders might agree to let the member attend the meeting but insist that a cult sub-leader be present. This is not recommended, but it becomes a point of negotiation, and is a step in the right direction. Your point is that you want your loved one to think for himself, and that may be less likely to happen if someone from the group is there.

As soon as your loved one agrees to a meeting, the time and place should be established immediately. Discuss with him the fact that if he tells the group, they will undoubtedly pressure him not to come, or find some last minute excuse to keep him from attending.

Get his commitment that he will fulfill the agreement, no matter what the group says. Rehearse with him possible responses to cult pressure, and help him to imagine the best possible, worst possible, and most likely outcomes. Ideally, he will decide not to even tell them, but if he is confronted, he will know how to respond. Get a handshake to solidify the commitment.

The alternative, more traditional approach is to have the rest of the counseling team ready and waiting nearby when you ask the cult member for consent. Such an approach is sometimes the only viable way to proceed. If warned in advance, the most destructive cults would never allow a member to attend such a meeting. Choose your words carefully when you present the plan to your loved one. As always, your attitude should be sincere, loving, and conversational. Talk about the cult involvement as a family problem, not just the member's problem. First, acknowledge your loved one's good intentions. Then, express your concern. If he is upset that you didn't tell him enough in advance, acknowledge that he has the right to be upset. Give him time to think and digest the situation. If he is angry, then apologize and ask for forgiveness. Explain that you trust him, but you don't trust the group and the way it seems to exert control through fear and guilt. Tell him that you wanted to give him the opportunity to think for himself, and ask him, "What would you have done in my position? How would you react in my place?" Ask him, "If we had called last week and told you what we wanted, would you even be here now?" If he says, "Yes," then apologize and say that you made a miscalculation. Tell him that you are glad that he is independent and able to be open-minded.

Customizing the approach

People who are leaders or sub-leaders in their group are often proud of their position and extremely confident that the cult is honorable and legitimate. In such situations, I find that a well-timed challenge can be fruitful:

- "If you are a responsible leader and believe in the group so strongly, then you should know your critic's issues and be able to refute them. Many people look up to you for guidance, and I am sure you will be able to articulate the group point of view effectively."

- "You've been telling me for ten years that you're not under mind control. I am asking you to prove it now. Meet with these people. Give us three days. Sit, listen, talk, and question. I really want to hear you and them discussing the pros and cons."

Rank-and-file members are typically more submissive, and will often respond better to you as an authority figure if you are a parent or older sibling. You can do some gentle questioning that appears to defer to cult authority:

- "I'm confused. On the one hand, I have many concerns about your well-being. On the other hand, you seem convinced that you've made your own decision, and that it was the right decision. Help me to better understand what's going on."

- "Who can I speak with to get permission for you to come home for a visit?"

A common strategy for dealing with a cult member who believes his group has "the Truth" is to present yourself as a potential convert: "Who knows? Maybe I'll have an experience with God, and I will join too, because it could mean my salvation." If he thinks that you might still be "saved," a door will be left open. Although it is tempting to express distaste for a mind control cult, try not to close the door with angry declarations, like "There's not a chance in a million years that I will ever join your group." Talking in such absolutes, you will probably lose the rapport and trust you may have established with your loved one's cult identity. You may even be cut off.

You can also appeal to your loved one on a more personal level. You might say, "If you love us, even if you think we're totally off-base, just do it anyway to allay our fears." Or, you might negotiate a quid pro quo agreement with your loved one. For example, if he asks, "Will you buy a car for me?" you can reply, "We would consider helping you if you would consider doing something to help us."

Telephone issues

You should also prepare yourself for the possibility that your loved one will want to make calls to the cult or receive phone calls from other cult members. This can create problems. I've seen interventions fall apart when the cult leader or sub-leader calls and says, "You're with the Devil. Get out of there! No matter what, don't listen to what they say!" Such declarations can make cult members so afraid that they pack up and walk out the door.

You don't want to make the cult member feel uncomfortable, so you should not forbid him to make or receive phone calls. You can talk with him in advance, help him to consider what the cult's response might be if he calls telling them about your request, and ask him to please take this time away from the group to think for himself. It is imperative that you literally rehearse with him what he will say to the cult, possibly by having a former member (or some other team member) role-play what the cult member should say. If he insists on calling, encourage him to limit the conversation as much as possible. He might say, "I'm fine. I'll call you in a few days." You might even suggest that a family member call and leave a message for him. Remember, the telephone line is his link back to the cult and the cult perspective. You want to do everything you can to weaken that link.

Seizing, or creating, the moment

If, after repeated requests, your loved one resists all of your efforts to help, you may have to actively choreograph the conditions for an intervention. By being imaginative and resourceful, you may create a situation that will help elicit the pre-cult self. For example, one of the most effective ways to reach a cult member is to find a former member of the group who was his friend, and have that person discuss a possible meeting. The success of such a request will always depend on several factors, such as who is asking, how it is asked, and the timing in terms of your loved one's involvement. Your loved one may have refused in the past, but a "no" does not have to mean a universal "no." If it had been a different person asking, or if it had been asked in a different tone of voice, or if it had been asked on a different day, the answer might have been "yes."

Another strategy is to ask the cult member to come home to do an intervention with another family member. For instance, I have seen families with loved ones in two different cults carry out successful interventions with both cult members. In such situations, you might say, "Jenny's in trouble. As you know she is involved with this guru, and she is about to move to India. Would you come and help us talk with her?" You can also ask a cult member to help with a drug or alcoholism intervention: "Dad's got an alcoholism problem. We need to do an intervention with Dad. Would you come home and do that?"

Sometimes, helping a cult member to think for himself is just a matter of getting him to step away from the group long enough for the authentic self to come up for air. Do everything within your power to give your loved one opportunities to take a break from the cult, and you may be amazed at what happens. The following story shows how a Team's persistence and flexibility can create success in unexpected ways. Please note that all names and identifying features appearing in the following story have been changed to protect the privacy of my clients.

Sally and Greg

Felicia and Larry Michaels were divorced the year after she became a member of the Jehovah's Witnesses. Larry loved Felicia but could not deal with her sudden personality change; it appeared to him that she had become a religious fanatic. She was awarded custody of their two small children, Greg and Sally. Many years later, once he realized it was a destructive cult, Larry called me and asked me to help plan an intervention with his children. After evaluating Larry's relationship with his son and daughter, I advised him to begin by approaching his fourteen-year-old son, Greg.

Larry asked Greg to join him on a five-day fishing trip in Canada, which we hoped would remind Greg of the old times when they fished together. While they fished, Larry talked about the good times they had, and coaxed the pre-cult Greg to express himself. Once Larry felt he had achieved an adequate level of rapport and trust, he was able to present hundreds of pages of original WatchTower documents that he had photocopied from the Library of Congress. His son was so moved by his effort that, after the trip, Greg agreed to meet with former members, and soon made the decision to leave the group.

We talked at length and started making plans to help his daughter Sally. It took months for Greg to build bridges with his mother and sister, because anyone who leaves the Jehovah's Witnesses is viewed as under Satan's control. We discussed a variety of possible places to do the intervention. We wanted to get her as far away from cult influences as possible. Larry decided to invite Greg and Sally to travel to the island of Jamaica with him. I recommended an ex-member named Rebecca to help us with the intervention. Rebecca is a sweet, compassionate person who appears very youthful. She is also a devout Christian who is comfortable talking about her faith.

Sally agreed to go. When she arrived, she was asked by her father to meet with me, and she refused. While Larry, Greg and I discussed alternative strategies, Rebecca decided to sit at the pool-side and wait. To her surprise, Sally sat down next to her. A conversation ensued, and Sally began proselytizing. Rebecca listened quietly for a few minutes. Then she remarked, "These things that you're saying sound familiar to me. You see, I was involved with a group similar to yours when I was your age." Rebecca's loving manner reached Sally, and she began building a relationship with her. They talked for hours. That evening, Sally agreed to meet with me, which ultimately led to a successful intervention. Within a year of Sally's decision to leave the JW's, Felicia decided to leave also.

C. Using family counseling as a focal point

Unlike exit-counseling, the Strategic Interaction Approach uses family counseling to help bring the cult member closer to other family members. By focusing on healing and improving communication within the entire family, we take pressure off the cult member, and identify more general underlying issues. A traditional family counseling session is held at the therapist's office for one or two hours. In the SIA intervention, we do long, sometimes marathon sessions, and often we do them at home. Loved ones who have participated in extended cult workshops are usually open to a multiple-day intervention.

They may be especially motivated to attend if the intervention is presented to them as a time to work on the family's problems: "We have been going to counseling to try to deal with some of the issues in the family. You are an important part of the family, and we'd love to have you there with us." Once you have developed rapport and trust, you might identify the loved one's cult involvement as one of the issues at hand: "We want to talk about all of these issues, including some things that have come up about your group involvement."

When participating in counseling sessions at home, I am able

to understand the family better by observing the home environment. Is the house orderly or chaotic? What are the decorations
like? Who are the people in the photographs? What do these pictures tell me? For example, if pictures of the father always show
him holding the same one of his three daughters, I might assume
he has a closer relationship with that daughter. Family members
will also have their own positive and negative associations with the
home environment. If the cult member or an important Team
member has particularly negative associations with home, the
intervention should probably be held somewhere else — perhaps at
a neighbor's or close friend's house.

During an SIA family counseling session, I ask the cult member
a series of questions to help me better understand his perspective:
"What was it like growing up in your family? How did you feel
about your father? Your mother? Your brother?" In addition to
identifying his personal family concerns, I am trying to develop
rapport, and also to elicit the pre-cult self.

My aim is to help the loved one shift his point of view. For
example, if the cult member mentions a specific family problem, he
is being drawn out of the cult mentality and into the family system.
For example, a cult member might tell her father, "Dad, you've
been going to a shrink for sixteen years to deal with your shyness,
and you're just as shy today as you were when you started." For the
father, this is an opportunity to model positive change by breaking
out of his rut. He might admit that he is stuck and wants to change
his behavior, and say, "You're right. What I've been doing isn't
working, so maybe I should see someone else—try something different."

Another issue that often comes up during counseling is conflict
over spirituality. For example, a member of a political cult may
complain that his Catholic parents are too rigid in their beliefs. If
the family is agnostic, a religious cult member may say that they
should have more faith. In both cases, I work to promote the idea

that we all have the right to believe different things. However, it helps to be able to step into each other's shoes to make sure that we are making healthy choices. Discussing within the family how the group uses social influence methods to promote beliefs can encourage the cult member to reality-test. The point is not to focus so much on the beliefs themselves but on the way the group exploits the four components of BITE. Ideally, both cult member and family will be motivated to find common areas of agreement, and to accept one another.

It is a good idea to take regular breaks. This gives the cult member time to take a walk, reflect or pray alone or, if he prefers, with the family. I have found some of the most significant conversations take place during the breaks.

THE THREE-DAY INTERVENTION

Although there is no such thing as a typical SIA intervention, it is helpful when planning an intervention to think in terms of the three-day model. Below I sketch the basic steps that I usually take each of the three days. To illustrate this model, I will describe a case that is representative of my approach. All names and identifying features have been changed in this story.

Jan Thompson, a young member of a yoga guru cult in southern California, had been put through very intense mind control techniques—everything from sleep deprivation, to immersion in freezing cold water, extensive sauna baths, and long periods of meditation and chanting. After she had been involved for over a year, her family flew to California to visit her. There, they were able to "befriend" the leader and obtain permission for Jan to come east for a visit home to get some "trust" money. That's when they asked me to step in and help plan an intervention.

As it turned out, the guru had been kicked out of another state where he had used a different name. I was able to track down more information about him and learned that he was using the more attractive women as prostitutes to raise money for the group. Of course, the members of Jan's family were extremely concerned, and wanted to act immediately. Fortunately, through mini-interactions, they had planted enough seeds in her mind that she was willing to meet with me.

Day One

Typically, most of day one is spent building rapport and trust, gathering information, getting everyone to connect as much as possible with the cult member, and laying the groundwork for the next two days. In some cases, we will begin general discussions of mind control and cults. We may watch videotapes of programs on social influence, such as Dr. Philip Zimbardo's "Discovering Psychology," or shows on social psychology experiments like the Milgram, Asch, or Stanford prison experiments. I usually share aspects of my own cult involvement, and try to highlight those points that would be most relevant to my client. It helps that I have over two decades of experiences to draw on, and it becomes crystal clear that I have "walked the walk."

Because the first full day of Jan's intervention involved family counseling issues, she really felt like she was being heard. We took turns listening as Jan and her family talked about their feelings, and then moved on to a few structured exercises. For example, I asked each person to say three things they liked about each other, as well as three things they would like to change. I asked to meet with each family member for a few minutes alone. When it came to Jan's turn, we wound up spending a lot longer, which allowed me to gain rapport and trust with her. She felt that I understood her and could advocate for her at times when confronting family dynamics.

Day Two

During day two, we delve more deeply into the cult mind control issue. If the three-part phobia cure has not been accomplished, I make sure to talk about phobias and do a phobia intervention with the person. I usually go into greater detail about my own cult experience, and ask probing questions about the person's experience with her group. This is a good time to introduce a former member of her group. If I've contacted any experts—such as a theologian, a Buddhist teacher or scholar, or a rabbi—I also try to bring them in on day two, if not sooner.

In Jan's case, I coached the family to start raising some of their questions and concerns on day two. Later, I asked to speak again with her privately, where she might feel more comfortable talking about her experiences. I also addressed her phobias. For Jan, day two marked the transition from family counseling to doing educational cult counseling. I showed her videotapes of other guru cults, and helped her understand how the practice of meditation had made her more susceptible to accept cult beliefs uncritically.

Day Three

On day three, we pursue more in-depth discussions about the specific beliefs of the group, such as theological questions that the cult member might have. Of course, day three builds on the progress made in the previous two days. Hopefully, by this time, the person is making important connections, and asking direct questions about her own group.

Since I had done research on the leader of Jan's group, I was able to present her with information about him that disturbed her greatly. It turned out that Jan had not yet been asked to perform any sexual activities, but was getting close to that point. She was aware that some of the women in the group spent time at a massage parlor, but the revelation of her leader's prostitution ring was nevertheless quite shocking to her. At the end of the third day, Jan's family was overjoyed when she announced that she had decided to stay home and receive additional follow-up counseling.

ALTERNATIVE STRATEGIES

It is possible that you are dealing with a situation in which the SIA, as I've described it, is unworkable. The cult member may be unreachable or unresponsive to the family's appeals. The family might be fragmented, and some family members may not be able to regain trust from the cult member for the time being. But if your efforts to communicate are not working, you have other options.

To begin with, you can organize a support system of families with loved ones in the same group. If the cult owns a business, as did Heaven's Gate, you can contact non-cult personnel in the business and conduct mini-interactions to educate them about the group and enlist their help. You can work with ex-members to create a cult awareness action group in your city, if one does not already exist. My hope is to do training around the world for those individuals, particularly former members, who want to be activists.

You can also use the media to draw public attention to the group's activities. Cult leaders often go to great lengths to create a positive image of the group. When Cathryn Mazer's family appeared at the Moonie center accompanied by NBC's *The Today Show*'s cameras to talk to their daughter, the cult began paying attention to their requests. The producer interviewed Cathryn, and it was clear that she was not exercising her free will. *The Today Show* decided to do a show featuring the family's plight and asked me to appear in the segment with the President of the American Unification Church. The resulting show was a public relations nightmare for the cult. The public saw a family being torn apart by a so-called religious group, one spouting so-called "family values", that would not allow Cathryn to see her own brother.

After the show, the family was contacted by the producer of another national television show that wanted to do a segment. I encouraged Cathryn's family to play hardball. I suggested they call the Moon leader they were dealing with and tell him about the invitation. I told them to tell the Moonies that if Cathryn were immediately put on a plane and sent home, the family wouldn't do the show. In the meantime, Cathryn was very upset about being kept from her family. She was sent home. She agreed to counseling, and went on *The Today Show* several months later. She was vibrant and articulate as she explained what had happened to her and warned the public about the dangers of cult mind control. She ended her appearance with an appeal to family members to "never lose hope."

Her family had broken new ground. They showed how the media could be used as a vital part of a rescue strategy. Our strategy worked because the media was willing to do the proper research, get the right personnel, and dramatically showed the cult influence on Cathryn and her family. A half-hearted effort by a less important, less popular show probably would not have worked. Also, it is important to note that the Moonies were vulnerable to this approach because of their high public profile as publishers of *The Washington Times* newspaper and owners of the University of Bridgeport, Connecticut. A small, unknown cult would not believe they had as much to lose by having a show done on them.

Remember to use the Internet to seek out information, to find others with similar concerns, and to spread the word about destructive cults. Visit different newsgroups that discuss cult-related subjects, such as alt.religion.unification, alt.religion.scientology and ex-cult.support. Search the Web for recent news about cults, contacts with ex-members and experts, and possible cult-generated Web sites.

When communication is cut off, some families have put up Web pages to publicize information about their loved ones. This is most effective when the page contains photographs of family, friends, pets, and home, and the message is positive: "We love you. We miss you. Please call, write a letter, or send an e-mail. We want to know that you're safe." Such a web site can also alert other cult watchers (and readers of this book) who might be able to be of assistance.

If you decide to design your own Web page, be careful not to merely attack the group. Even when a family member or friend has been critical for years, toning it down and taking a more balanced approach will be most effective. Recently, a cult member's daughter insisted on posting a Web page to expose the group's practices. I told her to start with a smiling picture of her mother and herself, and tell her story in a calm, rational way: "I love my Mom. I haven't seen her since last year. She has been told that she can't leave the group, that if she leaves, she will die. This is an example of phobia programming."

FINANCIAL ISSUES

The costs associated with helping a loved one in a cult can add up quickly, and money often becomes an obstacle. Families with limited financial resources face difficult decisions about expenses and possible sources of money to help. Although financing an intervention may seem hopeless at first, there is usually a way to make it possible. For some, this will mean getting a second job. For others, this will mean cashing in stock, dipping into a savings account or trust fund, or applying for a second mortgage.

A cult member's father once told me that, to him, the cost of an intervention effort is worth at least the price of tuition for a year of college. At a top private college, that can run $20,000 to $30,000. To many families, it makes sense to use money set aside for college, especially when a cult member has dropped out of school to follow the group. Creativity and persistence will help you find unique ways to fund an intervention, and it should cost less than the figure above. It might mean tracking down lost family members or friends who are willing to help. It may be necessary to first convince them that the person is under mind control. In certain cases, counselors are willing to negotiate flexible payment terms or lowered fees. In recent years, my pro-bono counseling efforts have gone primarily to counseling cult walk-outs who have no money or family.

Family members who work together and pool their resources can reduce expenses. In some cases, two or more families with loved ones in a cult will share time as well as money, conducting mini-interactions for one another and holding group workshops. Others have raised funds through public appeals for help (often on the Internet). Some have started second businesses, such as mail-order enterprises. A significant amount of money can be saved simply by cutting expenses. For instance, family members could make an effort to make more long-distance calls on weekends. A computer-literate Team member might teach others how to use free, Internet-based telephone programs. These days, the cost of computers is decreasing rapidly, and they can even be leased. The more work you do on your own, the less you will have to pay a counselor. By reading this book, you have already saved thousands of dollars on consultation fees.

If family members are truly in need—sick, unemployed, impoverished—there are many humanitarian organizations that might be willing to contribute money. Some families appeal to their church or temple for help. Another route is to hire a grant-writer that might try contacting appropriate foundations on behalf of the family. I hope that one day, Freedom of Mind Resource Center will be well-funded and able to assist those in dire financial need.

WARNING: Money is often a loaded subject for cult members as well as ex-members. In fact, some ex-members feel tremendous guilt regarding financial expenditures by their families to help them. Some people actually insist on repaying the family for the cost of the intervention. Nevertheless, family members are best advised to avoid discussing financial issues around the cult member. Such discussions usually lead him to one of two conclusions: either "The family is materialistic, and only cares about money," or "The family is paying too much, so I'll save them the expense by declining the invitation." If your loved one ever asks about the cost, respectfully refuse and say that money is not the issue: "We're not worried about that. We just care about you." I have unfortunately heard of parents using the issue of money to manipulate ex-members and induce guilt. This is very damaging and undermines not only the relationship but also the recovery efforts as well.

AFTER THE INTERVENTION

A successful intervention will help to connect with and liberate an individual's authentic identity. If it is done properly, at the end of a counseling intervention, everyone is tired but relieved. In the unlikely event the person says that he still wants to stay in the group, family members should express their disappointment, but remain encouraged that they have done what they could to help. Progress has been achieved. It is useful to summarize what the experience has meant for family members. If the cult member wants time and needs distance to reflect, try to maintain meaningful communication (telephone, letters, and visits), and continue building a new relationship with him. Remind him that he now has a valuable understanding of mind control and cult tactics. It is good to discuss the possibility that the cult might try to call him a hero for refusing to leave, and distort what happened to make it seem like the intervention was involuntary and coercive. Ask him to always remember what really happened, rather than accepting the group's distortion of what happened.

If your loved one decides to leave the group, there is still a lot of work to be done. Physically leaving a cult will not necessarily resolve all of a person's issues. Former cult members need time to readjust to life outside of the group, and to seek answers to the questions raised by their decision to leave. This period of soul-searching can be rewarding, but it is an arduous process, and family members should be available for support and encouragement. Most people who leave cults will benefit greatly from post-cult counseling sessions. Others will need more intensive help, and may seek psychotherapy or spend time in a halfway house like Wellspring, in Ohio, or Meadow Haven, in Massachusetts.

Destructive cults teach their members to block out information and suppress feelings. A person who walks out of a cult needs to reconnect with the world and with himself. Remind your loved one that knowledge is power and that emotions tell us important things about reality. Encourage him to educate himself about what happened to him by reading and reflecting, and to get in touch with his feelings — for example, by venting frustration in appropriate ways. The more he opens up to you, the sooner both of you will be able to identify any lingering problems that might be hampering the recovery process.

Dealing with common ex-member problems

The healing process can differ from person to person. For some people, making plans to get back to work or school as quickly as possible is a good decision. For most people, though, taking time to work through their problems is best. With the support of family and friends, they won't have to rush their healing process. Many ex-members want to help friends still in the cult, or assist other families who are dealing with a cult involvement. Soon after I left the Moonies, and despite my parent's initial protests, I decided to help others to re-evaluate their cult involvement. I found helping people to get out of the Moon cult was a real benefit in my own recovery. With each case during that first year, I was able to free myself a little bit more from the cult mind set. Listening to other people spout the same exact Moonie rhetoric as I had was very liberating. I am glad that I could turn a negative personal experience into a positive one for myself and so many others. My hope is that reading this book will inspire other former members to heal themselves, and reach out to help others.

Depression, nightmares, panic attacks

Even years after leaving a cult, dealing with cult issues can be traumatic. Former cult members suffer from a wide variety of difficulties as a result of the cult's manipulations. Most cult members feel depressed during the first few months of post-cult life. Some compare the experience to falling head-over-heels in love, only to be realize that their lover was two-faced and just using them. Others liken their involvement to a spiritual rape of their soul. Without proper counseling, they can still have intact phobias and a fragmented sense of self.

Nightmares are a common symptom of fear in former cult members. In severe cases, a person will experience panic and anxiety attacks, and some develop a form of post-traumatic stress disorder (PTSD). Psychosomatic symptoms, such as headaches, allergies, and asthma, can make matters worse. Ex-members who have panic attacks, eating or sleeping disorders, or persistent nightmares should definitely seek additional counseling as soon as possible.

Ex-members typically feel tricked, used, and psychologically defeated, and their pain can be so intense that it blocks out all hope for a better future. Family members should help their loved ones through this period of grieving by encouraging a balanced and hopeful perspective. Let them know that other people have made it through situations that were as bad and, perhaps, even more painful. Don't forget to encourage any positives, if the ex-member talks about them. Point out how the experience can be used to make them stronger and wiser. Be patient. Don't rush a person to go faster than they can go. It is common for the family to want the person to just "get over it." It isn't something that can heal quickly. Everyone has to go at their own speed.

Encourage independent decision-making

Cult members are expected to surrender autonomy, and often must ask permission for routine activities, like using the bathroom. As a result, ex-members can agonize over the smallest of decisions, like what to eat, what to wear, what to read, and when to sleep. After an intervention, they sometimes shift the devotion given to a cult leader onto a counselor or other Team member. Friends and family should also be sensitive to possible tendencies toward dependence on others or transference of loyalty.

It is very common for ex-members to ask for direction and advice. Ex-members are frequently caught in the "one right way" mode of thinking. Since one of your goals is to help your loved one act independently, be sensitive and gently encourage him to make his own choices. You can do this by avoiding the tendency to tell him what to do. Instead, ask, "What do you want to do?" or "Which do you think is the better choice? Why?" Facilitate the decision-making process by encouraging the person to make the best decision possible and to learn from the experience.

In time, the family can help a former member recover the ability to make decisions for himself, rather than depend on someone else for advice and direction. People need to learn to make timely decisions and live with their consequences. They need to develop confidence that they can make good decisions and that they will learn from bad experiences. For example, if they make the wrong choice when ordering something to eat, the worst that can happen is they don't like the taste of their food, have a stomach-ache, and waste money. Everyone makes mistakes—to err is human—but hopefully we learn from the experience.

Psychological strength

Long-term members often exhibit psychological impairments, such as a loss of concentration and memory. When I first left the Moon cult, I had great difficulty just reading a book. I had to retrain my brain, by reading, re-reading, and looking up words I had forgotten, to process information on my own. Like an atrophied muscle, my mind needed exercise to restore its former level of performance.

Trust

Another common problem is a lack of trust. Ex-members sometimes feel that they can never trust anyone again — least of all themselves. They fear intimacy and avoid commitment to people, jobs, and even hobbies, because they worry about taking another emotional risk. They need to have the tools to assess new people and situations, and to understand that when they were recruited into a cult, they didn't have those tools. They need to understand that they were vulnerable to cult influence because they didn't understand mind control and were deceived into an involvement. Now they know better. They need to forgive themselves, and trust that they have new tools to make good decisions.

Shame and guilt

Ex-members typically have strong feelings of shame and guilt. I felt "stupid" for getting involved with the cult, and at first didn't want people I met to know about my two years as a Moonie. I also felt guilty about all of the lies I told, and things I had done as a Moon leader, especially all of the people I had recruited. It was hard for me to face how much pain I had caused my family and friends.

Cult members need to be reassured that it is perfectly normal to regret having participated in harmful behaviors, such as deception, and in unethical or illegal activities, such as theft, fraud, and prostitution.

They should also realize that it is common to miss aspects of cult life, whether it be friends still in the group, or the feeling of being involved in something "special." The desire to help people still in the group needs to be balanced with the need to get on with their own lives. It is imperative that ex-members develop a strong grounding within themselves so that contact with cult members won't draw them back into the cult mindset.

Fear

Some cults teach their members that people who leave the group are the enemy and should be hurt. While such intimidation should be taken seriously, actual incidents of violence are rare. Fear of negative publicity usually keeps the group from retaliating. Ex-members need to realistically appraise the potential for cult retribution. Here they might draw upon the discussion of phobias in Chapter 10. In addition, I recommend that they read *The Gift of Fear*, by Gavin DeBecker.[3] An expert on violence and security issues, DeBecker teaches how to assess the warning signs in dangerous situations, and encourages people to pay attention to their "fear" intuition.

"Floating"

The extreme identity confusion caused by membership in a cult can follow an ex-member for years, causing flashbacks in which the person "floats" back to the time of his involvement. In an instant, the cult identity can be triggered by a stimulus, such as an image, sound, or smell, that was instrumental in their manipulation.

During my first year out of the cult (1976), the word "moon" would cause me to think "Father," see an image of Sun Myung Moon, and begin to think from within my cult identity.

This dissociative state, which is known as "floating," can be a significant obstacle for former cult members. Involuntary episodes are most common among people who were exposed to trance-inducing techniques, such as chanting, meditation, and speaking in tongues. Floating is particularly scary for those who lack an understanding of mind control. People who leave a cult without counseling are often confused and terrified by the experience, and begin to feel irrational guilt and fear over having left the group.

Undoing "triggers"

The initial panic caused when one discovers he was "floating" can usually be alleviated with a firm self-reminder that it is a natural symptom of mind control that can be healed. To gain control over "floating," a person must first identify the trigger, which could be internal (a thought or mental image) or external (a person or place). The next step is to learn a new response to the trigger by systematically calling forth the stimulus and creating a different association. For instance, I would repeat the word "moon" over and over, visualize the moon, and say to myself, "The earth has only one natural satellite, the moon." By reinforcing the actual meaning of "moon" rather than the cult connotation, I was able to neutralize and re-associate the trigger that caused me to float.

A trigger is an anchor for an experience and can involve one or more of the five senses. Fortunately, the mind is capable of one-trial learning, and ex-members can use this capability to undo cult triggers. What they need is to become conscious of how they process information using the five senses:

1. Visual images can be associated (participatory) or dissociated (observational). They can be seen in color or black-and-white, in focus or out of focus, in two or three dimensions, and from assorted perspectives—larger, smaller, from below, and from above. To neutralize a visual trigger, for example, a picture of the cult leader, the member might imagine watching himself looking at it (dissociated image), rather than looking at it directly (associated image). He can also practice adjusting its color, focus, and size.

2. Auditory information includes words, volume, tone, speed, timbre, and voice. Some ex-cult members cannot listen to certain pieces of music, for example Mozart sonatas, played by the cult. When I first left the Moonies, I could not listen to a Korean accent without becoming upset. The key to undoing auditory triggers is, first, to become conscious and, next, to make healthy associations, for example, by attending a Mozart concert with good friends, or by speaking to Koreans who are not cult members.

3. Kinesthetic (feeling) information is registered as pleasure or pain, heat or cold, smooth or rough, and internal or external. A kinesthetic trigger might be doing a bow at the waist or praying while sitting on one's knees. It could be a particular yoga posture, like sitting in the lotus position. By becoming aware and forming new associations—performing those actions in new settings with a different frame of mind—we can neutralize such triggers.

4. Olfactory (smell) information can be positive or negative, interesting or dull, sweet or sour. Olfactory triggers include the smell of foods, incense, scented candles. If a cult member worked in a fish-processing plant, it might be the smell of fish.

5. Gustatory (taste) information may be positive or negative, spicy or bland, sweet or tart. Cult members often develop aversions to foods they commonly ate when in the cult. For me it was fast foods, like McDonald's Big Macs, and Korean foods such as kim chee. As with the first three senses, a person can identify olfactory and gustatory triggers and make new associations.

This technique for undoing "triggers" is especially important to apply to cult "loaded language." Encourage your loved one to write down common cult words he finds himself using. Then ask him to go to a good dictionary and read the real definitions of the word.[4] Ex-members will be much better off if they can make new associations, rather than merely avoid words used in the cult. Especially for those who were in cults for many years, neutralizing the cult terms and using regular words to describe "reality" will help speed up the recovery process.

Ex-members will also benefit by making a conscious effort to use words that are productive. Depending on how it is framed, even well-meaning self-talk, like "Don't think that you're stupid" or "Don't worry that people are coming to get you," can create the opposite effect. A more effective approach is to think in the positive, for example, by remembering one's intellectual achievements or reassuring oneself that he knows how to protect himself.

Overcome Black-and-White, All-or-Nothing Thinking

If you observe your loved one exhibiting cult thinking, such as making black-and-white, all-or-nothing statements, gently point it out to him. It takes time for former members to realize that the world has "grays" and a full spectrum of color! Gently point out other possibilities if you see the ex-member looking for another set of absolute answers to fill the void created by their membership.

Don't dismiss spiritual experiences

Family and friends should be careful never to dismiss, minimize, or put down so-called "spiritual" experiences. A more effective response is to discuss alternative interpretations. Show how other ex-members you have talked with or heard about came to understand their cult experiences into their current worldview.

Nurture the authentic self

Families should encourage former members to recover their authentic self: their true values, beliefs, dreams, and goals. If the person disapproves of his pre-cult self, it is probably because the authentic self has not yet been fully realized. In these cases, a family member may help their loved one to build a new identity he can be proud of.

Part of restoring the authentic identity involves dealing with feeling the loss of believing you are part of an elite group. Ex-members often miss the "high" associated with cult beliefs that they were saving the world, creating the Kingdom of Heaven on earth, or achieving enlightenment. However, there are healthy substitutes for the emotional rush experienced by some cult members. When the energy and enthusiasm of an ex-member is channeled in positive directions, he often finds true fulfillment. For instance, maybe the person will find a benevolent, humanitarian organization which actually accomplishes some of the goals that motivated the person to join a cult in the first place. When discussing such possibilities, be sure to emphasize integrity, honesty, spirituality, and human service.

Ex-members need to know there is nothing "defective" about them. They often must be reminded that they are intelligent, and that there are millions of others who have gone through similar experiences. They should understand that when they joined the group, they made what they believed was the best choice at the time. Now they know more: they understand mind control. They know what questions to ask, what behaviors to watch out for, and how to depend on friends and family for reality-testing. Encourage the ex-member to understand that new resources, information, and perspectives can help him change and grow.

Modeling

Modeling can enable a person to examine and change behavior by helping to identify patterns and psychological roadblocks. It is useful, for instance, to be able to recognize, and articulate, the difference between what you do not want (a mediocre job) and knowing what you do want (a fulfilling career). This distinction is related to a person's motivational style, which, as we've discussed, can be either defensive (moving away from a negative) or assertive (moving toward a positive). Both strategies are natural and valuable, but assertive motivation is by far the best in allowing a person to break out of a rut and grow as a person. Former cult members should be asked to identify their own style and work on developing the "moving towards a positive" style. When setting goals (what you want to do and what you want to avoid), it is good to consider short- and long-term consequences of each choice.

When an ex-member feels stuck, this feeling is often related to his personal locus of control. Does he have an external reference (like depending on an authority figure) or an internal reference for direction in life? Even when a former member rejects his group's leadership, he can still harbor subconscious loyalty to a leader or surrogate authority figures. An essential step in breaking free from cult mind control is developing an internal locus of control which allows the person to make his own informed choices.

Time orientation is another perspective that former members should consider. It is impossible for a former member to heal if he feels stuck in the past (memories of cult life) or the present (adjusting to post-cult life). Family members should empower their loved one to see life not just in terms of the present, but of the short- and long-term future. Visualizing the positive possibilities in each will help him to identify worthwhile and achievable goals.

Insight can also be gained by working with the various parts of a person's identity, or sub-personalities, that were used to create the cult identity. If the idealist part of an ex-member's identity was used to manipulate him, he may end up adopting an extremely cynical attitude if this sub-personality is neglected after cult involvement. A former member can begin the process of self-discovery by seeking out, accepting, and communicating with different sub-personalities. For example, an ex-member whose "hero" part was co-opted by the cult must learn to value the good intentions represented by this sub-personality, such as fighting for one's beliefs. At that point, he can begin to integrate the "hero" into a post-cult identity.

A POWERFUL SELF-HEALING STRATEGY

I believe that to heal from destructive mind control, one must learn to control one's own mind. In fact, I am writing a recovery book in which I will present methods that I have used in my own recovery, and in my counseling with ex-members, to regain such mental control. Meanwhile, I offer the following exercise. It is one of the most important and effective self-healing strategies that I have ever encountered. Practice it in a step-by-step manner.

Step One

First, the former member starts by writing a detailed outline of his cult experiences—in essence, a time line beginning before his recruitment and ending with his departure from the group. This time line should include both positive and negative events, as well as people, places, and activities. By recording all of these memories, the person will be in a better position to process his involvement. Once the outline is in place, the ex-member should sort through his notes to trigger memories of additional positive, negative, and curious or "strange" experiences. The aim is to recover thoughts, feelings, and behaviors that might have been ignored or repressed while he was in the cult, and to assess values and beliefs that were distorted by the group.

Step Two

With this outline as a guide, former members visualize the scene of their recruitment from a dissociated or "observer" perspective, as if they were watching themselves on television. This differs dramatically from remembering it from an "associated" perspective—experiencing what they saw and felt at the time. Knowing that they can take control of their memories, and can choose to remember them from an observer perspective, is very powerful. Ex-members come to realize that they do not need to re-victimize themselves by re-experiencing their cult self each time they have a memory. The observer point of view should be the "default" setting for their cult experiences, the one that occurs automatically. If a person wants to re-experience the cult thoughts and feelings, all he needs to do is "step into" the picture again.

Step Three

The next step is perhaps the most significant part of the healing process. I suggest the client go back in time to crucial moments in his involvement and "re-do" them, with the new information, resources, and perspectives that he now has. He can say or do what he would do if he knew then what he knows now. During this exercise, he should keep in mind that:

- These negative things happened to a younger "you."
- You did the best you knew how at the time based on your knowledge and abilities.
- Now, you are older, wiser, and have more resources about mind control and cult practices.

By imagining how he would have acted differently, a person can integrate the new resources into the cult identity. For example, the cult member might imagine a different response to the cult recruiter. Instead of saying, "That sounds fascinating!" he can tell the person, "I'm not interested!" or "Leave me alone!" or "Go away before I expose the group publicly!" A critical piece in my own healing was going back to re-do a moment when Moon was telling leaders that there would come a time "when the Constitution would be amended to make it a capital offense for people to have sex with people other than the one assigned to them." Instead of agreeing wholeheartedly with Moon, I needed to tell Moon in front of the other leaders how crazy he was, and how I would never participate in a mass genocide, and that I was leaving the group. It felt so good to imagine that I could confront Moon and that I might persuade other leaders to come leave the group with me. It helped me transform and integrate my cult identity with my pre-cult and present self.

This technique of re-visualizing past problems with the added resources of the present is very effective and powerful. Cult members who have issues that stem from their childhood can envision the younger self taking power to act the way they would have wanted to. If necessary, they can work through major developmental stages to gain positive experiences. They can even return to past experiences with their mother, father, siblings, and friends so that they can learn to accept the mistakes of the past. The key to this technique is to build resources and enhance the individual's coping skills.

Help ease the transition to life outside the cult

The first year after leaving a cult should be viewed as a transitional period of healing where few (if any) major commitments — such as marriage or joining the military—are made. An ex-member must take one step at a time, and avoid taking on too much in an attempt to make up for lost time. Instead, he should plan manageable, practicable tasks and fulfill them, developing self-confidence and trust as he goes.

When a former member seems to be struggling for direction in post-cult life, vocational or pastoral counseling is a good choice. Many ex-members need practical advice about writing résumés, selecting schools to attend, subjects to pursue, how to make new friends, and how to communicate — in particular, how to talk about their cult experience. Open and supportive discussions with family and friends can help a loved one overcome the stigma of having been in a cult.

With the passage of time, former cult members will hopefully grow stronger and live happy, fulfilled lives. I believe that a key to a successful recovery depends on remembering, and reintegrating, the cult experience, rather than repressing it. Former members can take pride knowing that they have struggled for, and won, something very precious. Indeed, freedom is something that is often taken for granted until it is lost. It is my hope that everyone who has ever had a cult experience will never forget or deny that it really happened. It is by remembering that we may preserve freedom and work to make the world a better place.

Conclusion

We All Must Help!

My hope is that this book has helped you to understand how destructive mind control cults work. Even more important, I hope that it has encouraged you to take concrete actions to help your loved one and others in similar situations. My twenty-five years of first-hand experience have shown me the enormous misery and suffering that destructive cults have caused to people throughout the world. I am also aware of the present and future threat that mind control poses to people of all ages, races, religions, occupations, economic and educational backgrounds.

When a person is subjected to mind control, relatives and friends feel the effects. The impact ripples further. Co-workers and schoolmates may be affected if the cult instructs the member to proselytize or recruit. Physicians, mental health professionals, and clergy may find their efforts thwarted if the person they are trying to help belongs to a group that instills phobias against the medical, therapeutic, and religious "establishment." Innocent bystanders have been maimed and even killed by cults, like Aum Shinrikyo, which directed members to perform terrorist acts, and it may be only a matter of time before more cults practice biological terrorism. We can longer deny that the problem affects us all.

Yet many people are unaware of how cults exert their destructive influence. When I left the Moonies in 1976, the whole issue of cult mind control was shrouded in ignorance. Much has been revealed in the past twenty-five years—how cults instill phobias while preventing access to many of the tools people need to think for themselves. Unfortunately, few people have been exposed to this knowledge. As the events at Waco, Texas, have shown, many people think of cult members as fanatic, evil and deranged, to be treated with force rather than understanding.[1] Most people fail to recognize that those who join cults are usually intelligent, talented, idealistic, and motivated to contribute to the greater good. Like all decent human beings, they deserve respect and consideration.

I will never forget the simple gift of a cold drink on a hot day from a stranger as I sold flowers on a New York City street. By treating me with compassion, he helped to undo the Moonie-programmed belief that the "outside" world was evil. We should never pass up an opportunity to reach out to a cult member, whether he be someone we know or a stranger. It could help open the door to his freedom.

Over the past ten years, I have seen more long-term members come out of cults than ever before—a testament to the strength of the human spirit. Many other long-term cult members want to leave their group, but don't know where to go. Their families, who do not understand that their loved one is under mind control, may have cut them off because they were hurt by things that were said and done. I believe there are many long-term cult members who would walk out the minute they had the viable alternative of a job and a place to stay. Rejoining society and the workforce is especially difficult for someone who has been in a cult for twenty years. Outreach and job training programs, organized by a civic organization or church, could make a huge difference in the lives of long-term cult members.

I believe that the people who can make the greatest difference in helping to overcome the pervasive ignorance surrounding destructive mind control cults are my fellow former cult members.

I urge them, for their own and the greater good, to stand up and be counted. Get involved! Imagine what a positive impact it would have if thousands of engaged and educated former cult members started speaking openly about their experiences. Whenever a comment was made promoting a negative stereotype about cult members, they could expose the person's ignorance. Doing so might help save lives. Verbal and physical abuse of cult members by people who are ignorant of mind control is all-too-common, and unfortunately can push members even deeper into the group by reinforcing the cult belief that the outside world is evil. There is an added benefit. By standing up and speaking out about their experience, cult members may overcome their own residual feelings of shame or embarrassment. I encourage family, friends, and educated citizens to speak out too.

Sweeping attitudinal change will take time, but I believe there is reason to be optimistic. The excitement surrounding the Millennium is creating an atmosphere where the average person is getting informed about the potential for large-scale destructive cult activity. I hope that, through my own activities and by encouraging others to stand up and fight destructive mind control and the prejudice surrounding it, this new Millennium brings about a new age of freedom and tolerance. Hopefully, your reading of this book will help bring about that change.

To further the dream, I have compiled a wish list for the new Millennium. One of my aims in the coming years is to see that the non-profit Freedom of Mind Institute finds sufficient funding to achieve some of these wishes.

ACTIVISM FOR FREEDOM OF MIND

I would love to see more people, and especially former members and their friends and family, come forward and organize their own community. "Think globally, act locally," is an inspiring motto.

Local activist groups

In every city there should be an activist group with a web site
(featuring, among other things, a list of cult groups that are active
in the area), a local phone number with hot line, and a monthly
support group for former members and people trying to get loved
ones out of cults. Former cult members and their families would be
among the group's greatest resources. With their knowledge and
experience, they could advise others on how to help loved ones
leave cults and, possibly, participate in SIA teams. They might also
help each other in their own recovery process. Those who want to
remain anonymous could help in the background, for example, by
offering advice over the Internet, or by providing financial help to
those on the front lines.

Local missing persons bureau

In some cults, such as "The Brethren," members may be sent
far away so that they will not be found by their families. I would like
to see, in each city, a system for distributing "missing person
alerts," with pictures and vital information about the person. If
someone's loved one is known to be in a particular city, members of
that city's activist group might try locating and approaching the
person, for example, by attending a cult seminar.

Activist groups could coordinate their efforts to locate members with local police as well as civic organizations, mental health
professionals, religious institutions, and activist organizations in
other cities. One of the projects of Freedom of Mind Resource
Center will be to coordinate the efforts of activist groups who are
trying to locate missing people suspected of being in a cult.
Another project will be to train activists in the Strategic Interaction
Approach. If you want to set up an activist group in your community, the best way to start is by networking with others, either on
the Internet or by contacting the Institute for referrals.

THE GOVERNMENT

I believe that the government must do much more to protect citizens, cult members and nonmembers alike, from the effects of destructive mind control cults.[2]

Consumer bureau

As a first step, I would like to see a governmental agency established that serves to responsibly field consumer complaints concerning all kinds of non-profit organizations. I believe that any institution that benefits from tax-exempt status should be held accountable for its activities. Citizens should not have to support institutions that systematically practice deception, mind control, and fraud. If it can be proven that a group has deceived or defrauded its members and the public, it should lose its tax-exempt status. If a group abuses basic human rights, such as those espoused in the United Nations Universal Declaration of Human Rights, it should not have an exemption. With such a governmental entity in place, cult groups might be forced to change their policies, or else lose a great deal of money and status.

Investigation of cult lobbies

It is my sense that the big cults are exerting significant political influence through their lobbying efforts. To truly serve the public, the government must monitor and expose these cult lobbies. I would like to see an investigation of how cult groups are trying to influence specific legislation.

Public disclosure of past mind control research

Over the past four decades, the government, and particularly the CIA, has done a huge amount of research, much of it clandestine, in the area of mind control. I would like to see the reports of this research made available to the general public. Elected representatives should investigate the nature of the experiments performed, as well as their results, and make a definitive report to the citizens of this country about the evidence for mind control. Individuals in the military intelligence, or the CIA, should deliver an honest account to the public of what they believe mind control can and cannot achieve.

More funding for "open" mind control research in the future

I would like to see more federally-funded research on mind control. One area that needs attention is what I call the 'epidemiology of mind control cults.' Mind control can be dangerous to a person's physical and mental health, just like smoking, drinking, or HIV—the AIDS-causing virus. I want to see it treated like the public health threat that it is, with surveys done to ascertain prevalence, not only nationally, but in specific at-risk populations. For example, a study of college campuses might ask how many students have belonged, or been exposed, to a cult? I predict the numbers would be shockingly high. Another at-risk group is the elderly.

Public awareness campaigns

Based on its findings, the government might launch a campaign to raise awareness about the dangers of cults, just as it has done for smoking, seat belts, and drunk driving. The theme might be, "Think for yourself, take responsibility for your acts. Remember, only you can keep your mind free." Billboards, radio spots, television and newsprint advertising such a message would not only raise awareness but also save lives. We tried many years ago to introduce legislation to make November 18, Cult Awareness Day, in remembrance of the day that Leo J. Ryan and hundreds of others died in Jonestown. Perhaps, we could try again and call it "Freedom of Mind Day" not only to commemorate the suffering caused by cults but to celebrate our liberty.[3]

MENTAL HEALTH PROFESSIONALS

Psychiatrists, psychologists, social workers, mental health counselors, drug and alcohol counselors, suicide prevention specialists, social psychologists, family therapists...

There is a vital need for more research regarding all aspects of cult mind control. The scope of the problem needs to be identified. In addition, existing treatment approaches need to be evaluated and refined, and new ones, like the SIA, developed and implemented. Private, as well as public, funding might subsidize this research.

Basic research into mind control

I predict that a study of inpatients in mental hospitals will reveal that a significant percentage of them were once in a destructive cult. Research confirming this hypothesis is vital since such patients could be more susceptible to suicidal thoughts, resulting from cult phobias that go untreated. For the same reason, I would like to see a study of suicides and suicide attempts to see how many are linked to a cult involvement. I would also be curious to see how many prison inmates have been exposed to mind control through abusive families, gangs, or cults. I have been told that destructive cults are actively recruiting prisoners and converting them. This should be investigated.

Perhaps the one area of scientific research that holds the greatest promise for demonstrating the reality of mind control is functional brain imaging. Using the latest imaging techniques, researchers might try imaging a person performing a particular task while still in a cult, just after leaving a cult, and after cult counseling therapy. Identifying affected brain regions would not only provide definitive evidence of the power of mind control, but might also suggest therapeutic strategies.

Better diagnosis and treatment of patients with cult histories

When interviewing new clients, professionals should make sure to ask whether their clients have had, or currently have, a cult involvement. There is no doubt in my mind that most current and former cult members in the mental health system are not getting proper treatment. Many are inappropriately given medication, reinforcing the cult phobia that they "will go crazy" if they leave the cult.

Former cult members, particularly those who experienced prolonged states of altered consciousness, such as meditating many hours a day for years, should be given psychological tests, including dissociative disorder examinations. It would be interesting, and potentially valuable, to see whether people who are experiencing similar symptoms, for example, headaches and auras, practiced the same meditative techniques. Such knowledge could be used to develop new and more specific methods of treatment.

There should be more facilities set up modeled on the Wellspring Retreat, which has been using pioneering therapeutic approaches to help those who have been subjected to mind control. I have recommended the program to many people, who have since reported to me that they benefited greatly by their participation.[4]

More holistic treatment of patients with cult histories

I believe that holistic approaches can be very effective in helping ex-cult members. Art, music, and massage therapy, and methods of psychodrama can be extraordinarily useful. Art and music therapies are non-verbal means for expressing emotion and may be particularly effective for releasing painful memories. Massage therapy, which helps a person get in touch with his body, could be especially therapeutic for individuals who were taught by their cults to deny their feelings, or have "out of body" experiences. In the hands of a skilled practitioner, patients would learn to pay attention to what their body is feeling, areas of tension, as well as how to relax. Again, research evaluating the relative merits of various holistic therapies is needed.

Training in the Strategic Interaction Approach

One of my goals in writing this book has been to teach the fundamentals of the SIA. In the future, I would love to see more mental health professionals receive SIA training and I plan to hold workshops for this purpose. While I hope to appeal to all mental health professionals, I would like to make a special plea to former cult members. Those with at least a master's degree in counseling have the ideal background for doing SIA counseling. Those without the degree could build a rewarding career by obtaining counseling training. Of course, anyone with a dedication to helping others can make a difference. Once trained, these counselors could establish recovery centers for former cult members in every large city.

RELIGIOUS INSTITUTIONS AND CLERGY

It is essential that every major religious institution become proactively involved in the fight for freedom of mind.

Preventive education and counseling

Leaders of legitimate faiths should establish preventive education programs, as well as counseling programs to help those already affected. In seminaries, curricula should include courses on how to counsel people in mind-control groups. Religious leaders should speak out against groups that give their religion a bad name. For example, they might show how extremist Bible cults impugn Christian principles with their unrelenting injunctions and lack of forgiveness and understanding. Buddhists might show how individuals like Frederick Lenz, who professed meditation as a means to money and success, are perverting true Buddhist philosophy and practice.

Interfaith declaration for ethical proselytizing

I would like to see religious leaders get together and write a document outlining ethical means of proselytizing. The contract would guarantee that anyone interested in a particular group be provided with the following: a full disclosure of the teachings of the group, a full disclosure of the leader's background, a declaration of what membership will entail (for example, fasting, celibacy), and a guarantee not to harass anyone who is not interested in joining. A group's refusal to agree to the charter would be grounds for suspicion.

LEGAL PROFESSIONALS

One of the potentially most effective instruments for change is the law. We need to utilize and, if necessary, change aspects of our system of justice to protect people from destructive mind control cults, and to exact retribution when they have been harmed.

Hold cults legally accountable for their actions

I would love to hold a series of conferences for lawyers and judges with the aim of identifying whether particular cult practices fall within the limits of the law. It is my hope that, eventually, a case may reach the Supreme Court that will set a new legal precedent concerning the practices of mind control cults. As it is, there has yet to be a case decided by the Supreme Court that establishes what actually constitutes mind control, for example, whether or not physical coercion is necessary. Nor has it been legally determined whether a predominance of experts in the field say that mind control exists. Until this happens, the entire question of whether mind control theory meets the United States Supreme Court's test for the admissibility of expert testimony will not be resolved. In the meantime, lawyers might work with families of loved ones, and with ex-members, to develop proactive legal strategies for the purpose of exposing the wrongdoings of cults.

New legal measures and procedures

Judges might give renewed consideration to how cult members are prosecuted by the legal system. Like Patty Hearst, members may have committed crimes while under the influence of mind control.

In the case of cult members whose physical or mental health is at risk, I would like to see some type of legal option by which families could gain access to a loved one for the purpose of medical evaluation.

Citizen involvement in the legal system

We can all learn to use the legal system to hold cults account-able for their actions. For example, any organization that conducts business is regulated by State and Federal laws requiring minimum wages and standard working conditions and hours. There are non-profit groups, such as Cheryl Larsen's Group Research Institute (www.groupresearch.org), that draw attention to questionable cult activities, like failing to compensate their followers who work in their businesses, refusing to pay taxes, and keeping records from their members. You might also contact the Attorney General's office or register a complaint with the Better Business Bureau. Be forewarned that your name may go on public record.

Legal defense fund

Some cults sue their former members and critics in order to create an atmosphere of fear. We need to establish a legal defense fund to support people who are courageous enough to challenge destructive groups. Lawyers who are educated about issues concerning cult mind control might be prepared to take cases on contingency fees only (usually 30% of a damages award), so that former cult members who are penniless have legal recourse. FACTNet.org has created a huge database to assist attorneys in litigation with Scientology. Some lawyers with experience in this area might be willing to work pro bono in addition to their compensated work.

THE MEDIA

Members of the media have traditionally served a vital watch-dog function—exposing major social problems and political injustices. They not only educate, but can also motivate people to make personal and societal changes.

More in-depth coverage of the cult mind control phenomenon

More than almost any other institution, the media stands to make a difference in how people think about cults, and may actually save people from the costly mistake of joining one. Unfortunately, in recent years, news media seem to be focusing more on profits, on what will sell, and less on what will make a social difference. In particular, there seems to be a conscious avoidance of cult stories that might result in costly litigation by cult groups.

There are some excellent exceptions. In 1991, *Time* magazine published a cover story, called "Scientology: The Cult of Greed."[5] Scientology sued *Time* and ultimately lost when Richard Behar was found to have done a responsible job of reporting. *The New York Times* has written major stories that expose wrongdoings of several cult groups. Likewise, major television shows, such as *60 Minutes*, *Dateline*, and *20/20* , have done numerous stories on different cult groups. When Oklahoma City was bombed, David Koresh's compound in Waco was besieged, and thirty-nine members of Heaven's Gate committed suicide, there was intense media coverage.

My major complaint with the media is that they have focused too much on a particular cult group's wacky beliefs and not enough on explaining their coercive mind control techniques. Stories typically focus on the content of a particular cult's practices and beliefs, and do not delve into how intelligent people are indoctrinated into accepting them. I suspect that one reason they have not done so is that advertisers, who themselves employ psychological influence techniques, may prefer not to have their own secrets revealed.

Virtually every day, a cult story is being reported somewhere in the world. No doubt, there will be many more as we enter the 21st century. One of my hopes for the new Millennium is that the media will become a major force to educate the public about its susceptibility to the social and psychological influence techniques practiced by such groups.

A FINAL PLEA

Anything that has the power to hurt has the power to heal. The knowledge of how to influence people, used ethically and responsibly, can be used to preserve and enhance our free will, individuality, and uniqueness. It is my hope that this book has given you that knowledge and, also, the inspiration to use it to join in the fight for freedom. I sometimes feel like a David battling a Goliath with a slingshot, my wits, and my faith as, I imagine, do the many others who have struggled for their own and others' freedom. It is at the most personal, grassroots level that ex-members, families and friends do battle, often with wealthy, powerful, multinational, destructive groups. Now, aided by new technologies, the giant is getting even bigger. Cult mind control has led to a new kind of imperialistic power—subjugation of peoples, not just for the physical and natural resources of their countries, but for control of their minds. In this new Millennium, it is imperative that everyone come and join the effort to protect that most precious of human resources—our minds and spirits.

Resources

This is only a partial list of resources in the United States. In order to get the latest information, please go to our web site. If you need help, I would strongly recommend that you read the information on the key web sites first, before calling on the telephone or e-mailing. There are precious few people and resources to handle this huge problem.

Freedom of Mind Resource
Center, Inc.
PO Box 45223,
Somerville, MA 02145-0002
617-628-9918
www.freedomofmind.com

Leo J. Ryan Foundation
PO Box 1180
Bridgeport, CT 06601-1180
203-338-9776
www.cultinfo.org
help@cultinfo.org

American Family Foundation
(AFF)
PO Box 413005, Suite 313
Naples, FL 34101-3005
Tel: (941) 514-3081
www.csj.org
aff@csj.org

The Lisa McPherson Trust
(*This book is dedicated to Lisa*)
PO Box 191
Clearwater, FL 33757-0191
www.lisamcp1hersontrust.net
ed@lisamcphersontrust.net

Cult Information Service-
New York /New Jersey
PO Box 867
Teaneck, NJ 07666
201-833-1212
www.members.aol.com/shaw-dan/cis.htm

Arnold Markowitz
Jewish Board of Family Services
Cult Clinic
120 West 57th St.
NY, NY 10019-3371
212-632-4640

Reverend Bob Pardon (SIA
trained, with mainstream
Christian orientation)
The New England Institute of
Religious Research &
Meadow Haven Retreat and
Recovery Center
PO Box 878
Lakeville, MA 02347-0878
508-947-9571
www.ultranet.com/~neirr/
neirr@neirr.org

Paul Martin, Ph. D.
Wellspring Retreat and Resource
Center
PO Box 67
Albany, OH, 45710
740-698 6277
www.wellspringretreat.org
liz@wellspringretreat.org

Monica Pignotti, MSW
New York, NY
212 683 0378
pignotti@worldnet.att.net

Steve Dubrow-Eichel, Ph.D.
RETIRN- Re-Entry Therapy,
Information, and
Referral Network
9877 Veree Road
Philadelphia, PA 19115
215-698 8900
www.retirn.com
steve@retirn.com

Joe Szimhart
Cult Expert, Exit Counselor,
Media Consultant
610-326-2322
www.users.fast.net/~szimhart
szimhart@fast.net

Janja Lalich
Community Resources on
Influence & Control (CRIC)
PO Box 1199
Alameda, CA 94501
510- 522-1556
janja@crl.com

Dr. Karen Magarian
Womanspirit Consulting
PO Box 25978
Los Angeles, CA 90025
888-WMN-SPRT

Hal Mansfield
Religious Movement Resource
Center
629 S Howes Street
Fort Collins, CO 80521
970-490-2032
www.lamar.colostate.edu/~ucm/
rmrc1.htm
intruder@pageplus.com

Larry Zilliox- Private Investigator
Investigative Research Specialists
1390 Chain Bridge Rd. #10
McLean, VA 22101
703-356 5922
zilliox@aol.com

Cheryl Larsen
Group Research Institute
PO Box 136
NY, NY 10009
www.groupresearch.org

The James Randi Educational
Foundation
201 S.E. 12th St.
Fort Lauderdale, FL 33316-1815
954-467-1112
www.randi.org
jref@randi.org

Watchman Fellowship- A mainstream Christian counter-cult
resource
P.O. Box 13340
Arlington, Texas 76094
Voice: 817-277-0023
www.watchman.org/
towfi@aol.com

Endnotes

Introduction

1. The acronym CARP, which stands for Collegiate Association for the Research of Principles, alludes to a fish, an early symbol of Christianity. To my knowledge, this group never researched anything but, instead, was used to recruit students into the Moonies.
2. I use the masculine pronoun throughout the book for the sake of simplicity.
3. McKean, Kip. *They Hated the Dreamer*, AudioTape #6353, August 1989.
4. According to cult researchers at the American Family Foundation.

Chapter 1

1. Taken from the mirror of the original Heaven's Gate site. Heaven's Gate—How and When It May Be Entered. www.heavensgatetoo.com.
2. Heaven's Gate Exit press release, heavensgatetoo.com/ressrel.htm.
3. The Maeder's real names are used with their permission.
4. Major Offenses and Lesser Offenses. www.heavensgatetoo.com/book/2-6.htm.
5. Lenz took an overdose of Valium and was found drowned, with his dog's collar around his neck, in Conscience Bay, Long Island, on April 13, 1998. For more information, see www.freedomofmind.com/groups/rama/rama.htm
6. One of the most volatile controversies in the world of psychotherapy focuses on two fallacious viewpoints: the so-called "recovered memory" camp, those who believe that most adult problems are the result of repressed childhood sexual abuse; and the "false memory" camp, those who believe that memories cannot be repressed and, therefore, any newly uncovered traumatic memories must have been implanted by therapists. Both labels are deceiving. There is no recognized school of "recovered memory" therapy (and every memory is "recovered," that is what makes it a memory.) Nor is "false memory syndrome" recognized by the mental health profession. Researchers have yet to demonstrate that memories about traumatic events that never occurred can be implanted in subjects in a controlled setting. Anecdotal evidence suggests that under certain conditions, false beliefs about the past may be implanted in some people. I have had many former cult members tell me that they came to harbor images of experiences that never occurred. One of the most disturbing developments of the controversy is that it has engendered a strong anti-therapy backlash. Responsible therapists who have helped patients recover from real childhood sexual abuse have had lawsuits leveled against them. For the most extensive review of this heated controversy, see Brown, Scheflin & Hammond, *Memory, Trauma Treatment and the Law*. NY: W.W. Norton

& Company, 1998. See also Brown, Scheflin & Whitfield, "Recovered Memories: The Current Weight of the Evidence in Science and in the Courts", *Journal of Psychiatry & Law* p. 5-156, Spring, 1999. Brown and Scheflin suggest that some people claiming false memory syndrome may suffer from a factitious disorder characterized by a need to obtain attention or approval from healers. See Brown & Scheflin, "The Interrelationship Between Factitious and Dissociative Disorders," *Journal of Psychiatry & Law* (in press).
7. See www.metacrawler.com, www.dogpile.com, www.askjeeves.com. There are others, too.
8. Described in more detail in chapter 11.

Chapter 2

1. Lifton, Robert J. *Thought Reform and the Psychology of Totalism*, NY: W.W. Norton and Company, Inc., 1961.
2. Kenrick, Douglas T., Neuberg, Steve L., & Cialdini, Robert B. *Social Psychology: Unraveling the Mystery*. MA: Allyn and Bacon, 1999.
3. Deutsch, Morton. "Field Theory." In *International Encyclopedia of Social Sciences*. NY: Macmillan Company and Free Press, 1968.
4. Hunt, Morton. *The Story of Psychology*, NY: Doubleday, 1993, p. 411.
5. Ibid. p. 412
6. Ibid. p. 412
7. Packard, Vance. *The Hidden Persuaders*. NY: David McKay, 1965.
8. Zimbardo, Philip, ed. *The Psychology of Mind Control*. Palo Alto, CA A Course Reader, Stanford University, 1996.
9. Hunter, Edward. *Brainwashing*. NY: Farrar, Straus & Cudahy, 1956.
10. Schein, Edgar with Schneier, Inge & Barker, Curtis. *Coercive Persuasion*. NY: W.W. Norton & Company, 1971.
11. Lifton, Robert Jay. *Destroying the World to Save It: Aum Shinrikyo, Apocalyptic Violence, and the New Global Terrorism*, NY: Metropolitan Books, 1999. See also Zablocki, Benjamin, "The Blacklisting of a Concept: The Strange History of the Brainwashing Conjecture in the Sociology of Religion", *Nova Religio: The Journal of Alternative and Emergent Religions*, Vol. 1, No. 1, October 1997; Anthony, Dick, & Robbins, Thomas, "Law, Social Science and the "Brainwashing" exception to the First Amendment", *Behavioral Sciences and the Law*, Vol. 10, 1992; and Robbins, Thomas & Anthony, Dick, eds., *In Gods We Trust: New Patterns of Religious Pluralism in America*. Transaction Press, 1990.
12. Singer, Margaret & Lalich, Janja. *Cults in Our Midst*, Jossey-Bass 1997.
13. Festinger, Leon, Rieken, Henry W. & Schachter, Stanley. *When Prophecy Fails: A Social and Psychological Study of a Modern Group that Predicted the Destruction of the World*. NY: Harper & Row, 1956.
14. My thanks to Reverend Buddy Martin for suggesting the acronym BITE.
15. Dick Joslyn interview, May 26, 1997. With permission of Mr. Joslyn.
16. Pardon, Robert & Barba, Judith. *Messianic Communities: Journey from*

Orthodoxy to Heresy. Lakeville, MA: New England Institute of Religious Research, 1995.

17. Brown, Janelle. "A web of their own: Scientologists say their Internet filter protects the faithful. Critics call it cult mind-control." *Salon Magazine*, July 15, 1998.

18. NLP was modeled after the therapeutic techniques of psychiatrist Milton Erickson. The founders of NLP, John Grinder and Richard Bandler, describe their use of trance in several books. See Bandler, R. & Grinder, J., *Trance-Formations: Neuro-Linguistic Programming and the Structure of Hypnosis.* CA: Real People Press, 1981.

19. Investigation of Korean-American Relations. Report of the Subcommittee on International Organizations. U.S. Government Printing Office, October 31, 1978.

20. Reverend Bob Pardon told me about this boy.

21. Members are told to never reveal their mantra, which is viewed as highly personal and secret (see www.trancent.org/secrets/checking/steps). However, a list of mantras now published on the internet at www.minet.org/steps reveals that mantras are assigned to initiates according to their age and the year of initiation. In other words, the unique mantra is not unique at all.

22. West, Louis Jolyon & Martin, Paul. "Pseudo-Identity and the Treatment of Personality Change in Victims of Captivity and Cults", in Steven Jay Lynn and Judith Rhue S., eds., *Dissociation: Clinical and Theoretical Perspectives*, pp. 268-288. New York, NY: The Guilford Press, 1994.

23. American Psychiatric Association, *Diagnostic and Statistical Manual of Mental Disorders*, 4th edition. Washington, D.C. 1994.

24. Schein, Edgar with Schneier, Inge & Barker, Curtis. *Coercive Persuasion.* NY: W.W. Norton & Company, 1971.

25. In statistical terms, they exhibited a normal distribution of personality types.

26. Interestingly, the type is Extrovert, Sensing, Feeling, Judging—a type which is often thought of as a "super-salesman."

27. Yeakley, Flavil R., Norton, Howard W., & Vinzant, Gene & Don E., eds. *The Discipling Dilemma.* Nashville, TN: Gospel Advocate Press, 1988.

Chapter 3

1. Patrick, Ted, with Dulack, Tom. *Let Our Children Go!* NY: E.P. Dutton and Company, Inc., 1976.

2. Several ex-members of this cult have written books about their involvement. See Williams, Miriam, *Heaven's Harlots: My Fifteen Years As a Sacred Prostitute in the Children of God Cult.* NY: William Morrow, 1998. Davis, Deborah Berg. *The Children of God: The Inside Story.* Grand Rapids, MI: The Zondervan Publishing House, 1984. McManus, Una. *Not for a Million Dollars.* Impact Books, 1980.

3. The term "deprogramming" has been used to describe voluntary interventions, though it is mostly used to describe a forced process.

4. I have publicly criticized forceful deprogramming since 1980. To discredit me,

cults lie to members as well as the public. The truth is that I was involved in approximately one dozen deprogrammings between 1976 and 1977 for members of the Moonies. Most of these were successful. Two of them were not. The fact is that I have never been arrested, criminally prosecuted, or even sued by anyone that I have met or counseled.

5. Personal correspondence, summer 1999.

6. Some exit-counselors now refer to themselves as "Thought Reform Consultants."

Chapter 4

1. King, Dennis. *Get the Facts on Anyone*. Arco Publications, 1999.

2. The book can be ordered from Investigative Research Specialists at 703-356-5922 or www.extremistgroups.com.

3. Laxer, Mark. *Take Me For A Ride: Coming of Age in a Destructive Cult*. Outer Rim Press, 1993; Margulis, Zachary, "The Code Cult of the CPU Guru", *Wired Magazine*, January 2, 1994; Diamond, David, "Street Brawl in the Twilight Zone", *Wired Magazine*, September 7, 1999.

4. Norman Geisler Lecture, "The Rise of the Cults," The New England Institute for Religious Research, November 2, 1991.

5. Parry, Robert. *The Dark Side of Reverend Moon: Buying the Right*. Consortium News, 1997.

Chapter 5

1. Identifying features in this story have been changed to protect my client's privacy.

2. Gurdjieff was quite a controversial personality. Both men wrote books about a mystical "school" to develop one's spirit. I believe there are other Gurdjieff and Ouspenky "schools" which do not use deception and destructive mind control.

3. I mentioned this case in Chapter 1.

4. These questions will be covered in future chapters, particularly chapter 11.

5. This is one point where I disagree with Margaret Singer and others. According to my model, the military uses many components of mind control. What the military does not do is deceive a new recruit (some vets have argued with me about this because they said their recruiter lied to them). The structural checks and balances operating in the military provide some protection of an individual's authentic self.

Chapter 6

1. Bonher, Kate and Trump, Donald. *The Art of the Comeback*, Times Books. 1997.

2. Keirsey, David. *Please Understand Me II: Temperament, Character, Intelligence*. Prometheus Nemesis Book Co., 1998..

3. Go to www.keirsey.com.

4. Keirsey, David & Bates, Marilyn. *Please Understand Me: Character and*

Temperament Types. Prometheus Nemesis Books, 1984.

5. Thanks to Reverend Bob Pardon for suggesting this paragraph.

6. American Bible Society. *The Holy Bible,* revised standard edition, 1994.

7. Moses, Jeffrey. *Oneness: Great Principles Shared By All Religions,* NY: Fawcett Books, 1992.

8. Smith, Huston. *The World's Religions.* San Francisco, CA: Harper, 1992.

9. Burns, David. *Feeling Good: The New Mood Therapy.* NY: Avon, 1999.

10. Alman, Brian & Lambrou, Peter. *Self-Hypnosis: The Complete Manual for Health and Self-Change.* NY: Brunner/Mazel, 1991.

11. A basic book on meditation is Leshan, Lawrence. *How to Meditate: A Guide to Self-Discovery,* NY: Bantam Books, 1984.

Chapter 7

1. The Reichmanns kindly gave permission to use their names.

2. Pardon, Robert & Barba, Judith. *Messianic Communities: Journey from Orthodoxy to Heresy.* Lakeville, MA: New England Institute of Religious Research, 1995.

3. JoEllen Griffin's name while in the group was "Diynah." She left with her husband Roger Griffin, who was one of the highest ranking leaders to walk away. For most of his eighteen years in the group, he held the positions of household head, shepherd, teacher, elder, and, during the last few years there, apostolic worker. Their e-mail address is RGDAD1@aol.com.

4. For more information about online privacy, see http: //www.epic.org /privacy/tools.html

5. Kornfield, Jack. *A Path With Heart: A Guide Through the Perils and Promises of Spiritual Life.* NY: Bantam Doubleday, 1993.

6. Consult my Web site and other counter-cult sites for ways to contact ex-members.

7. Licensed social worker and former Sea Org member Monica Pignotti wrote me: "Another aspect of the mind control around definitions is the way that a Scientology supervisor asks for definitions when testing a student. The student is asked to define a word, or answer a question and if there is any hesitation at all, the person is "flunked" for a "com lag." In light of what you say about the importance of allowing for time in between the asking of questions, and giving the person plenty of time to think and reflect on the answer, it becomes obvious that in demanding instant answers, this is yet another way that Scientologists are trained not to think, but to respond to programmed cues."

8. A family that cared enough for a loved one would not go to the lengths of initiating a deprogramming and then stand idly by and allow a rape or beating to occur. It just wouldn't happen!

9. Hansen, Susan. "Did Scientology Strike Back?" *American Lawyer,* June 1997.

10. See www.zimbardo.com for Professor Zimbardo's full résumé.

11. American Psychiatric Association. *Diagnostic and Statistical Manual of Mental Disorders,* 4th edition. Washington, D.C., 1994.

12. *The Lancet* and *American Journal of Psychiatry* reviews are on the freedomof-mind.com web site.

13. Reid, T.R. "U.S. Visitors Boost Cause of Japanese Cult; Lawyer Says Police Imperil Religious Rights of Sect." *Washington Post Foreign Service*, May 9, 1995; Watanabe, Teresa. "Alleged Persecution of Cult Investigated," *Los Angeles Times*, May 6 1995.

14. *Milwaukee Journal*, Dec. 3, 1988.

15. See www.cultawarenessnetwork.org/referral/page01.

16. Zablocki, Benjamin, "The Blacklisting of a Concept: The Strange History of the Brainwashing Conjecture in the Sociology of Religion", *Nova Religio: The Journal of Alternative and Emergent Religions*, Vol. 1, No. 1, October 1997, p. 98.

17. Taken from the expert testimony of J. Gordon Melton in Lee vs. Duddy et al. See www.hightruth.com/experts/melton.

18. See www.freedomofmind.com for more information about these respected doctors.

Chapter 8

1. Names and other identifying details have been altered to protect the individual's right to privacy.

2. Many Christians believe that they are "born again" as they give their life to Jesus. However, there is a vast difference between having a personal experience of transformation and being socially influenced by other people, in the context of a high-pressure, emotionally-charged, and manipulative environment.

3. For the first time since my childhood, I have found a rabbi and a temple that I feel comfortable joining. My wife and I are members of the non-aligned Temple Beth Zion in Brookline, Massachusetts. Rabbi Moshe Waldoks is an exceptional spiritual leader. Misia and I were honored to have him perform our wedding ceremony. If you are curious and want to know more, see www.templebethzion.org

4. Cooper, Paulette. *The Scandal of Scientology*. NY: Tower Publications, 1971.

5. Monica Pignotti, former six-year Sea Org member of Scientology, told me this.

Chapter 9

1. Klienke, C.L. "Compliance to requests made by gazing and touching experimenters in field settings". *Journal of Experimental Social Psychology*, 13, 218-223. 1977.

2. E-mails count too, but should only be used if the cult member has a private electronic address.

Chapter 10

1. Statistic from the Anxiety Disorders Association of America.

2. King, Stephen. *Talisman*, NY: Viking Press, 1984; IT, New American Library, 1990.

3. Castaneda, Carlos. *A Journey to Ixtlan*, NY: Washington Square Press, 1992;

Tales of Power. NY: Pocket Books, 1992.

4. Wilson, Reid. *Don't Panic: Taking Control of Anxiety Attacks.* San Francisco, CA: HarperCollins, 1996.

5. I first learned about these techniques in 1980-81, during a one-year training in Neuro-Linguistic Programming (NLP). I have encountered these techniques in other therapeutic contexts, including my training at the Milton Erickson Foundation. I have since become disillusioned with many aspects of NLP.

6. Patricia Campbell Hearst Shaw continues to seek a Presidential pardon for her involvement with a bank robbery while a cult member. I believe she deserves one.

Chapter 11

1. Some of these ideas are drawn from Mckay, Matthew, & Fanning, Patrick. *Self Esteem.* St. Martins Mass Market Paperbacks, 1994.

2. I first learned and used this model of Thinker, Feeler, Doer or Believer as a Moonie in 1974. I've discovered that a person is all four of these, but these orientations can be ranked—for example, believer first, then feeler, doer, thinker. Religious cult identities are always believer first, then doer or feeler, and lastly, thinker.

3. Jon Atack was a nine-year Scientology member and reached the 24th of the 27 available levels of the Bridge (OT5). His book, *A Piece of Blue Sky*, is the best ever written on the group. He is a brilliant, multi-talented man who I am proud to call my friend.

Chapter 12

1. Hong, Nansook. *In the Shadow of the Moons.* NY: Little Brown, 1999.

2. Real name used with permission. John M. Knapp is currently pursing his doctorate in social psychology and is the founder of www.trancenet.org.

3. De Becker, Gavin. *The Gift of Fear.* Dell Books, 1999.

4. The act of looking up words in a dictionary will probably be a negative trigger for an ex-Scientologist because the ritual of looking up words is part of the group's method for restructuring thoughts. Nevertheless, I have found that encouraging ex-Scientologists to reclaim the use of language is an indispensable part of their healing.

Chapter 13

1. In the face of revelations that the FBI did use firebombs on the Branch Davidian compound, even President of the United States Bill Clinton commented that he did not see why people were getting so upset "because a bunch of religious fanatics committed suicide." *The New York Times*, August 31, 1999.

2. I am afraid that very little has been learned since the tragedy at Waco. Six years after the government assault and siege, which resulted in the fiery deaths of men, women and children, a responsible investigation has yet to be accomplished. My efforts during the siege fell on deaf ears. Congressman Joe Kennedy's office sent

letters to F.B.I. Director Sessions and Special Agent Jamar in charge of the oper-
ation, asking that they talk with me. Massachusetts Attorney General Scott
Harshbarger's office faxed a letter, written by me, to Attorney General Reno warning of the dangers of the situation, and offering concrete alternatives weeks before
the final deadly assault. A copy of my book *Combatting Cult Mind Control* was
reportedly given to Presidential Advisor Webster Hubbell by Eleanor Acheson
more than a week before the final assault. On television shows and in a lecture at
Harvard in 1994, I detailed what could have been done to resolve the standoff
peacefully. Six years later, I have yet to receive even a telephone call from anyone
in the government asking me for my perspective. A transcript of my Harvard lecture is on www.freedomofmind.com.

3. Ex-Scientologists and concerned citizens gather on December 5 to commemorate the birthday of Lisa McPherson. The Church of Scientology was indicted by
the State of Florida on criminal charges relating to her untimely death. The formal charges are abuse and/or neglect of a disabled adult, and practicing medicine
without a license. The criminal trial is scheduled for March 2000 and additionally a civil suit is scheduled for June 2000. A nonprofit organization called the Lisa
McPherson Trust has been set up in her name. See the resources section of this
book.

4. Martin, Paul, & Langone, Michael, & Dole, Arthur & Wiltrout, J. "Post-cult
symptoms as measured by the MCMI before and after residential treatment",
Cultic Studies Journal, 9, 219-249, 1992.

5. Behar, Richard. "Scientology: The Thriving Cult of Greed and Power. Ruined
lives. Lost fortunes. Federal crimes. Scientology poses as a religion but really is a
ruthless global scam. Aiming for the mainstream", *Time Magazine*, May 6, 1991.

Bibliography

General

Allen, Steve. *Beloved Son: A Story of the Jesus Cults*. Indianapolis, IN: The Bobbs-Merrill Company, 1982.

Andres, Rachel & Lane, James R., eds. *Cults & Consequences: The Definitive Handbook*. Los Angeles, CA: Jewish Federation of Greater Los Angeles, 1988.

Appel, Willa. *Cults in America: Programmed for Paradise*. NY: Holt Rinehart & Winston, 1983.

Conway, Flo & Siegelman, Jim. *Snapping: America's Epidemic of Sudden Personality Change*. NY: Stillpoint Press, 1995.

——————————. *Holy Terror*. NY: Doubleday, 1982.

Hassan, Steven. "Spiritual Responsibility and Cult Awareness". *New Age Journal* March/April 1999.

——————————. *Combatting Cult Mind Control*. Rochester, VT: Park Street Press, 1988, 1990.

Hearst, Patricia Campbell with Moscow, Alvin. *Every Secret Thing*. NY: Pinnacle Books, 1982.

Hunter, Edward. *Brainwashing*. NY: Farrar, Straus & Cudahy, 1956.

Huxley, Aldous. *Brave New World Revisited*. NY: Harper & Brothers, 1958.

Kaminer, Wendy. *I'm Dysfunctional, You're Dysfunctional: The Recovery Movement and Other Self Help Fashions*. NY: Vintage Books, 1992.

Kamentsky, Ellen. *Hawking God: A Young Jewish Woman's Ordeal in Jews for Jesus*. MA: Sapphire Press, 1992.

Kent, Stephen A. & Krebs, Theresa. Academic compromise in the social Scientific study of alternative religions, *Nova Religio*, Vol 2 (1), October 1998.

Kramer, Joel & Alstad, Diana. *The Guru Papers : Masks of Authoritarian Power*. CA: North Atlantic Books, 1993.

Mehta, Gita. *Karma Cola: Marketing the Mystic East*. NY: Simon & Shuster, 1979.

Orwell, George. *Nineteen Eighty-four*. Middlesex, England: Penguin, 1954.

Patrick, Ted, with Dulack, Tom. *Let Our Children Go!* NY: E.P. Dutton and Company, Inc., 1976.

Pressman, Steven. *Outrageous Betrayal: The Real Story of Werner Erhard from Est to Exile*. NY: St. Martin's Press, 1993.

Randi, James. *The Faith Healers*. NY: Prometheus Books, 1989.

Ross, Joan & Langone, Michael. *Cults: What Parents Should Know.* NJ: Lyle Stuart, 1989.

Rudin, James & Rudin, Marcia. Prison or Paradise? *The New Religious Cults.* Philadelphia, PA: Fortress Press, 1980.

Schecter, Robert E. & Noyes, Wendy L. *Cultism on Campus: Commentaries and Guidelines for College and University Administrators.* American Family Foundation, 1987.

Shirer, William L. *The Rise and Fall of the Third Reich.* Greenwich, CN: Fawcett, 1960.

Singer, Margaret & Lalich, Janja. *Cults in Our Midst.* San Francisco, CA: Jossey-Bass 1997.

——————. *Crazy Therapies: What Are They? Do They Work?* San Francisco, CA: Jossey-Bass, 1996.

Sklar, Dusty. *Gods and Beasts: The Nazis and the Occult.* NY: Thomas Y. Cowell, 1977.

Stoner, Carolle, & Parke, Joanne. *All God's Children: The Cult Experience(Salvation and Slavery?* NY: Penguin Books, Inc., 1979.

Storr, Anthony. *Feet of Clay: Saints, Sinners, and Madmen: a Study of Gurus.* NY: The Free Press. 1997

Thomas, Gordon. *Journey into Madness: The True Story of Secret CIA Mind Control and Medical Abuse.* NY: Bantam Books, 1989

Wilber, Ken. *The Marriage of Sense and Soul: Integrating Science and Religion.* NY: Broadway Books, 1999.

Psychology

Addis, M., et al. "The Cult Clinic Helps Families in Crisis". Social Casework, *The Journal of Contemporary Social Work*, 1984.

Adorno, T.W., Frenkel-Brunswil, Else, Levinson, D.J. & Sanford, R.N. *The Authoritarian Personality.* The American Jewish Committee, NY: Harper, 1950; Norton Library, 1969.

Alman, Brian & Lambrou, Peter. *Self-Hypnosis: The Complete Manual for Health and Self-Change.* NY: Brunner/Mazel 1991.

American Psychiatric Association. *Diagnostic and Statistical Manual of Mental Disorders,* 4th edition. Washington, D.C., 1994.

Anderson, S.M. "Identifying coercion and deception in social systems". In *Kilbourne's Scientific Research and the New Religions: Divergent Perspectives,* edited by B. Kilbourne. San Francisco, Pacific Division of the American Association for the Advancement of Science, 1985.

Anderson, S.M. & Zimbardo, Philip G. "Resisting Mind Control", *USA Today,* November 1980.

Asch, S.E. "The doctrine of suggestion, prestige, and imitation in social psychology". *Psychology Rev.* 55, 1948

——————. "Effects of group pressure upon the modification and distortion of judgements". In Harold Guetzkow, ed., *Groups, leadership, and men.* Pittsburgh, PA: Carnegie Press, 1951

——————. *Social Psychology.* NY: Prentice-Hall, 1952

Bandler, Richard & Grinder, John. *Patterns of the Hypnotic Techniques of Milton H. Erickson, M.D.* Cupertino, CA: Meta Publications, 1975

——————. *Trance-Formations: Neuro-Linguistic Progamming and the Structure of Hypnosis.* CA: Real people Press, 1981

Bandura, A. *Principles of Behavior Modification.* NY: Holt, Rinehart & Winston, 1969.

Bateson, G. *Steps to an Ecology of Mind.* NY: Ballantine Books, 1972.

Brown, J.A.C. *Techniques of Persuasion.* Middlesex, England: Pelican, 1963.

Brown, Daniel, Scheflin, Alan & Hammond, D. Corydon. *Memory, Trauma Treatment and the Law.* NY: W.W. Norton & Company, 1998.

Brown, Daniel, Scheflin, Alan & Whitfield, C.L. "Recovered memories: The current weight of the evidence in science and in the courts," *Journal of Psychiatry & Law*, 5-156, Spring 1999.

Brown, Daniel & Scheflin, Alan. "The Interrelationship Between Factitious and Dissociative Disorders," *Journal of Psychiatry & Law*, in press.

Brownfield, Charles A. *The Brain Benders.* NY: Exposition Press, 1972.

Burns, David. *Feeling Good: The New Mood Therapy.* Avon 1999.

Cialdini, Robert B. *Influence: The New Psychology of Modern Persuasion.* NY: William Morrow and Company, 1984.

Clark, John G. "We are all cultists at heart", *Newsday*, November 30, 1978.

——————. "Cults". *Journal of the American Medical Association*, Vol. 242, No.3. July 20, 1979.

Clark, J.G., Langone, M.D., Schecter, R.E. & Daly, R.C.B. *Destructive Cult Conversion: Theory. Research, and Treatment.* American Family Foundation, 1981.

Conway, Flo & Siegelman, Jim. "Information Disease: Have Cults Created a New Mental Illness?" *Science Digest*, January 1982.

——————. "Information disease: Effects of covert induction and deprogramming." *Update*, Vol. 10, No.2, June 1986.

——————. "University study concludes mind control can cause lasting and damaging alterations of thought: University of Oregon researchers studied 400 former members of 48 cults", *Cult Awareness Newsletter,* December, 1985.

Csziksentmihalyi, Mihaly. *Flow: The Psychology of Optimal Experience.* NY: HarperCollins, 1991.

Dellinger, R. *Cults and Kids: A Study of Coercion*. Nebraska: Boys Town, 1985.

Dennett, Daniel C. *Consciousness Explained*. NY: Little Brown & Co., 1992.

Dilts, Robert, & Grinder, John, & Bandler, Richard, & Bandler, Leslie C., & Delozier, Judith. *Neuro-Linguistic Programming: The Structure of Subjective Experience. Volume 1*. Cupertino, CA: Meta Publications, 1980.

Ellul, Jacques. *Propaganda: The Formation of Men's Attitudes*. NY: Alfred A. Knopf, 1965.

Engler, Jack & Goleman, Daniel. *The Consumer's Guide to Psychotherapy*. NY: Simon and Schuster, 1992.

Erickson, M.H. & Rossi, Ernest, eds. *The Collected Papers of Milton H. Erickson on Hypnosis*. NY: Irvington, 1980.

Volume I: The Nature of Hypnosis and Suggestion;

Volume II: Hypnotic Alteration of Sensory, Perceptual and Psychophysiological Processes;

Volume III: Hypnotic Investigation of Psychodynamic Processes;

Volume IV: Innovative Hypnotherapy.

Erickson, Milton H., Rossi, Ernest L. & Rossi, Sheila I. *Hypnotic Realities: The Induction of Clinical Hypnosis and Forms of Indirect Suggestion*. NY: Irvington Publishers, 1976.

Farber, I.E. & Harlow, Harry F. & West, Louis Jolyon. "Brainwashing, Conditioning, and DDD". *Sociometry*. Vol. 20 No. 4, December, 1957.

Festinger, Leon, Rieken, Henry W. & Schachter, Stanley. *When Prophecy Fails: A Social and Psychological Study of a Modern Group that Predicted the Destruction of the World*. NY: Harper & Row, 1956.

Frank, Jerome D. *Persuasion and Healing*. NY: Schoken Books, 1961.

Freud, Sigmund. *Group Psychology and the Analysis of the Ego*. NY: W.W. Norton, 1959.

Fromm, Erich. *Escape from Freedom*. NY: Avon Books, 1965.

Glass, Leonard L. & Kirsch, Michael A. & Parris, Frederick N. "Psychiatric disturbances associated with Erhard Seminars Training: A report of cases; Additional cases and theoretical considerations". *American Journal of Psychiatry*, March 1977 and November 1977.

Goldberg, Lorna & William. "Group work with former cultists". *Social Work*, March 1982.

Goldfied, Marvin R., & Merbaum, Michael. eds. *Behavior Change Through Self-Control*. NY: Holt Rinehart & Winston, 1973.

Gordon, David & Meyers-Anderson, Maribeth. *Phoenix: Therapeutic Patterns of Milton H. Erickson*. Cupertino, CA: Meta Publications, 1981.

Greek, Adrian & Anne. *Mind Abuse by Cults and Others*. Portland, OR: Positive

Action Center, 1985.

Haley, Jay. *Uncommon Therapy: The Psychiatric Techniques of Milton H. Erickson, M.D.* NY: Norton, 1973.

Halperin, David. ed. *Psychodynamic Perspectives on Religion, Sect and Cult.* NY: John Wright, 1983.

Heller, Randy K. *Deprogramming for Do It Yourselfers: A Cure for the Common Cult.* Medina, OH: Gentle Press, 1982.

Herman, Judith M.D. *Trauma and Recovery.* NY: Basic Books, 1997.

Hersch, Tom. "The phenomenology of belief systems". *Journal of Humanistic Psychology*, Vol.20, No.2, 1980.

Hochman, John. "Iatrogenic symptoms associated with a therapy cult: Examination of an extinct 'New Psychotherapy' with respect to psychiatric deterioration and 'Brainwashing.'" *Psychiatry*, Vol.47, 1984.

Hoffer, Eric. *The True Believer.* NY: Harper & Row, 1951.

——————. *The Ordeal of Change.* NY: Harper & Row, 1963.

Hunt, Morton. *The Story of Psychology.* NY: Anchor Books, Doubleday, 1993.

Jung, C.G. *Psychology and Religion.* New Haven, CT: Yale University Press, 1938.

Key, Wilson Bryan. *Subliminal Seduction.* NY: Signet Books, 1973.

Kaslow, Florence & Sussman, Marvin. "Cults and the family". *Marriage and Family Review*, Vol. 4, Numbers 3 & 4. NY: The Haworth Press, 1982.

Keirsey, David. *Please Understand Me II: Temperament, Character, Intelligence.* Prometheus Nemesis Book Co. 1998.

Kenrick, Douglas T., Neuberg, Steve L., & Cialdini, Robert B. *Social Psychology: Unraveling the Mystery.* MA: Allyn and Bacon, 1999.

Kilbourne, Brock, ed. *Scientific Research and New Religions: Divergent Perspectives.* San Francisco, CA: Pacific Division of the American Association for the Advancement of Science, 1985.

Kilpatrick, William Kirk. *Psychological Seduction: The Failure of Modern Psychology.* NY: Thomas Nelson Publishers, 1983.

Klienke, C.L. "Compliance to requests made by gazing and touching experimenters in field settings". *Journal of Experimental Social Psychology*, 13, 218-223. 1977.

LaBarre, Weston. *They Shall Take Up Serpents: The Psychology of the Southern Snake-Handling Cult.* NY: Schoken Books, 1969.

Langone, Michael, ed. *Recovery from Cults.* NY: W.W. Norton & Company, 1993.

Lankton, Stephen R. & Lankton, Carol H., *The Answer Within: A Clinical Framework of Ericksonian Hypnotherapy.* NY: Brunner/Mazel, 1983.

Leary, Timothy. *Neuropolitique.* NE: Falcon Press, 1988.

Levine, Saul. *Radical Departures: Desperate Detours to Growing Up.* San Diego, CA: Harcourt Brace Jovanovich. 1984

Lewin, Kurt. "Frontiers in Group Dynamics: Concept, Method, and Reality in Social Science". *Human Relations*, 1947.

Lifton, Robert Jay. *Destroying the World to Save It: Aum Shinrikyo, Apocalyptic Violence, and the New Global Terrorism.* NY: Metropolitan Books 1999.

——————. *Thought Reform and the Psychology of Totalism.* NY: W.W. Norton and Company, Inc., 1961.

Lisman, Michael & Tanenhaus, Sara. *Cults as Restrictive Groups: Assessing Individuals During Recruitment, Indoctrination and Departure.* Unpublished manuscript. California State University, Sacramento, 1988.

Machovec, Frank J. *Cults and Personality.* IL: Charles C Thomas, 1989.

Mahoney, Michael J. & Thoreson, Carl E. *Self-Control: Power to the Person.* Monterey, CA: Brooks/Cole Publishers, 1974.

Marks, John. *The Search for the Manchurian Candidate; The CIA and Mind Control.* New York Times Books, 1979.

Martin, Paul, Pile, Lawrence, Burks, Ron & Martin, Stephen. "Overcoming the Bondage of Victimization: A Rational/Empirical Defense of Thought Reform (a response to 'Overcoming the Bondage of Victimization' by Bob and Gretchen Passantino." *Cultic Studies Journal*, 15 (2), 1998.

Martin, Paul & Langone, Michael, Dole, Arthur & Wiltrout, J., "Post-cult symptoms as measured by the MCMI before and after residential treatment," *Cultic Studies Journal*, 9, 219-249, 1992.

McKay, Matthew, & Fanning, Patrick. *Self Esteem.* St. Martins Mass Market Paperbacks, 1994.

Meerloo, Joost A. *Rape of the Mind.* NY: Grosset & Dunlap, 1961.

Milgram, Stanley. *Obedience to Authority.* NY: Harper & Row, 1974.

——————. Behavioral study of obedience. *The Journal of Abnormal and Social Psychology.* Vol. 67, No.4, 1963.

Miller, Jesse. S. "The utilization of hypnotic techniques in religious cult conversion," *Cultic Studies Journal*, 3 (2), 1986.

Mithers, Carol L. *Therapy Gone Mad: The True Story of Hundreds of Patients and a Generation Betrayed.* Reading, MA: Addison-Wesley, 1994.

Morse, Edwin L. & Julia C. "Toward a Theory of Therapy with Cultic Victims", *American Journal of Psychotherapy*, Vol. XLI, No. 4, October, 1987.

Mostache, Harriet. Searching: *Practices and Beliefs of the Religious Cults and Human Potential Groups.* NY: Stravon Educational Press, 1983.

Northruo, Bowen. "Treating the Mind-Psychotherapy Faces A Stubborn Problem; Abuses by Therapists; Role Imparts Power That Is Easy to Misuse; Field is Tricky One to Regulate; The Damage a Victim Suffers," *The Wall Street Journal*, Vol. CCVIII, No. 85.

Ofshe, Richard & Waters, Ethan. *Making Monsters: False Memories, Psychotherapy and Sexual Hysteria*. NY: Scribner. 1994.

Ofshe, Richard & Singer, Margaret. "Attacks on peripheral versus central elements of self and the impact of thought reforming techniques". *Cultic Studies Journal*, Vol. 3, No. 1, 1986.

Packard, Vance. *The Hidden Persuaders*. NY: David McKay, 1965.

Pinker, Steven. *How the Mind Works*. NY: W.W. Norton & Company, 1999.

Randi, James. *Flim Flam! Psychics, ESP, Unicorns and other Delusions*. Buffalo, NY: Prometheus Books, 1986.

Reich, Wilhelm. *The Mass Psychology of Fascism*. NY: Pocket Books, 1976.

Robbins, Thomas & Anthony, Dick, eds. *In Gods We Trust: New Patterns of Religious Pluralism in America*. Transaction Press. 1990.

Rose, Stephen. *The Conscious Brain*. NY: Vintage Books, 1976.

Rosen, R.D. *Psychobabble*. NY: Avon Books, 1975.

Rudin, Marcia. "Women, elderly, and children in religious cults". *Cultic Studies Journal*, 1(1), 8-26. 1984.

Sargent, William. *Battle for the Mind*. London: Pan Books, 1951-1959.

——————————. *The Unquiet Mind*. London: Pan Books, 1967.

——————————. *The Mind Possessed*. Penguin Books, 1975.

Satir, Virginia. *Conjoint Family Therapy*. Palo Alto, CA: Science and Behavior Books, 1964.

——————————. *Helping Families to Change*. Hays, KS: The High Plains Comprehensive Community Mental Health Center, 1972.

——————————. *Peoplemaking*. Palo Alto, CA: Science and Behavior Books, 1972.

Schein, Edgar with Schneier, Inge & Barker, Curtis. *Coercive Persuasion*. NY: W.W. Norton & Company, 1971.

Shapiro, Eli. "Destructive Cultism". *American Family Physician*, February, 1977.

Shapiro, Francine & Forrest, Margot *EMDR: The Breakthrough Therapy for Overcoming Anxiety, Stress, and Trauma*. NY: Basic Books, 1998.

Singer, Margaret. "Coming out of the cults". *Psychology Today*. January 1979.

——————————. "Cults: What are they? Why now?" *Forecast for Home Economics*, May/June 1979.

——————————. "Consultation with families of cultists". In Wynne, L.C., Mc Daniel, S.H. and Weber, T.T. Systems Consultation: *A New Perspective for Family Therapy*. NY: Guilford Press, 1986.

———————. "Group Psychodynamics". In Berkow, Robert, ed. *The Merck Manual of Diagnosis and Therapy*. Rahway, N.J.: Merck Sharp & Dohme Research Laboratories, 1987.

Singer, Margaret & West, Louis J. "Cults, Quacks and Non-Professional Therapies". In *Comprehensive Textbook of Psychiatry*. Vol. 3. Baltimore, MD: Williams and Wilkins, 1980.

Spero, M.H. "Psychotherapeutic procedure with religious cult devotees". *The Journal of Nervous and Mental Disease*, 1982.

Sprecher, Paul. "The Cult as a Total Institution: Perceptual Distortion, Consenual Validation, and Independent Decision Making. Delivered to the panel". *Taking the Cult to Court, Conference on Law & Society*, Washington D.C. June 13, 1987.

Skinner, B.F. *Beyond Freedom and Dignity*. NY: Alfred A. Knopf, 1971.

Temerlin, M. K. & Temerlin, J.W., "Psychotherapy cults: An Iatrogenic Perversion". *Psychotherapy: Theory, Research and Practice*, 1982.

Tobias, Madeline & Lalich, Janja. *Captive Hearts, Captive Minds: Freedom and Recovery from Cults and Abusive Relationships*. Alameda, CA: Hunter House, 1994.

Verdier, Paul A. *Brainwashing and the Cults*. CA: The Institute of Behavioral Conditioning, 1977.

Watzlawick, P. Weakland, J. & Fisch, R. *Change*. NY: W. Norton, 1974.

West, Louis Jolyon & Martin, Paul. "Pseudo-Identity and the Treatment of Personality Change in Victims of Captivity and Cults", in Steven Jay Lynn and Judith Rhue, Eds., *Dissociation: Clinical and Theoretical Perspectives*, pp. 268-288. NY: The Guilford Press, 1994

West, Louis Jolyon. "Contemporary Cults—Utopian Image, Infernal Reality". *The Center Magazine*, March/April, 1982.

West, Louis Jolyon & Delgado, Richard. "Psyching Out the Cults' Collective Mania". *Los Angeles Times*, October 26, 1978.

Wilson, Reid. *Don't Panic: Taking Control of Anxiety Attacks*. NY: HarperCollins, 1996.

Wolinsky, Stephen & Ryan, Margaret. *Trances People Live: Healing Approaches in Quantum Psychology*. Bramble Press, 1992.

Yapko, Michael. *Suggestions of Abuse; True and False Memories of Childhood Sexual Trauma*. NY: Simon & Schuster, 1994.

Zablocki, Benjamin. "The Blacklisting of a Concept: The Strange History of the Brainwashing Conjecture in the Sociology of Religion", *Nova Religio: The Journal of Alternative and Emergent Religions*, Vol. 1, No. 1, October, 1997.

Zeig, Jeffrey. Ericksonian *Approaches to Hypnosis and Psychotherapy*. NY: Brunner/Mazel, 1982.

Zimbardo, Philip. *The Psychology of Mind Control*. Palo Alto, CA: Stanford

University Course Reader, 1996.

—————-. "Now that cognitive science has put the head back on the body of psychology, we might consider implanting a little soul", *Psychology Today*, May, 1982.

Zimbardo, Philip & Ebbeson, Ebbe B. *Influencing Attitudes and Changing Behavior.* Reading, MA: Addison-Wesley, 1970.

Religious and Spiritual Orientation

Amercian Bible Society. *The Holy Bible.* Revised Standard Edition, 1994

Batchelor, Stephen. Buddhism Without Beliefs: *A Contemporary Guide to Awakening.* NY: Riverhead Books, 1997.

Bjornstad, James. *The Moon is Not the Son.* Minneapolis, Minnesota: Bethany Fellowship, Dimension Books, 1976.

Burks, Ron & Vickie. *Damaged Disciples: Casualties of Authoritarian Churches and the Shepherding Movement.* Grand Rapids, MI: Zondervan, 1992.

Bussell, Harold. *Unholy Devotion: Why Cults Lure Christians.* Grand Rapids, MI: Zondervan Publishing House, 1983.

Cohen, Daniel. *The New Believers: Young Religion in America.* NY: Ballantine Books, 1975.

Eisenberg, Gary D. *Smashing the Idols: A Jewish Inquiry into the Cult Phenomenon.* Northvale, NJ: Jason Aronson, 1988.

Enroth, Ronald. *Churches That Abuse.* Grand Rapids, MI: Zondervan, 1992.

————————. *Youth, Brainwashing and the Extremist Cults.* Grand Rapids, MI: Zondervan, 1977.

Groothius, Douglas R. *Unmasking the New Age: Is there a New Religious Movement Trying to Transform Society?* Downers Grove, IL: InterVarsity Press, 1986.

Hunt, Dave. *The Cult Explosion.* Irvine, CA: Harvest House, 1980.

James, William. *Varieties of Religious Experience.* Britain: Fontana, 1960

Kornfield, Jack. *A Path With Heart: A Guide Through the Perils and Promises of Spiritual Life.* NY: Bantam Doubleday, 1993.

Langford, Harris. *Traps: A Probe of those Strange New Cults.* Decatur, GA: Presbyterian Church of America, 1977.

Larsen, Bob. *Larson's Book of Cults.* CA: Tyndale House, 1982.

LeBar, Reverend James J. *Cults, Sects, and the New Age.* Huntington, IN: Our Sunday Visitor, 1989.

LeShan, Lawrence. *How to Meditate: A Guide to Self-Discovery.* NY: Bantam Books, 1984.

Levitt, Zola. *The Spirit of Sun Myung Moon.* Irvine, CA: Harvest House, 1976.

MacCollum, Joel A. *Carnival of Souls.* NY: Seabury, 1978.

Martin, Paul. *Cult Proofing Your Kids.* Grand Rapids, MI: Zondervan, 1993.

Martin, Rachel. *Escape: The True Story of a Young Woman Caught in the Clutches of a Religious Cult.* Denver, CO: Accent Books, 1979.

Martin, Walter. *The New Cults.* Santa Ana, CA: Vision House, 1980.

——————————. *Kingdom of the Cults.* Minneapolis, MN: Bethany House, 1984.

May, Rollo. *Man's Search for Himself.* NY: Delta Books, 1978.

Needleman, Jacob & Baker, George, eds. *Understanding the New Religions.* NY: The Seabury Press, 1978.

Smith, Huston. *The World's Religions.* CA: Harper San Francisco, 1992.

Surya Das, Lama. *Awakening the Buddha Within: Tibetan Wisdom for the Western World.* NY: Broadway Books, 1998.

Yamamoto, J. Isamu. *The Puppet Master: A Biblical Perspective and Inquiry into Sun Myung Moon.* Downers Grove, IL.: InterVarsity Press, 1977.

Yeakley, Flavil R., ed Norton, Howard W. & Vinzant, Gene & Done E., *The Discipling Dilemma.* Nashville, TN, Gospel Advocate Press, 1988.

Political

Clarkson, Frederick. *Eternal Hostility: The Struggle between Theocracy and Democracy.* Monroe, ME: Common Courage Press, 1997.

Diamond, Sara. *Spiritual Warfare: The Politics of the Christian Right.* Boston, MA: South End Press, 1989.

Legal

American Bar Association Commission on Mental Health and Physical Law. "Cults in American society". *Cultic Studies Journal,* 12 (1).

Anthony, Dick & Robbins, Thomas. "Law, social science and the 'brainwashing' exception to the First Amendment", *Behavioral Sciences and the Law,* Vol. 10, 1992.

Aronin, Douglas. "Cults, deprogramming, and guardianship: A model legislative proposal". *Columbia Journal of Law and Social Problems,* 17, 1982.

Assembly of the State of New York. "Public Hearing on the Treatment of Children by Cults", August 9-10, 1979.

Brandon, Thomas S. "New religions, conversions, and deprogramming: New frontiers of religious liberty". *The Center for Law and Religious Freedom,* January 1982.

Delgado, Richard. "Religious Totalism: Gentle and Ungentle Persuasion Under the First Amendment". *Southern California Law Review,* Volume 51, Number 1, 1977.

———————. "Ascription of criminal states of mind: Toward a defense theory for the coercively persuaded ('brainwashed') defendant." *Minnesota Law Review*, Vol. 63, No. 1. November, 1978.

———————. Religious totalism as slavery. *New York University Review of Law and Social Change*, 1979-80.

———————. a response to Professor Dressler. *Minnesota Law Review*, Vol. 63, No. 2. January, 1979.

———————. "Cults and Conversion: The Case for Informed Consent". *Georgia Law Review*, Volume 16, No.3. Spring 1982.

———————. "When religious exercise is not free: Deprogramming and the constitutional status of coercively induced belief." *Vanderbilt Law Review*, 1984.

Dressler, Joshua. "Professor Delgado's 'brainwashing' defense: Courting a determinist legal system," *Minnesota Law Review*.

Driesen, George & Georgiades, Peter. "Comments on Stender Article". *Cultic Studies Journal*, Vol. 4, No. 1

Greene, Ford. "Appellant Molko's Response to Briefs by Amicus Curiae National Council of Churches of Christ, Christian Legal Society, and the American Psychological Association". Supreme Court of the State of California, March 18, 1987.

Greene, Robert H. "People v. religious cults: Legal guidelines for criminal activities, tort liability, and parental remedies". *Suffolk University Law Review*.

Hansen, Susan. "Did Scientology Strike Back?" *American Lawyer*, June 1997.

Kandel, Randy & Francis, "Litigating the Cult-Related Child Custody Case", *Cultic Studies Journal*, Vol. 4, No.2/Vol. 5, No.1. Double Issue.

Karlin, Robert A. & Orne, Martin T. "Hypnosis and the Iatrogenic Creation of Memory: On the need for a per se exclusion of testimony based on hypnotically influenced recall". *Cultic Studies Journal*, Vol. 14, No. 2

Landa, Susan. "Children and cults: a practical guide". *Journal of Family and Law*, 29, 591-622. (1991).

Lemoult, John E. "Deprogramming members of religious sects". *Fordham Law Review*, 1978.

Levy, Lawrence Esq.. "Prosecuting an Ex-Cult Member's Undue Influence Suit", *Cultic Studies Journal*, Vol. 7, No. 1

Lucksted, Orlin D. & Martell, Dale F. "Cults: A conflict between religious liberty and involuntary servitude?" *FBI Law Enforcement Bulletin*, 1982.

Nievod, Abraham Ph.D., J.D. "Undue influence in contract and probate law", *Cultic Studies Journal*, Vol. 10, No. 1.

Robbins, Thomas. "Cults, brainwashing and deprogramming: The view from the law journals." Unpublished manuscript.

Rosedale, Herbert, Esq. "Women and Cults: A Lawyer's Perspective". *Cultic*

Studies Journal, Vol. 12, No. 2

—————————. "Letter to Mr. Ira Glasser," Executive Director, American Civil Liberties Union, 1984.

—————————. "Legal Analysis of Intent as a Continuum Emphasizing Social Context of Volition". *Cultic Studies Journal*, Vol. 6, No. 1.

Scheflin, Alan W. "False memory and Buridan's Ass: A Response to Karlin and Orne". *Cultic Studies Journal*, Vol. 14, No. 2

—————————. *Trance on Trial*. NY: Guilford Clinical and Experimental Hypnosis Series, 1989.

(See Psychology section for other Scheflin works).

Shapiro, Robert N. "'Mind control' or intensity of faith: The constitutional protection of religious beliefs." *Harvard Civil Liberties Law Review, 1978.*

—————————. "Of robots, persons, and the protection of religious beliefs." *Southern California Law Review,* 1983.

Shepherd, William C. "The prosecutor's reach: Legal issues stemming from the new religious movements". *Journal of the American Academy of Religion.*

Singer, Margaret Ph.D. Undue Influence and Written Documents: Psychological Aspects. *Cultic Studies Journal,* Vol. 10, No. 1.

Stender, Fay Esq. "Some rigors of our times: The first amendment and real life and death. One ACLU member looks at Guyana, Nazis, and pornography." *Cultic Studies Journal*, Vol. 4, No. 1.

Unknown law student "Cults, deprogrammers, and the necessity defense." *Michigan Law Review*, Vol. 80, No. 2 December, 1981.

Van Hoey, Sarah. "Cults in Court". *Cultic Studies Journal*, Vol. 8, No. 1.

Wilshire, David MA, MP. "Cults and the European Parliament: A Practical Political Response to an International Problem". *Cultic Studies Journal*, Vol. 7, No. 1.

Zoning Board of Appeals, Town of New Castle, New York, Society of Neighbors. *Petition to Deny Application of the Moon Organization to Operate an Indoctrination Center;* Legal Decision; Appendix and footnotes.

Author unavailable. "Cults, deprogrammers, and the necessity defense". *Michigan Law Review*, Vol.80.

Amway

Butterfield, Steve. *Amway: The Cult of Free Enterprise.* Montreal, Quebec: Buffalo Black Rose Books, 1986.

Carter, Ruth. *Amway Motivational Organizations: Behind the Smoke and Mirrors.* Winter Park, FL: Backstreet Publishing, 1999.

Fitzpatrick, Robert L. & Reynolds, Joyce K. *False Profits.* Charlotte, NC: Herald

Press, 1997.

Andrew Cohen and Moksha Foundation

Tarlo, Luna. *The Mother of God.* Brooklyn, NY: Plover Press, 1997.

Aum Shinrikyo

Kaplan, David E. & Marshall, Andrew. *The Cult at the End of The World.* NY: Crown, 1996.

Lifton, Robert Jay. *Destroying the World to Save It: Aum Shinrikyo, Apocalyptic Violence, and the New Global Terrorism.* NY: Metropolitan Books, 1999.

Reid, T.R. "U.S. Visitors Boost Cause of Japanese Cult; Lawyer Says Police Imperil Religious Rights of Sect", *Washington Post Foreign Service,* May 9, 1995.

Watanabe, Teresa. "Alleged Persecution of Cult Investigated", *Los Angeles Times,* May 6, 1995.

Charles Manson

Atkins, Susan & Slosser, Bob. *Susan Atkins: Child of Satan- Child of God.* Plainfield, NJ: Logos International, 1977.

Bugliosi, Vincent & Gentry, Curt. *Helter Skelter: The True Story of the Manson Murders.* NY: Bantam, 1974.

The Children of God (Family of Love)

Davis, Deborah Berg. *The Children of God: The Inside Story.* Grand Rapids, MI: The Zondervan Publishing House, 1984.

Kent, Stephen A. "Lustful prophet: a psychosexual historical study of the Children of God's leader, David Berg". *Cultic Studies Journal,* 11(2), 1994.

McManus, Una. *Not for a Million Dollars.* Impact Books, 1980.

Williams, Miriam. *Heaven's Harlots: My Fifteen Years As a Sacred Prostitute in the Children of God Cult.* NY: William Morrow, 1998.

Wallerstein, Herbert J. *Final Report on the Activities of the Children of God to Honorable Louis J. Lefkowitz, Attorney General of the State of New York,* Charity Frauds Bureau, September 30, 1974.

David Koresh/ Waco

Breult, Marc. *Inside the Cult; A Members Exclusive Chilling Account of Madness and Depravity in David Koresh.* NY: Signet Books, 1995.

Linedecker, Clifford L. *Massacre at Waco, Texas : The Shocking Story of Cult Leader David Koresh and the Branch Davidians.* NY: St. Martins Press, 1998.

Reavis, Dick J. *The Ashes of Waco: An Investigation.* NY: Syracuse University Press 1998.

Thibodeau, David & Whiteson, Leon. *A Place Called Waco: A Survivor's Story.* NY: 1999.

Wright, Stuart A., ed. *Armageddon in Waco: Critical Perspectives on the Branch Davidian Conflict.* Chicago, IL: University of Chicago Press, 1996.

Eckankar

Lane, David Christopher. *The Making of a Spiritual Movement: The Untold Story of Paul Twitchell and Eckankar.* Del Mar, CA: Del Mar Press, 1983.

International Church of Christ

Bauer, Rick & Bauer, Sarah. *Toxic Christianity.* Bowie, MD: Freedom House Ministries, 1994.

Giambalvo, Carol & Rosedale, Herbert, eds. *The Boston Movement: Critical Perspectives on the International Churches of Christ.* (2nd Edition) Bonita Springs, FL: American Family Foundation 1996.

Jones, Jerry. *What Does the Boston Movement Teach?* Bridgeton, MO: Mid-America Book and Tape Sales, 1990.

Jehovah's Witnesses

Bergman, Jerry R. *Jehovah's Witnesses and the Problem of Mental Health.* Clayton, CA: Witness Inc. 1992.

Franz, Raymond. *Crisis of Conscience.* Commentary Press, 1984.

————. *In Search of Christian Freedom.* Commentary Press, 1992.

Harrison, Barbara Grizutti. *Visions of Glory: A History and a Memory of Jehovah's Witnesses.* NY: Simon and Shuster, 1978.

Magnani, Duane & Barrett, Arthur. *Dialogue with Jehovah's Witnesses.* CA: Witness Inc.

Penton, James A. *Apocalypse Delayed: The Story of the Jehovah's Witnesses.* University of Toronto Press, 1985.

Reed, David A. *Blood on the Altar: Confessions of a Jehovah's Witness Minister.* NY: Prometheus Press 1996.

————. *Jehovah's Witnesses: Answered Verse by Verse.* Grand Rapids, MI: Baker Book House, 1986.

Watters, Randall. *Thus Saith the Governing Body of the Jehovah's Witnesses.* Manhattan Beach, CA: Bethel Ministires, 1982, 1996.

Krishna (ISKCON)

Daner, Francine Jeane. *The American Children of Krishna: A Study of the Hare Krishna Movement.* NY: Holt, Rinehart, and Winston, 1976.

Hubner, John & Gruson, Lindsey. *Monkey on a Stick: Murder, Madness and the Hare Krishnas.* NY: Harcourt, Brace & Jovanovich, 1988.

Levine, Faye. *The Strange World of Hare Krishna*. NY: Fawcett, 1973.

Muster, Nori. *Betrayal of the Spirit: My Life Behind the Headlines of the Hare Krishna Movement*. Chicago, IL: University of Illinois Press, 1996.

Yanoff, Morris. *Where is Joey? Lost among the Hare Krishnas*. Chicago, IL: Swallow Press, 1981.

Lenz (Rama)

Diamond, David. "Street Brawl in the Twilight Zone". *Wired Magazine*, September 7, 1999.

Laxer, Mark. *Take Me For A Ride: Coming of Age in a Destructive Cult*. Bowie, MD: Outer Rim Press, 1993.

Margulis, Zachary. "The Code Cult of the CPU guru". *Wired Magazine*, January 2, 1994.

Lyndon LaRouche

King, Dennis. *Lyndon LaRouche and the New American Fascism*. NY: Doubleday, 1989.

——————. *Get the Facts on Anyone*. Arco Publications, 1999.

Messianic Communities (Twelve Tribes)

Pardon, Robert & Barba, Judith. *Messianic Communities: Journey from Orthodoxy to Heresy*. Lakeville, MA: New England Institute of Religious Research, 1995.

Militia/ Hate groups

Dees, Morris with Corcoran, James. *Gathering Storm: America's Militia Threat*. NY: HarperCollins, 1997.

Noble, Kerry. *Tabernacle of Hate: Why They Bombed Oklahoma City*. Prescott, Ontario: Voyageur Publications, 1998.

The Moon Organization

Anderson, Scott & Anderson, Jon Lee. *Inside the League*. NY: Dodd Mead, 1986.

Boettcher, Robert. *Gifts of Deceit—Sun Myung Moon, Tongsun Park and the Korean Scandal*. NY: Holt, Rinehart and Winston, 1980.

Edwards, Christopher. *Crazy for God: The Nightmare of Cult Life*. Englewood Cliffs, NJ: Prentice-Hall, Inc., 1979.

Freed, Josh. *Moonwebs: Journey into the Mind of a Cult*. Toronto, Ontario: Dorset Publishing, 1980.

Greene, Ford, esq. *The Outline of Rev. Moon's Hand in Central America: The Unification Church, the World Anti-Communist League, CAUSA and John Singlaub*. Unpublished manuscript, 1987.

Heftmann, Erica. *The Dark Side of the Moonies.* Australia: Penguin Books, 1982.

Hong, Nansook. *In the Shadow of the Moons.* NY: Little Brown, 1999.

Horowitz, Irving Louis, ed. *Science, Sin and Scholarship: The Politics of Reverend Moon and the Unification Church.* Cambridge, MA: The MIT Press, 1978.

Investigation of Korean-American Relations. *Report of the Subcommittee on International Organizations.* U.S. Government Printing Office. Stock number 052-070-04729-1. October 31, 1978.

Kemperman, Steve. *Lord of the Second Advent.* Ventura, CA: Regal Books, 1981.

Lofland, John. *The Doomsday Cult.* NY: Irvington Publishers, 1977.

Parry, Robert. "The Dark Side of Rev. Moon: Buying the Right". *Consortium News,* 1997.

Racer, David G. *Not for Sale: The Rev. Sun Myung Moon and One Amercian's Freedom.* St. Paul, MN: Tiny Press, 1989.

Underwood, Barbara and Underwood, Betty. *Hostage to Heaven: Four Years in the Unification Church by an Ex-Moonie and the Mother Who Fought to Free Her.* Portland, OR: Clarkson N. Potter, 1979.

Wood, Allen Tate & Vitek, Jack. *Moonstruck: A Memoir of My Life in a Cult.* NY: William Morrow & Company, 1979.

U.S. v. Sun Myung Moon and Takeru Kamiyama (Moon conviction of conspiracy and filing false tax returns, Kamiyama of aiding and abetting filing of false returns, obstruction of justice and perjury) 718 Federal Reporter, 2nd Series Nos. 755,765,766 and 1153, Dockets 82-1275,82-1279, 82-1277,82-1357 and 82-1387 United States Court of Appeals, Second Circuit. Argued March 23rd, 1983. Decided Sept 13, 1983.

Mormons (Church of Latter-Day Saints)

Heinerman, John & Shupe, Anson D. *The Mormon Corporate Empire.* Boston, MA: Beacon Press, 1985.

Wise, William. *Massacre at Mountain Meadows.* NY: Thomas Crowell, 1976.

MSIA and John-Roger

McWilliams, Peter. *LIFE 102:* What to Do When Your Guru Sues You. Los Angeles, CA: Prelude Press. 1994

The People's Temple (Jim Jones)

Kilduff, Marshall & Javers, Ron. *The Suicide Cult: The Inside Story of the Peoples Temple Sect and the Massacre in Guyana.* NY: Bantam Books, 1978.

Layton, Deborah. *Seductive Poison: A Jonestown Survivor's Story of Life and Death in the Peoples Temple.* Anchor Books, 1998.

Mills, Jeannie. *Six Years With God.* NY: A&W Publishers, 1979.

Reiterman, Tim & Jacobs, John. *Raven: The Untold Story of the Rev. Jim Jones and His People*. NY: Dutton, 1982.

White, Mel. *Deceived: The Jonestown Tragedy*. Old Tappan, NJ: Fleming H. Revel Company, Spire Books, 1979.

Wooden, Kenneth. *The Children of Jonestown*. NY: McGraw-Hill, 1981.

Yee, Min S., Layton, Thomas N. *In My Father's House: The Story of the Layton Family and the Reverend Jim Jones*. NY: Holt, Rinehart and Winston, 1981.

Rajneesh (Osho)

Belfrage, Sally. *Flowers of Emptiness: Reflections on an Ashram*. NY: Seaview Books, 1980.

Gordon, James S. *The Golden Guru: The Strange Journey of Bhagwan Shree Rajneesh*. Lexington, MA: The Stephen Greene Press, 1987

McCormick, Win, ed. *The Rajneesh Chronicles* Portland, OR: New Oregon Publishers, 1987.

Milne, Hugh. *Bhagwan: The God That Failed*. NY: St. Martin's Press, 1987.

Strelley, Kate. *The Ultimate Game: the Rise and Fall of Bhagwan Shree Rajneesh*. NY: Harper & Row, 1987.

Sai Baba

Beyerstein, Dale, ed. *Sai Baba's Miracles: An Overview*. India: Skeptics, 1994.

Premanand, B. *Science Versus Miracles*. India: Skeptics, 1994

Satanic Cults

Kahaner, Larry. *Cults that Kill: Probing the Underworld of Occult Crime*. NY: Warner Books, 1988.

Kent, Stephen A. "Deviant scripturalism and ritual satanic abuse. Part one: possible judeo-christian infuences". *Religion*, 23, 229-241. 1993.

——————————. Part two: possible masonic, mormon, magick, and pagan influences. *Religion*, 1993.

Lyons, Arthur. *Satan Wants You: The Cult of Devil Worship in America*. NY: The Mysterious Press, 1988.

Scott, Gini G. *The Magicians: A Study of Power in a Black Magic Group*. Oakland, CA: Creative Communications Press.

Smith, Margaret. *Ritual Abuse: What It Is, Why It Happens and How to Help*. CA: Harper SanFrancisco, 1993.

Terry, Maury. *The Ultimate Evil*. NY: Doubleday & Co., 1987.

Warnke, Mike. *The Satan Seller*. Plainfield, NJ: Logos International, 1972.

Scientology

Atack, Jon. *A Piece of Blue Sky: Scientology, Dianetics and L. Ron Hubbard Exposed.* NY: Lyle Stuart, 1990.

Behar, Richard. "Scientology:The Thriving Cult of Greed and Power. Ruined lives. Lost fortunes. Federal crimes. Scientology poses as a religion but really is a ruthless global scam — and aiming for the mainstream". *TIME* magazine, May 6, 1991.

Brown, Janelle. "A Web of their own: Scientologists say their Internet filter protects the faithful. Critics call it 'cult mind-control'." *Salon Magazine* July 15 1998.

Cooper, Paulette. *The Scandal of Scientology.* NY: Tower Publications, 1971.

Corydon, Bent & Hubbard, L. Ron Jr. *L. Ron Hubbard: Messiah or Madman?* Secaucus, NJ: Lyle Stuart, 1987.

Evans, Dr. Christopher. *Cults of Unreason.* NY: Delta, 1973.

Kaufman, Robert. *Inside Scientology.* NY: Olympia, 1972.

Kent, Stephen A. "The Globalization of Scientology: Influence, Control and Opposition in Transnational Markets", *Religion* Article number 1998.0154, 1999. available at www.idealibrary.com.

Lamont, Stewart. *Religion, Inc.* London: Harrap, 1986.

Malko, George. *Scientology—The Now Religion.* NY: Delacorte Press, 1970.

Miller, Russell. *Bare Faced Messiah: The True Story of L. Ron Hubbard.* Great Britain: Penguin Books Ltd., 1987.

Vosper, Cyril. *The Mind Benders: The Book They Tried to Ban.* Great Britain: Neville Spearman Ltd., 1973.

Wallis, Roy. *The Road to Total Freedom: A Sociological Analysis of Scientology.* NY: Columbia University Press, 1977.

Soka Gakkai (formerly NSA)

Batchelor, Stephen. *The Awakening of the West: The Encounter of Buddhism and Western Culture.* Berkeley, CA: Parallax Press, 1994.

Fujiwara, Hirotatsui. *I Denounce Soka Gakkai* Tokyo, Japan: Nisshin Hodo Co. 1970.

Kitagawa, Joseph H. *Religion in Japanese History.* NY: Columbia University Press, 1966, 1990.

Tono, Reverend Kando. "...the background, meaning, content and spirit..." Kando Tono, PO Box 1868, Grand Central Station, New York, NY 10163, 1981.

Synanon

Gerstel, David U. *Paradise Incorporated: Synanon.* Novato, CA: Presidio Press, 1982.

Mitchell, Dave & Cathy, & Ofshe, Richard. *The Light on Synanon*. Seaview Books, 1980.

Yablonsky, L. *The Tunnel Back: Synanon*. NY: Macmillan , 1965.

Transcendental Meditation

Lazarus, A. "Psychiatric problems precipitated by transcendental meditation". *Psychological Reports*, 1976.

Persinger, Michael A., Carrey, Normand J. & Suess, Lynn A. *TM and Cult Mania*. North Quincy, MA: The Christopher Publishing House, 1980.

Scott, R. D. *Transcendental Misconceptions*. San Diego, CA: Bobbs-Merrill Co, 1978.

The Way International

Morton, Douglas V. & Juedes, John P. *The Integrity and the Accuracy of the Way's Word*. St. Louis, MO: Personal Freedom Outreach, 1980.

Williams, J. L. *Victor P. Wierwille and the Way International*. Chicago, IL: Moody Press, 1979.

Index

About the Author

Steven Hassan has been on the front lines of the mind control and destructive cult issue for over twenty-three years. He is a licensed Mental Health Counselor and holds a Master's degree in counseling psychology from Cambridge College. In 1988, he authored the critically acclaimed book *Combatting Cult Mind Control: The #1 Best-selling Guide to Protection, Rescue and Recovery from Destructive Cults* (Park Street Press), favorably reviewed in *The Lancet* and *The American Journal of Psychiatry.*

Mr. Hassan has pioneered a new approach to helping victims of mind control called the Strategic Interaction Approach. Unlike the stressful and media-sensationalized "deprogramming," this non-coercive approach is an effective and legal alternative for families to help cult members. It teaches family and friends how to strategically influence the individual involved in the group. During his years of work Mr. Hassan has helped thousands of persons victimized by cult-related mind control. He has provided numerous training workshops and seminars for mental health professionals, educators and law enforcement officers, as well as for families of cult members.

Deceptively recruited into the Moon organization at the age of nineteen while a student at Queens College, Hassan spent twenty-seven months recruiting and indoctrinating new members, fundraising, political campaigning and personally meeting with Sun Myung Moon during numerous leadership sessions. Mr. Hassan ultimately rose to the rank of Assistant Director of the Unification Church at National Headquarters. Following a serious automobile accident, he was deprogrammed by several former members at his parents' request. Once he realized the insidious nature of the organization, he authorized police officials to take possession of his personal belongings, which included a massive set of private speeches documenting Moon's secret plan to "take over the world."

During the 1977-78 Congressional Subcommittee Investigation into South Korean CIA activities in the United States, he consulted as an expert witness.

Mr. Hassan has established Freedom of Mind Resource Center, Inc. as an educational organization dedicated to upholding human rights, promoting consumer awareness, and exposing abuses of destructive cult groups. The Web site for FMRC is http://www.freedomofmind.com and has material being added regularly. The newly established nonprofit The Freedom of Mind Institute will do research, publish material, offer training for mental health professionals, and sponsor educational conferences. Its Web site is http://www.freedomofmind.org.

Mr. Hassan has appeared on innumerable television and radio shows including *Nightline, 60 Minutes, Dateline NBC, The Oprah Winfrey Show, Good Morning America, Today Show, CBS This Morning,* and *Larry King Live.* Quoted extensively in newspaper and magazine articles, Mr. Hassan has continuously sought to educate the public through the media. In his commitment to fight against destructive cults, Mr. Hassan devotes a major portion of his time and energy to actively consult individuals and organizations. He has addressed hundreds of campus, religious and professional organizations throughout the world.

Get Involved! Make a Difference!

Please sign up for our e-mail mailing list and be kept up to date on the latest news and resources. Become an activist! Educate members of your community.

If you are a former member consider sharing your story with others. Make information available about your former group! Help those cult members, ex-cult members, families, and friends who still have a problem. Speak to the media.

If you are a professional—an attorney, computer expert, member of the media, educator, mental health expert, politician—we need your talent and expertise!

If you have a family member or friend in a destructive group, get involved with the larger issue. You can help others while helping yourself!

If you wish to start a local activist group, a support group of former members, a family and friend support group, please do!

The Freedom of Mind Institute
PO Box 45223
Somerville, MA 02145
www.freedomofmind.org

To order additional copies of Releasing the Bonds, please go to our Web site or to order by credit card (Visa, Mastercard or Discover) please call 1 800 860-2139.